CORPORATE COMMU

Corporate Communication: A Marketing Viewpoint offers an overview of the framework, key concepts, strategies and techniques from a unique marketing perspective. While other textbooks are limited to a managerial or public relations perspective, this book provides a complete, holistic overview of the many ways communication can add value to an organization. Step by step, this text introduces the main concepts of the field, including discipline and function frameworks, corporate identity, corporate and employer branding, corporate social responsibility, stakeholder management, storytelling, corporate associations, identification, commitment and acceptability.

In order to help reinforce key learning points, grasp the essential facts and digest and retain information, the text offers a comprehensive pedagogy, including: chapter summaries; a list of key words and concepts; case studies; and questions at the end of each chapter. Principles are illustrated through a wealth of real-life examples, drawn from a variety of big, small, global and local companies such as BMW Group, Hidria, Lego, Mercator, Krka, Barilla, Domino's Pizza, Gorenje, Si.mobil, BP, Harley-Davidson and Coca-Cola.

This exciting new textbook is essential reading for all professional corporate marketing and communication executives, as well as undergraduate and postgraduate students of marketing and public relations, not to mention managers who need a complete and accurate view of this increasingly important subject.

Klement Podnar (PhD) is a professor at the Faculty of Social Sciences at the University of Ljubljana, where he teaches Corporate Communication, Basics of Visual Communication and Marketing. He serves on several editorial boards of international journals and is as an associate editor of the *Journal of Promotion Management*. His research has been published in a number of international journals including: *Journal of Business Research, European Journal of Marketing, Corporate Communication: An International Journal* and *Journal of Marketing Communications*. Klement Podnar is the organizer of several international conferences and cofounder of the International CSR communication conference.

CORPORATE COMMUNICATION

A marketing viewpoint

Klement Podnar

Routledge
Taylor & Francis Group

LONDON AND NEW YORK

First published 2015
by Routledge

2 Park Square, Milton Park, Abingdon, Oxon OX14 4RN
and by Routledge
711 Third Avenue, New York, NY 10017

Routledge is an imprint of the Taylor & Francis Group, an informa business

British Library Cataloguing in Publication Data
A catalogue record for this book is available from the British Library

Library of Congress Cataloguing in Publication data
Podnar, Klement.
   [Korporativno komuniciranje. English]
   Corporate communication: a marketing viewpoint / Klement Podnar.
      pages   cm
   Includes bibliographical references and index.
   1. Communication in organizations.   2. Corporate culture.   3. Corporate image.
   4. Organizational behavior.   5. Marketing–Management.   I. Title.
   HD30.3.P625 2015
   658.4′5–dc23
   2014016817

ISBN: 978-1-138-80470-8 (hbk)
ISBN: 978-1-138-80472-2 (pbk)
ISBN: 978-1-315-75278-5 (ebk)

Typeset in Bembo
by Out of House Publishing

Printed and bound by CPI Group (UK) Ltd, Croydon, CR0 4YY

CONTENTS

List of figures   *viii*

Introduction   1

1 Corporate communication framework   4
   1.1 The concept of corporate communication   4
   1.2 Overview of corporate communication   5
   1.3 Duality of organizations   8
   1.4 Focus of corporate communication: identity,
        image and reputation   9
   1.5 Corporate communication in organizations   10

2 Corporate identity   17
   2.1 Understanding corporate identity   17
   2.2 Goals and corporate identity   20
   2.3 Managing corporate identity   22
   2.4 The role of branch identity   23
   2.5 Articulation of corporate identity   25
   2.6 Communicating corporate identity   27

3 Corporate brand and branding   32
   3.1 Definition of corporate brand   32
   3.2 Purpose and consequences of corporate brands   34
   3.3 Corporate branding   35
   3.4 Identity and position of corporate brands   36
   3.5 Company's brand architecture   38

3.6 Organizational structure of corporate brands   40
3.7 Corporate rebranding   42

4 Employer branding   **49**
4.1 Corporate brand and employees   49
4.2 Employer branding   50
4.3 Internal branding programmes   53
4.4 Internal branding and organizational identity and culture 56

5 Ethical branding and corporate social responsibility **63**
5.1 Ethical branding and its misuses   63
5.2 Understanding corporate social responsibility   65
5.3 Societal expectations as the foundation of corporate
     social responsibility   67
5.4 Implementation of corporate social responsibility   69
5.5 Communicating corporate social responsibility   71
5.6 Reporting corporate social responsibility   74

6 Stakeholder management and communications   **81**
6.1 Stakeholder paradigm   81
6.2 Public and public sphere   82
6.3 Categories of stakeholders   83
6.4 Distribution of power among stakeholders   84
6.5 Criteria for classification of stakeholders   85
6.6 Stakeholder management   87
6.7 Stakeholder behaviour   89
6.8 Communication with stakeholders   90

**7 Storytelling and issue management in times of
    change and crises**   **96**
7.1 Definition of corporate story   96
7.2 Framework and structure of the corporate story   98
7.3 Plurality of corporate stories and their role in times of
     organizational changes   101
7.4 Communication in crisis   104

8 Corporate communications   **114**
8.1 Purpose of corporate communications   114
8.2 Management as the company's spokesperson   115
8.3 Company's celebrity endorsers   118
8.4 Corporate visual identity (CVI)   120
8.5 Corporate and institutional advertising   122
8.6 Informal communications   125

9 Corporate associations: identity traits and corporate image **136**
9.1 Corporate associations 136
9.2 Perception of a company 137
9.3 Identity traits 139
9.4 Corporate image 141
9.5 Measuring corporate image 144
9.6 Critiques of corporate image 147
9.7 Achieving desired corporate image 149

10 Corporate associations: reputation and trust **157**
10.1 Corporate reputation 157
10.2 Dimensions of corporate reputation 159
10.3 Corporate reputation management 161
10.4 Perceived external prestige of a company 162
10.5 Consequences of corporate reputation 163
10.6 Forms and roles of trust 165
10.7 Definition of trust 166
10.8 Dimensions of trust 167
10.9 Consequences of bad reputation and mistrust 168

11 Organizational identification **177**
11.1 Identification: main characteristics 177
11.2 Identifications in the work environment 179
11.3 Corporate and group identification of employees 182
11.4 Consumer identification 184
11.5 Brand communities 187
11.6 Effects of organizational identification 188

12 Organizational commitment and social acceptability **197**
12.1 Influence of organizational identification on commitment 197
12.2 Understanding organizational commitment 198
12.3 Dimensions of commitment 200
12.4 Effects of commitment 203
12.5 Social acceptability 204

Conclusion **212**

Author index *215*
Subject index *221*

FIGURES

I.1 Book chapters in the classical communication model 3
1.1 Framework of corporate communication 6
2.1 Dimensions of the identity of organization 19
3.1 Basic types of brand architecture 40
4.1 Steps in formation of the employer brand 54
5.1 The framework of communicating corporate social responsibility 73
6.1 Criteria for stakeholder classification 87
7.1 Key protagonists and factors of a corporate story 100
8.1 Key tasks of corporate communication 115
9.1 Corporate image structure 140
10.1 Reputation dimensions 160
11.1 Forms of organizational identification and their consequences for the company 184
12.1 Types of commitment to a company 201

INTRODUCTION

The phrase **corporate communication**, and company departments dealing with it, first emerged at the beginning of the twentieth century when corporations started to realize that success is much more than merely selling products and services. In times when the development of capitalism revealed many of its dark sides and when large corporations, together with their owners and founders, came under fire because of corporate scandals, companies realized that, alongside their main activities and usual care for consumers, they also needed to communicate with other publics. The icons of American-style capitalism, for example, JP Morgan and the Guggenheim and Rockefeller families, did not hire professionals merely to polish their media image (even though this aspect should not be neglected) but also to manage relationships with trade unions, employees, government representatives and journalists, all those who could strongly influence their image and, consequently, their property. Railroad, oil, tobacco, financial, telecommunication and other companies learned that in order to do business successfully, they needed to monitor and influence political, economic and technological circumstances and regulations, and the first step was to communicate to the public in such a way to gain its affection. We are talking about the people (such as Ivy Ledbetter Lee and Edward L Bernays) who are now seen as the pioneers of modern public relations, and the events that designate its birth.

Across the Atlantic, in times of rapid industrialization and in the context of modernism, European companies similarly began to understand that to be competitive in the market, a recognizable and consistent appearance was needed. Pioneers of modern industrial and graphic design such as Peter Behrens, Lucian Bernhard, Ted McKnight Kauffer, Adolphe Mouron Cassandre and others not only designed the first graphic images but constructed whole systems of visual identity, which included the company logo, internal and external architecture, market communications and even advertised products. Companies such as AEG, London Transport,

Olivetti, Bosch, Shell and Braun were among the first to realize that a strategically managed visual identity could give them a competitive edge over their rivals.

In the USA, as well as in Europe, the era of public relations and marketing began, which flourished significantly after WWII. In this period, many new brands were born, among which some corporate brands became more and more significant. For companies and their stakeholders, these represented the most important value, though intangible, in the modern day business world. So what was born from the need for a better public image and a consistent company identity, and then developed across different boards and company sectors, such as public relations, HR, marketing and other departments responsible for market communications, in the States as well as in Europe, has finally grown by the end of the twentieth century into the idea of integrated organizational communications and their management. This is the tool needed to construct and present a company's identity, the basic element of reputation in the political, economic, social and technological global environments in which companies as social entities are operating. It seems that never before in the history of companies and their competitive appearance on the market, were the functions of marketing, PR and HR so similar and close to one another, and the need for their integrated application in the creation of competitive advantage has never been expressed more clearly than now with the concept of corporate communications.

This book was written for under- and postgraduate students of Marketing Communications and Public Relations as a basic guide into the field of corporate communications. The contents are focused only on one part of this rapidly developing field and are based on scientific literature and the author's wide experience. The work presents all the basic concepts that are not only possible tools for managing corporate identities and their communications, but also raise questions concerning the future development of corporate communications. The book is also aimed at practitioners responsible for corporate communications in profit and non-profit organizations, public relations managers, marketing staff, human resources managers, communications agencies and others who in their professional careers deal with corporate communications and manage company or brand identities – most prominently members of the board and chief executives. This book was written not only for academic purposes but also to be useful reading for practitioners in corporate communications and marketing.

There is, of course, the need to explain the term **corporate**. The word derives from the Latin word **corpus** that denotes a body or a body of people. The term is used for different social entities such as groups of people, profit or non-profit organizations, regions or countries. In the context of this book, however, the term is used for profit organizations, corporations.

The book can be read beginning to end or one chapter at a time, depending on the information that the reader is looking for, because chapters are written as complete and independent units. The Introduction is followed by a chapter presenting corporate communications as an interdisciplinary research field and as one of the key functions within a company. The third chapter deals with corporate

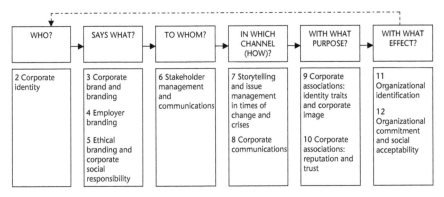

FIGURE I.1 Book chapters in the classical communication model

identity with which companies express who they are. The following chapters discuss the question 'What do companies try to say about themselves?' by discussing the concepts of corporate branding, employer branding and social responsibility. Chapter 6 deals with stakeholders and explains to whom and in what manner companies should communicate. In the seventh chapter, the book deals with ways and channels of communication. The structure of a corporate story is presented and its use and application in times of change and crisis are discussed. The next chapter is closely connected to the preceding one: it presents specific aspects of corporate communications such as chief executives, celebrities, visual identity, corporate advertising and word of mouth. These are 'communication means' and are, together with other communication tools, an important part of corporate storytelling. The book continues with a discussion of the purposes of corporate communications, among which are corporate associations which play an important role in attributing identity traits to a company, constructing its image, building corporate reputation and gaining trust. The last chapter deals with the desired effects of corporate communications, namely stakeholders' identification with a company that leads to their commitment or (at least) to a social acceptability of the company's actions. The book concludes with a short discussion of what has been said in the book and a few closing remarks.

An attentive reader will see that the structure of the chapters follows the classical communication model of Harold Lasswell who defined the model with the following questions: **'Who says what, to whom, in which channel, with what effect?'** The selection of this structure for the book demonstrates that everything we do in business starts and ends with communication or can be studied from the communication perspective. The author of this book wishes that you, dear reader, will recognize the practical value of good theory, and hopes that at least part of your trust in the author, which was demonstrated by picking this book up, has paid off.

1

CORPORATE COMMUNICATION FRAMEWORK

CONTENTS

This chapter presents various definitions of corporate communication. It underlines the integrative role of corporate communication and distinguishes it from similar disciplines dealing with organizational communications. Further, we highlight how important a good understanding of the duality of organizations is for a holistic approach to corporate communications. We also present the main focuses and tasks of corporate communication in an organization.

1.1 The concept of corporate communication

David Bernstein (1986, 1999), who is one of the first scholars to understand the concept of corporate communication in a modern way, warns that companies should adopt a holistic approach to the understanding of their communication, because they communicate continuously with their various audiences. A similar suggestion was made by Aberg (1990) in his model of total communications.

Both authors take into account the famous Watzlawick's axiom that one cannot not communicate, meaning that everything that an entity says, does or make (or doesn't say, do or make) is communication (Watzlawick 1976). That is why companies and other entities must assume control over and manage all their communications.

The basic idea of **corporate communication** (CC) is a synchronization of different aspects of communications by an entity and the integration of messages that this entity is sending to its audiences. An early definition of corporate communication says that CC is an 'integrated approach to all communication produced by an organization, directed at all relevant target groups' (Blauw 1986). Jackson (1987) similarly defines corporate communication as the total communication activity generated by a company to achieve its objectives. Corporate communications are defined by van Riel as the 'instrument of management by means of which all consciously used forms of internal and external communication are harmonized as effectively and efficiently as possible, so as to create a favourable basis for relationships with groups upon which the company is dependent' (van Riel 1995, 26). Corporate communication is a set of activities involved in managing and orchestrating all internal and external communications with a purpose to create favourable starting points with stakeholders on whom the entity depends (van Riel and Fombrun 2007, 25). Corporate communications is an umbrella term for all forms of behaviour and communication that are performed (within or outside of an organization) by a certain corpus (van Riel 1995).

Corporate communication is the aggregate of all messages, either from official or informal sources, that are transmitted through a variety of media, and by which the entity conveys its identity to its stakeholders (Gray and Balmer 1998, 696). Corporate communication can be a method of the overall presentation of the organization to external and internal publics, because it constructs and expresses the identity of the organization (Gray and Balmer 1998).

Although authors tend to use the term corporate communication mostly in an organizational context, the term corporate should not be understood as an adjective derived from **corporation**, but should be interpreted in relation to the Latin word **corpus**, denoting a body or, in a figurative sense, meaning 'relating to the total' (van Riel 1995, 26). In this broader sense, the application of the term corporate communication can be expanded outside profit-oriented organizations offering products and services, to a number of other organizations such as NGOs, political parties, not-for-profit organizations, government institutions and even broader – to cities, towns, regions, countries or people who are active in the public sphere and have, in terms of their activities and recognition, a character of institutions or brands.

1.2 Overview of corporate communication

Van Riel (1995, 1997) writes that corporate communication is not just another discipline, but a new view on the complete area of communication. That is why corporate communication should be understood as an **umbrella term** for a field that combines knowledge of various disciplines concerned with organizational communications. 'Corporate communication takes into account both the total of marketing communication and the large range of forms of organizational communication and management communications' (van Riel 1995, 21). This opinion is shared by several other authors who deal with corporate communication in connection with management, business and organizational communications, and public relations (Argenti 1996; Dolphin 1999; Argenti and Forman 2002).

In the academic sphere, corporate communication is understood as a framework for a **holistic approach** to individual fields in communications of organizations and for integration of knowledge and findings of different disciplines and traditions, including (see Figure 1.1):

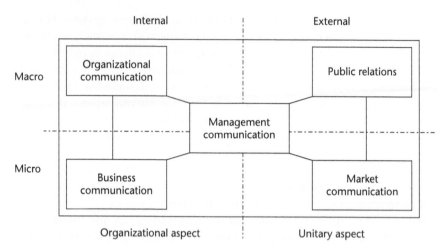

FIGURE 1.1 Framework of corporate communication

- **Business communication.** Applied science dealing with the construction and application of modes of expression, symbols and signs that accompany profit-oriented activities, related to offering products and services for satisfying human needs and desires (Reinsch 1991a, 1991b). Business communication is principally a link among participants of a business process that helps to accomplish a specific business task. This discipline deals with topics such as communication skills, use of technology and media in the communication process, types of business communications (e.g. interview, meeting, presentation, speech, written communications), use of business communications (e.g. negotiations, communication of salespeople, counsellors), and the aesthetics and ethics of business communications.
- **Organizational communication.** This focuses on analytical and critical capabilities that enable the interpersonal, collective and total understanding of the organization through a communication perspective. The main focus of the discipline is studying vertical, horizontal and transversal information flows in an organization, studying the content and meanings of messages, analysing the communication climate, and studying organizational development and personal training for competent communication activity on a systemic level (Greenbaum *et al.* 1988). Organizational communication is primarily understood as the glue that holds the organization together (Ivancevich and Matteson 1996) and influences the success of the organization's activities.
- **Management communication.** This combines the knowledge of business and organizational communications and transfers it to the management context. This discipline tries to explain structural, systemic and functional aspects of communications and to provide knowledge of communication techniques among managers in the internal and external environment of the organization. Argenti writes that the basic domains of management communication

are 'communication strategy; skills, including writing and speaking; process, including teamwork and interpersonal behavior; the global environment, which focuses on cross-cultural communication; and function, which gets us to the connection with corporate communication' (Argenti 1996, 83). Every communication – written or oral, personal or impersonal – that is used for reaching a (measureable) goal and is undertaken by managers, regardless of their hierarchical position, is management communication.

- **Public relations.** This is a discipline and a management function that deals with planning, execution and evaluation of organizational communications with internal and external publics, or with managing communications between an organization and its strategic stakeholders (Grunig and Hunt 1995, 6). The main objective of public relations (PR) is to establish and sustain mutually beneficial relationships between an organization and the public, upon which the success of the organization depends (Cutlip *et al.* 2000, 6). The basic resources of PR are, among others, relations with media and its instruments (press conferences, announcements, press materials, publicity, etc.), lobbying, organization of events, crisis communication, annual and other reports, internal newsletters and publications, speeches and presentations, donations and special programmes for relations with employees, local communities and the financial public aimed at informing, persuading and involving different stakeholders.

- **Marketing communication.** This is an instrument aimed at involving consumers in an exchange relationship with an organization. Each marketing communication is target-oriented in the sense that it directly or indirectly supports the selling of the product (Burnett and Moriarty 1997, 4). Marketing communication includes all communication activities by a company to inform, present, persuade and remind buyers and business partners in the target market about their activities and offer (Podnar *et al.* 2007). Everything that draws the buyer's attention to a selected offer can be, in a broader sense, understood as marketing communication, which is a 'strategic business process used to plan, develop, execute and evaluate coordinated, measurable, persuasive brand communication programmes over time with consumers, customers, prospects and other targeted, relevant external and internal audiences' (Schultz and Schultz 1998, 18). Classic tools of marketing communication are various forms of advertising, sales promotion, direct marketing, personal selling, etc.

Corporate communication emphasizes the **interdisciplinary view on communication** of organizations and sees communication as a resource that enables the existence, motivation and development of an organization. Because of its interdisciplinary design, we must keep in mind that the term organization can be understood in different ways, which reflects its duality – in business and organizational communications, **organization** denotes a group of people with a common goal, whereas PR and marketing communications implicitly define an organization as an independent social subject (Podnar and Kline 2003). We need to keep in mind the duality of organizations in order to understand better the interdisciplinary field of corporate communication, its individual disciplines and different theoretical approaches, and to deal in full with the phenomenon of comprehensive communication of such entities as companies.

1.3 Duality of organizations

We speak of an organization when there are people who can communicate with each other, are ready for cooperation and are capable of achieving common objectives (Lewis 1975, 19). This is a basis to the understanding of an organization that, on a group level, presupposes that individuals have a common primary goal – group members function as a unit in order to achieve their primary goal. Every individual within a group has a defined function that contributes to the achieving of the goal or purpose. It would be impossible or nonsensical if each individual did their work separately from other individuals, because every person in the group is in some way connected to other group members. That is why the organization is seen as a network of interdependent relations that have been created as a means for achieving certain goals and is understood as a series of functionalized groups with different goals and purposes. Organizations are not monolithic entities but coalitions of cooperating individuals and groups with different aims. Individuals negotiate their goals, actions and meanings to achieve a common direction, but they never cast aside their own interests and goals (Putnam 1983, 37). But, as highlighted by Handy (1974), an organization is not only a collectivity of individuals. It does not only exist within the intersubjective level – it is more than that. It is a phenomenon that is created during the process of generic subjectivity and is reflected as an independent (socially) functioning unit. The functionalists see the organization as a social fact or a concrete entity, therefore on the level of generic subjectivity. From a deterministic point of view, the structure of an organization remains static and determines the goals and activities of its members. An organization can be seen unitarily; it is a cooperative system that pursues certain interests and goals. Individuals are only a means of purpose-rational activities demanded by technological success and organizational efficiency (Putnam 1983, 36).

Therefore, to understand the concept of organization, one must be aware of its duality – on the one hand, an organization is a **group of people** joined together by a common goal, and on the other, it is an autonomous **social subject**. Although both paradigms seem to be contradictory, we can reason that they point to different but in a way complementary aspects of the organization and its apparent social reality. The first definition sees the organization as an *independent subject*, separated from its members, whereas the second sees an organization as a collective or an *aggregate of individuals* joined together by a common goal. From an outside observer's point of view, in the first definition the organization is addressed as 'it', whereas in the second it is addressed as 'they' (Podnar 2000, 175). The organization is either a *community* of individuals created and expressed on the intersubjective level, or a social actor or *pseudo-person* created in the process of generic subjectivity. The latter definition reflects the recognition that organizations without individuals (members) and their actions do not exist. Moreover, organizations have, despite the self-activity of their members, economic and political powers above and beyond those of the particular individuals that comprise them (Thompson and McHugh 1995, 5).

Corporate communication understands the duality of the organization as a complete and undividable unit, as two sides of the same coin that need to be taken into consideration when planning, implementing, influencing and explaining communication phenomena. In this way, corporate communication justifies its integrative role, not only as a function inside an organization, but on a theoretical level as well.

1.4 Focus of corporate communication: identity, image and reputation

As opposed to individual communication disciplines, corporate communication does not focus on studying different forms and functions of communication. Central to corporate communication are questions of how different forms of communication can best be synchronized to produce unified and integrated messages. It deals with the expressiveness of the organization in the communication process dyad that takes place in communications with the audiences that an organization communicates with. In this way, organizations establish, sustain and modify their own identity and their image in the eyes of communication and/or exchange partners. Corporate communication concentrates on the integrated communication system of an organization that van Riel and Fombrun (2007) define as a multiple tactical and strategic resource that an organization uses to communicate with stakeholders, transmitting messages and content about itself, in order to create beneficial micro and macro environments for its activities and to influence stakeholders and their attitudes.

Coordination and integration of communications should not be a goal in itself, but it helps to find solutions to problems of efficiency and effectiveness in organizations (van Riel 1997, 301). That is why corporate communication should always be based on the business strategy and its practical implementations. Despite the growing importance and popularity of decentralization, van Riel claims that it is still necessary to achieve agreement among most members of the organization about the way companies should profile their own sustainable 'corporate story' (van Riel 1997, 302). The primary function of corporate communication is to define how the company wishes to be understood and perceived by their stakeholders (Argenti 1998, 56).

Corporate communication is therefore in the function of corporate identity and represents a link between identity, image and reputation (Birkigt and Stadler 1986). The term **identity** represents a mix of characteristics of a corpus that make the corpus unique – uniform inwards and diverse outwards. **Image** is a personal impression or mental picture about a perceived entity, while **reputation** represents evaluated and simplified judgement on the entity made by individuals through time.

Identity, image and reputation are central concepts within corporate communication. Without considering those concepts, both from internal as well as external viewpoints, corporate communication loses its sense and meaning.

With respect to identity, image and reputation, corporate communication is not only a means of transfer but it also creates identity. Christensen and Cheney (2000) claim that projected identity is not a static constant but a dynamic variable and is, above all, a narrative that influences the creation of corporate image and reputation in the minds of internal and external receivers. Projected identity helps to create expressivity of the organization, as well as helping the sender to manifest their own identity. On these grounds, receivers create their own image about the sender that leads to a long-term evaluation of the sender's reputation (Podnar 2000).

The focus of corporate communication is less on the development of various communication skills but more on studying relationships among corporate identity, image and reputation, and examining various factors and influences. It is related to other specialized disciplines, such as corporate and internal branding, stakeholder theory, narrative theory, organizational identification and culture, organizational change theory, social responsibility of companies, and others. Only in this way can we approach, from a corporate point of view, the challenge of the classical communication model, which, with the questions 'Who says what, to whom, with what purpose, and with what effect?', makes the perfect framework to study corporate communication.

1.5 Corporate communication in organizations

If people responsible for corporate communication in organizations share the above holistic view of corporate communication, they can in fact be the linking element and pursue the overall strategic goals of the organization rather than strictly particular ones. We must keep in mind that a corpus speaks of itself through the following elements (Birkigt and Stadler 1986):

- *Verbal messages* – pieces of information that can be best controlled by the organization. Verbal messages enable the most unambiguous expression of desired content, regardless of whether they are used to inform, persuade, explain or excuse.
- *The use of symbols* and other signs that function as recognizable signs or identifiers of the organization and carry broader semantic meanings.
- *Behaviour of the organization* – the most complex but also the most important element, because it is the main indicator of whether the organization respects and holds its promises and commitments.

From a managerial point of view, these elements surpass the tasks of corporate communication because they interfere with many different departments and services within the organization that are responsible for specialized forms of communication with different spheres and markets.

It does not seem reasonable to substitute the fragmented communication system with a centralized one because specialization guarantees higher effectiveness and we can legitimately expect that communication with consumers would be best managed by the marketing department, similarly as the PR department would be the best department to communicate with media, and the HR department would be the best to communicate with employees. Nonetheless, exaggerated specialization of departments and services in the company can lead to many ivory towers, with each sending out their own narrowly focused information, being unable to see more than their own tasks and or know (let alone pursue!) the needs and goals of the organization as a whole. That is why the task of corporate communication must be to coordinate various departments with regard to the key issues and to achieve a consistent and coordinated performance. Another primary and important task of corporate communication is to find content that represents the desired, real and relevant basis for all future forms of communication. These corporate stories or comprehensive narrative about the organization or its aspects should not be mistaken for uniformity of communication.

The **main concern of corporate communication** is to design a unified groundwork, upon which complementary activities are to be built, supporting one another and representing a totality that would be more than a sum of its parts. During the implementation of specific activities by individual departments, the task of corporate communication is to ensure that such activities would be in accordance with previously defined groundwork and that there are no discords, contradictions or miscommunications. Further, the task of corporate communication is to surpass traditional contradictions and rivalries among individual departments that deal with different specialized forms of communication. If necessary, corporate communication must intervene in borderline cases where traditional departments or functions overlap, for example, internal marketing and internal branding, or employee relations and internal communication programmes. Corporate communication is also a bridge between the management board and traditional departments in an organization, such as marketing and market communications, human resources and public relations. If necessary, corporate communication can take over the task of communicating in the name of the management board or can serve as a support to board members when they communicate with different publics. Public appearances of the chair of the board are, in particular, a very important form of corporate communication because the chair strongly personifies the organization.

If we were to emphasize the concrete **operational tasks of corporate communication**, there are some that need to be mentioned:

- articulation of the company's identity, desired image and the corporate brand;
- responsibility for corporate identity and orchestrated communications;
- coordination of brand architecture;
- identification and ranking of key stakeholders and winning their positive attitude toward organizational goals and interests;

- fortification of the organizational community inside and outside the formal borders of the organization;
- creation, organization and coordination of communication processes and integration of activities of different departments;
- management of coordination groups;
- measuring image and reputation and other effects of corporate communication with different internal and external publics.

To conclude, corporate communication is a tool that helps the organization to articulate its identity, manage its communications, fortify the commitment of stakeholders, create recognizable and persuasive images in the minds of individuals and groups, develop a powerful corporate brand and increase the intangible capital, as a consequence of a good reputation.

CASE: THE BMW GROUP

The company BMW was founded in 1916 under the name Bayerische Flugzeugwerke AG (BFW). A year later, the name changed to Bayerische Motoren Werke GmbH and in 1918 to Bayerische Motoren Werke AG (BMW AG). At first, the company specialized in manufacturing engines for military aircrafts. The first BMW motorcycle was constructed in 1923 and in 1928 the company entered the car market. Today, the BMW Group is one of the largest manufacturers of motor vehicles. It owns the brands BMW, Mini, Rolls-Royce Motor Cars and Husquarna. The corporation's mission, valid to 2020, is to be the world leader in premium class products and services for individual mobility. The BMW Group operates in more than 140 countries with cars, motorcycles and financial services. Its research & development centres are located in Germany, USA, Austria, Japan and China, while there are 24 BMW factories in 13 countries and numerous subsidiaries around the globe. In 2009, the group sold around 1.3 million cars and 87,000 motorcycles to reach a revenue of €51 billion. The group employs over 96,000 people. For the sixth year in a row, BMW Group ranked first in its branch on the Dow Jones Sustainability Index (DJSI), which reflects its strategic orientation toward social responsibility and sustainable development. This orientation is, besides high quality and superior technology in all spheres of activity, the main recognizable attribute of the company. The global activities of the BMW Group are managed and coordinated in its headquarters in Munich, located in the famous BMW 'four-cylinder' tower, designed by the architect Karl Schwanzer. The tourist attraction the BMW Museum and the customer experience, exhibition and distribution centre, BMW Welt, are located next to the tower. The corporation has six divisions, managed by members of the management board: production; human resources management and industrial relations; sales and marketing; finance; development; and procurement and suppliers.

The board is headed by the Chair, who directly supervises the Corporate and Governmental Affairs service. This is a centralized organizational function that covers the whole spectrum of the company's communications, from business to finance, and sustainable development issues. BMW's corporate communication service is divided into the department for brand and technology communication, the department for corporate communication strategy, the department for internal communication and the department for political communication. Giving statements about the company as a whole is the domain of corporate communication. Also, any statements given by representatives of the BMW Group must be coordinated with the department responsible for the topic in question. The corporate communication service is responsible for carrying out analysis of the business environment and advises the management and specialized company functions in defining and communicating business policies. It is also responsible for creating the communication strategy on a global scale and monitoring its execution. It carefully defines communication goals, policies and strategies, key corporate messages, complete visual identity of all individual parts of the company, takes care of the company's publications, electronic media and all other company messages. Guidelines and instructions are given through regional managers of corporate communication to the local level, down to the PR representatives in individual countries or subsidiaries. In this way, the corporation sends different groups of stakeholders a unique message or image. It may seem that the corporate communication service is primarily responsible for communicating topics that concern the company as a whole (corporate values, technology, organizational culture, training, sponsorship and donations, sustainability and social responsibility) and addresses shareholders, employees, business partners, financial and local communities, media, trade unions and general public, while communication of individual product brands and consumer communication is primarily the domain of the marketing department, but corporate communication is also involved in activities and communication support on the level of the product. In this way, the product level inside corporate communication comprises the communication of car and motorcycle brands BMW and Mini and communication of technology and sports that are related to or supported by the BMW Group. All communications of the BMW Group are carefully planned and integrated on the corporate as well as on the product level.

Key terms

Corporate communication. An integrated and holistic approach to all communication produced by an entity (such as organization); a synchronization of different aspects of communications by an entity and the integration of messages that this entity is sending to its audiences through its behaviour, symbols and messages. It is an umbrella term for all forms of behaviour and communication that are performed (within or outside) by a certain corpus.

Business communication. Applied science dealing with the construction and application of modes of expression, symbols and signs that accompany profit-oriented activities, related to offering products and services for satisfying human needs and desires.

Organizational communication. Focuses on analytical and critical capabilities that enable the interpersonal, collective and total understanding of the organization through a communication perspective. The main focus of the discipline is studying vertical, horizontal and transversal information flows in an organization.

Management communication. Combines the knowledge of business and organizational communications and transfers it to the management context. This discipline tries to explain structural, systemic and functional aspects of communications and to provide knowledge of communication techniques among managers in the internal and external environment of the organization.

Public relations. A discipline and a management function that deals with planning, execution and evaluation of organizational communications with internal and external publics, or with managing communications between an organization and its strategic stakeholders.

Marketing communications. This is an instrument aimed at involving consumers in an exchange relationship with an organization. Each marketing communication is target-oriented in the sense that it directly or indirectly supports the selling of the product, service and/or any other brand.

Duality of organization. Refers to an organization or a group of people joined together by a common goal and as an autonomous social subject at the same time. The second view sees the organization as an independent subject, separated from its members, whereas the first view sees an organization as a collective or an aggregate of individuals joined together by a common goal. From an outside observer's point of view, in the first definition the organization is addressed as 'it', whereas in the second it is addressed as 'they'.

REVIEW QUESTIONS

- To what extent do corporate communications differ from other communication fields such as business, organizational, management, marketing communications and public relations?
- Discuss the meaning of duality of an organization and its consequences for corporate communication management.
- What is the function of corporate communication and what is the relation between corporate identity, corporate image and corporate reputation?

- What should be the main concerns of corporate communication in organizations?

Explore the BMW Group website. Prepare the organizational chart and identify the main responsibilities of its corporate communication. Pick an organization you know and explore in what way its communication with customers, employees, press, financial audiences differ from the BMW communication with different stakeholders.

References

Aberg, Leif Eric Gustav. 1990. Theoretical model and praxis of total communications. *International Public Relations Review* 13 (2): 256–261.

Argenti, Paul A. 1996. Corporate communication as a discipline: toward a definition. *Management Communication Quarterly* 10 (1): 73–97.

——1998. *Corporate Communication*. Second edition. Boston: McGraw-Hill.

Argenti, Paul A. and Janis Forman. 2002. *The Power of Corporate Communication: Crafting the Voice and Image of Your Business*. Boston: McGraw-Hill.

Bernstein, David. 1986. *Company Image and Reality: A Critique of Corporate Communications*. London: Cassell Ltd.

——1999. Corporate communication – the new kid on the block. *Corporate Reputation Review* 2 (3): 279–284.

Birkigt, Klaus and Marinus Stadler. 1986. *Corporate Identity: Grundlagen, Funktionen, Fallbeispiele*. Verlag: Moderne Industrie.

Blauw, Ed. 1986. *Het Corporate Image, vierde geheel herzine druk*. Amsterdam: De Viergang.

Burnett, John and Sandra E. Moriarty. 1997. *Introduction to Marketing Communication: An Integrated Approach*. New York: Prentice Hall.

Christensen, Lars Thøger and George Cheney. 2000. Self-absorption and self-seduction in the corporate identity game. In *The Expressive Organization: Linking Identity, Reputation, and the Corporate Brand*, eds. Majken Schultz, Mary Jo Hatch and Morgens Holten Larsen. New York: Oxford University Press, Inc., 246–270.

Cutlip, Scott M., Allen H. Center and Glen M. Broom. 2000. *Effective Public Relations*. London: Prentice Hall International.

Dolphin, Richard. 1999. *The Fundamentals of Corporate Communication*. Oxford: Butterworth-Heinemann.

Gray, Edmund R. and John M. T. Balmer. 1998. Managing corporate image and corporate reputation. *Long Range Planning* 31 (5): 695–702.

Greenbaum, Howard H., Phillip Clampitt and Shirley Willihnganz. 1988. Organizational communication, an examination of four instruments. *Management Communication Quarterly* 2 (2): 245–282.

Grunig, James E. and Todd Hunt. 1995. *Tehnike odnosov z javnostmi*. Ljubljana: Državna založba Slovenija.

Handy, Charles B. 1974. *Understanding Organizations*. Harmondsworth, Middlesex: Penguin Books.

Ivancevich, John M. and Michael T. Matteson. 1996. *Organizational Behavior and Management*. Fourth edition. Chicago: Irwin.

Jackson, Peter. 1987. *Corporate Communication for Managers*. London: Pitman.

Lewis, Phillip V. 1975. *Organizational Communication: The Essence of Effective Management*. Columbus, OH: Grid.

Podnar, Klement. 2000. Korporativna identiteta, imidž in ugled. In *Vregov zbornik*, ed. Slavko Splichal. Ljubljana: Evropski inštitut za komuniciranje in kulturo, Fakulteta za družbene vede, 173–181.

Podnar, Klement and Miro Kline. 2003. Corporate communication: theoretical framework. *Družboslovne Razprave* 19 (44): 57–73.

Podnar, Klement Urša Golob and Zlatko Jančič. 2007. *Temelji marketinškega načrta*. Ljubljana: Fakulteta za družbene vede.

Putnam, Linda. 1983. The interpretative perspective: an alternative to functionalism. In *Communication and Organizations: An Interpretative Approach*, eds. Linda Putnam and Michael E. Pacanowsky. London: Sage, 31–55.

Reinsch, Lamar N., Jr. 1991a. Editorial: boundaries and banners. *The Journal of Business Communication* 28: 97–99.

Reinsch, Lamar N. 1991b. What is business communication? *The Journal of Business Communication* 28: 305–310.

Schultz, Don E. and Heidi F. Schultz. 1998. Transitioning marketing communication into the twenty-first century. *Journal of Marketing Communication* 4 (1): 9–26.

Thompson, Paul and David McHugh. 1995. *Work Organisations: A Critical Introduction*. Basingstoke; London: Macmillan.

van Riel, Cees B. M. 1995. *Principles of Corporate Communication*. Hemel Hempstead; London: Prentice Hall.

——1997. Research in corporate communication: an overview of an emerging field. *Management Communication Quarterly* 11 (2): 288–309.

van Riel, Cees B. M. and Charles J. Fombrun. 2007. *Essentials of Corporate Communication: Implementing Practices for Effective Reputation Management*. London; New York: Routledge.

Watzlawick, Paul. 1976. *How Real is Real? Confusion, Disinformation, Communication. An Anecdotal Introduction to Communications Theory*. New York: Vintage Books.

2

CORPORATE IDENTITY

CONTENTS

This chapter focuses on the identity of the organization, that is, on corporate identity. The chapter starts by discussing the influence of corporate identity on the organization's success, and continues with an examination of the role of organizational goals in the formation of identity. We present the main steps in identity management and discuss the influence of branch identity. Further, we present several ways of how corporate identity can be articulated and the role of corporate communication in these processes. The chapter concludes with issues of durability and changeability of identity.

2.1 Understanding corporate identity

Many definitions of corporate identity focus on attributes that distinguish one entity from another, give an entity consistency and continuity, and contribute to its differentiation, stability, unity and visibility (van Riel 1995; Podnar 2003). Some narrow definitions, originating mainly from a designer point of view, search for identity attributes mainly in graphic symbols (Marquis 1970, 3; Selame and Selame 1975). Corporate identity is said to be a visual statement of a company, or of any other corpus, stating who and what they are and how they see themselves. According to Selame (1968) and Selame (1975, 1984), the key element of corporate identity was the identity sign or symbol because it was the symbol that represented the basis and the common thread of the complete and consistent visual identity and integrated appearance. However, even authors with a designer background claimed from the very beginning that visual representation must be based on a company's real identity, which is much more than just a symbol and involves all characteristics of the specific organization, including the people that the organization consists of.

Authors who deal with issues of corporate identity from organizational theory and human resources points of view find key identity attributes in employees and the internal organizational structure. Identity relates to permanent conceptions of employees about what makes the organization special, including organizational structure and actions, as a result of group dynamics, organizational culture and construction of reality in the organization. In this way, a company's identity becomes a strategic and management issue.

The communication approach defines corporate identity as a 'sum of all the factors that define and project what an organization is, and where it is going – its unique history, business mix, management style, communication policies and practices, nomenclature, competences, and market and competitive distinction' (Downey 1986/87, 7). Besides corporate symbols, all other controlled and uncontrolled communications are seen as identity projectors, including the actual behaviour of the organization and its employees, which is the most visible sign of what the company is. Corporate identity relates to the overall behaviour, appearance, reality and symbolism of the corpus (Olins 1979, 16). The issues of corporate identity involve a broader management process, through which major changes in the concrete operation of a company are implemented.

The modern understanding of the concept posits that identity should not only be considered from many different viewpoints, but should also be studied holistically. Scholars have concluded that all social actors, regardless of whether they are aware of it or not, have their own more or less expressed identity that represents the reality of the organization. That is why **corporate identity** can be defined as a mix of actual characteristics of a specific corpus that contribute to its uniqueness. Identity characteristics are real, central and relatively constant attributes that distinguish one entity from another. Identity is the reality of the entity; it is 'what the entity really is'. Identity is a strategically planned, internally and externally implemented representation that relates above all to the entity's distinctive and unique characteristics. At the same time, it is an extensive and coordinated presentation of what the organization is, where it is going and in what respects it is different. As such, identification relates to the mutually dependant characteristics of the organization that make it specific, stable, coherent and recognizable.

In terms of a company, its identity is composed of three major components that construct its tangible reality. These are:

- **concrete characteristics**, such as size (in terms of revenue, income, number of employees etc.), the company's products, organizational structure, geographical distribution of branches;
- **modes of actions**, such as applied style, clarity of mission and goals, aggressiveness of strategy, the level of control centralization, fairness in relation to stakeholders, communications;
- **consistency between employees and the organization**, expressed through team spirit, and commitment, loyalty, proactivity and anticipation of employees.

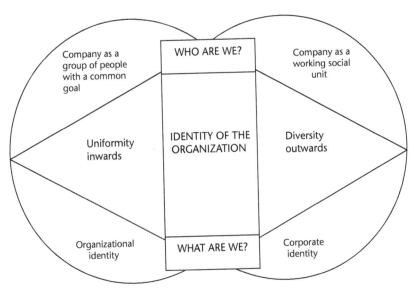

FIGURE 2.1 Dimensions of the identity of organization

In sum, corporate identities are built up from the 'physical', operational and human characteristics of organizations which ought to be closely interrelated ... Corporate identity ought, therefore, to be a tangible business reality: it provides valuable raw material and forms the platform for all messages to be communicated by an industrial organization about itself, both inside and outside (*Topalian 1984, 57*) and thus represents itself as a social actor that participates in exchanges.

Identity of the organization relates to those attributes that make it uniform inwards and diverse outwards (see Figure 2.1). **Diversity outwards** means that, besides their separate legal existences, each company develops its own series of characteristics that make the company recognizable. Corporate identity relates not only to characteristics that enable recognition of the organization, but configures a system that makes an organization unique and different from others. The emphasis is on the identification, articulation and development of unique capabilities of a company; of such attributes that enable the company to develop value on the market, that make the company incomparable and explicitly different from other companies in the branch of industry. It is an answer to the question: What or who is the organization? A company with its own identity, which is recognizable outwards, takes the position of an exchange partner in the relationships with its stakeholders, including the employees. It takes the position of a pseudo-person with whom the individuals and groups of individuals participate in exchange relationships. But at the same time, the company's identity is also oriented inwards. **Uniformity inwards** means that corporate identity provides employees with the possibility of personal and group identification, which functions as a glue that holds together different organizational departments and strategic units, but also individuals and groups in the organization.

2.2 Goals and corporate identity

If warning signals occur in a company, such as a decrease in profitability, over-quick production of new products (and their rapid failure), incompetent management response on bad business performance, and unproductive business meetings (with recurring topics such as mutual accusations, repeated discussions, lack of new views, desperate moves, etc.), this is a clear message that the company has a serious **identity crisis** and is losing its strategic compass. At that point, it is high time that the company started to find relevant answers to questions about its identity. Articulation of identity is the first step that has to be made in order to encourage consumers and other stakeholders to think about the company and create relationships with it that are rewarding for both sides. Also, a (re)consideration of identity must be made when the company enters the market or when it comes to a point where the existing identity does not comply with current trends.

The **corporate identity programme** is, in an ideal context, a systemic approach to managing the attributes and tangible assets of a company (Martineau 1984, 184). It encompasses a number of activities, from in-depth research of internal and external perceptions about what the company and its key assets are, to marketing, investment and other strategies. The management of corporate identity is aimed primarily at gaining strategic advantage in the environment in which the corpus operates. If the corpus is a company, we speak of the identification, articulation and development of the unique capabilities of a company, and of attributes that give the company advantages on the market and make the company explicitly and relevantly different from other companies.

However, differentiation is not the only advantage that comes with a strategically managed corporate identity. It also puts the company in a position where it can clearly see itself with the eyes of different stakeholders and is a basis on which understanding, credibility and support are created among key publics. All of that affects external stakeholders, but corporate identity also performs tasks inside the company, such as those pointed out by Downey (1986/87).

- It gives management the possibility to discover, or understand better, the key factors that motivate the company and its employees to believe and behave as they do. Well-managed corporate identity can help companies implement changes in their organizational culture and to integrate new cultures more easily in the case of acquisitions or mergers.
- Strategic planners get insights into basic values, beliefs and motivations that can be just as important a factor as financial results are in acquisitions or mergers.

Such observations can prevent mixing the water of one company with the oil of another.

- Management gets clear information about the ways in which to communicate competence and distinctiveness across the range of divisions, business units, product and service applications. Reputation from the corporation or of any of its parts can be used to enhance other parts, and thus the whole.
- Employees have a clearly defined, internally consistent and unique story about the company, which is also a useful platform for corporate advertising.
- Human resources managers understand better the characteristics of employees who will integrate well in the company's culture. Such knowledge is useful when selecting new candidates for employment. At the same time, employees are more committed to the company if they can understand its purpose, mission and specialties.

The **tasks of corporate identity management** are to improve visibility, to reflect strategic (re)directions, to integrate the company's goals with the corporate culture, to create a platform for growth and success, to occupy a desired position and image in the eyes of key stakeholders, to articulate key identity attributes (which are the basic elements of corporate communication), to change, link and fortify existing identity, to make stakeholders identify with the organization, to fortify and invest in reputation, etc. (Stone and Heany 1984, 16–17).

It is the company's main articulated goals that, besides its physical, human and technological resources, reveal the company's identity to the greatest extent. The main goals of the company say much about what the company is trying to be. They influence the company's overall performance and shape the company's character. No other management aspect requires so much wisdom and sense than the definition of the company's main goals. **Definition of goals** strongly affects corporate identity and, in this way, influences the company's long-term success (Newman 1953).

In order to avoid confusion and an identity crisis, the management must at all times have very clear answers to the following questions.

1. What is the **desired position** of the company within its field? The management team has to decide in which domain(s) it will operate, which functions the company will perform, whether it will specialize or diversify, in which quality and price classes it will operate, and what the scope and size of the business will be.
2. Does the company strive for **stability or dynamism?** What is the company's attitude toward change? These decisions are about the level of progressiveness, the constant search for new possibilities of improvement, the level of aggressiveness, the extent of power with which the company will pursue its goals, the extent to which it is ready to take risks, and the division of control over the company and its business.
3. What kind of a **citizen** does the company want to be? What kind of philosophy does it pursue in the relation with the surrounding environment?

What is its relation to key stakeholders and the community in which it operates? What is its attitude toward social and economic responsibility to the environment?

4. What is the desired **management type and philosophy?** This question deals with issues such as centralization and decentralization in decision making, qualities and characteristics of key personnel, the level of durability of planning, and the rigour of control.

2.3 Managing corporate identity

The key question in terms of corporate identity management is what the organization is. Only after the organization has a clear picture about who it is, what its responsibilities and priorities are, and how it should be managed, can it express its identity. When discussing **corporate identity management** (Ackerman 1988) with which to achieve strategic advantage, we are talking about identification, articulation and development of the unique capabilities of the company. From a management point of view, corporate identity is simply a mix of the company's unique attributes that enable the company to develop advantages on the market that make the company incomparable and explicitly and relevantly different from other companies in the industry. It is not enough, however, only to manage corporate identity; we must also understand and consider the factors that influence it.

The **corporate identity mix** is, by analogy with humans, composed of three dimensions (Balmer and Soenen 1997).

- *Mind*, which includes elements that are results of more or less conscious decisions: the company's vision and philosophy, strategy, provision of services and products, financial success, brand architecture, ownership structure, the company's history, etc.
- *Soul*, which encompasses elements that are hard to see, comprehend and manage, and are consequences/results of social interactions. These are the values which are characteristic of the company, existing subcultures inside the company, internal image, perceptions about and identifications with the company by the employees.
- *Voice*, which includes uncontrolled communication (direct communication of employees with customers, employee behaviour, and indirect communication) and controlled communication (management, organizational and integrated marketing communication, visual identity and the company's attitude toward important social and economical issues, such as the environment and unemployment issues).

The **corporate identity management mix** includes three additional elements (Balmer and Soenen 1997):

- *Environment*, which considers the political, economic, social and technological environment, existing and potential competition, image of the country of origin, and national, regional and local cultures.
- *Stakeholders*, an element that considers individuals who are members of different groups of stakeholders, from consumers, employees, management, shareholders, pressure groups, media, financial, public, state, regulative authorities, distributers, suppliers, professional organizations, competition, etc.
- *Image and reputation*, where beside the overall company reputation, we must also consider the reputation of the management, of the industry, of partners and of the country. It is also important to keep in mind that different groups of stakeholders have different expectations, on which they construct reputation. We must emphasize, however, that being reputable should not be an end in itself, but only a means of survival and achieving a competitive edge.

Managing corporate identity is a complex procedure and senior managers should involve middle management and other employees in the process, in which, at least indirectly, other stakeholders also participate, such as target consumers (who are desired exchange partners), competition (management needs to monitor their activities and react to them), shareholders (planning the spheres of activity), etc.

The process of **corporate identity management consists of five steps**, according to Ackerman (1988).

1. *Conducting a value analysis* with the key question: In what way does the company create value on the market? Value analysis uses methods such as interviews with strategically important people inside and outside the organization, content analysis of documents and organizational history, market research, etc.
2. *Formulating a positioning strategy*, which means articulation of the unique capabilities of the company and its communication with employees and other internal and external audiences.
3. *Developing a corporate identification system* used to translate corporate identity into verbal and designer language, which is manifested through graphic images, corporate communication, and the processing and execution of services.
4. *Devising an audience management programme* that will strengthen personal relationships with internal and external stakeholders to achieve strategic goals through them.
5. *Implementing and monitoring the identity management programme* to achieve as much as possible in the shortest amount of time, and to measure the effects in real time.

2.4 The role of branch identity

The process of determining identity attributes does not start by formulating unique characteristics but rather it starts with a quality analysis of existing identities inside and outside the organization. Of vital importance is a thorough analysis of the **branch or industrial identity**, which can be defined as a mix of properties or characteristics that can be implicitly or explicitly demanded by customers and other stakeholders, which are common to all companies inside a particular branch, and which a particular company has to have in order to operate competently inside the respective branch or industry (Podnar 2004, 378). This concerns those identity characteristics that are pivotal, common and distinguishing for all companies in a particular branch. Contrary to corporate identity that focuses on searching for unique characteristics, branch identity emphasizes uniformity or similarity among companies. In this book, branch is understood as a group of companies and other institutions that offer interchangeable services or products (Kotler *et al.* 1996).

The emphasis is on **shared, not distinguishing characteristics** of companies within a branch. These are basic traits that give the company an implicit licence to operate. The branch in which the company is active has its own characteristics and attributes, which, together with perceptions of the company's stakeholders about the branch, directly influence the company's identity. The branch is a solid ground on which the company can develop uniqueness. A company cannot competently participate in a branch if it does not meet basic requirements that allow for such operation. Furthermore, besides being a basis on which to construct corporate identity, the branch identity is also the context of the former. Associations about the branch directly affect the perceptions about companies in this branch. The associations are transferred and the results of the transfer are expectations, requirements and attitudes of different publics toward the actors in the branch. The reverse is also possible: the identities of individual companies influence the branch identity. Characteristics that are shared by all actors inside the industry become a standard for any potential company who would like to join the sector.

The role of branch identity can differ according to the specific branch. In some branches, the borders to which an individual company can express its own corporate identity are strictly defined, which can hinder the company from creating a unique identity. In branches where branch identity is clearly expressed, companies may have difficulties communicating uniqueness, especially if goals, strategies, behaviour and communications of competing companies are almost identical. That is why an analysis of branch identity must pay much attention to its content, strength and complexity (He and Balmer 2005).

- *Content* refers to characteristics and meanings that are recognized as typical of a specific branch.
- *Complexity* refers to the number of characteristics per specific branch.
- *Strength* refers to the intensity of the influence exerted by a specific branch in comparison with other branches (external strength) or by individual parts or characteristics within a specific content (internal strength).

It is worth highlighting, however, that just as corporate identity changes in time, branch identity also develops. That means that the content, complexity and strength of the branch identity are always dynamic and changing, and past developments in the branch determine its future character.

The analysis of branch identity, most often carried out by analysing the content of all communication by every actor in the branch, media publications, commentaries and perception studies of different stakeholders, enables us to learn about the corporate identities of competing companies. By differentiating between branch attributes and the distinguishing attributes of competing companies, a company can identify the untaken market position. This position can then be filled with its own identity presuming that the company has the capabilities to do so. Such analysis, in combination with sufficient knowledge of the organization's internal environment, its competences, visions of employees and management, and corporate identity, can be an important factor in becoming a competent and competitive company in the given market and business environment.

2.5 Articulation of corporate identity

A company's identity is simply a mix of the company's characteristics which, when combined, are more than just a sum of its components. An important step toward corporate identity is that the management makes a thorough consideration about the key characteristics for the company in order to make it successful and reputable. It is advisable, though, to make a distinction between the existing corporate identity and the desired future corporate identity (Balmer and Soenen 1999, 81).

To solve this identity-related dichotomy, we can use the **ACID test**, developed by one of the most visible scholars in this field, John Balmer. The ACID test is a tool that presupposes and, through research questions, addresses different types of identities (Balmer and Soenen 1999).

- **Actual identity**: what the organization is.
- **Communicated identity**: what and how the company communicates.
- *Conceived or perceived identity:* how the organization is perceived by its different publics (or audiences) and what its image and reputation are.
- **Ideal identity**: the optimum positioning of the organization in its market by taking cognizance of its strengths, capabilities and environmental consideration.
- **Desired identity**: the identity which the chief executive and management board wish to acquire.

The ACID test should be applied in three steps: the first step is to reveal the five types of identity; the second step is to compare all of the types and search for discrepancies; while the third step includes the analysis of the situation, based on which possible improvements can be suggested.

When searching for appropriate identities, management can use the so-called 'cobweb' method. This means that senior managers form a work group to identify as many possible identity traits. The work group than meets to articulate and rank up to eight characteristics that are key for the company's success, regardless of whether the company already has these characteristics or not. These eight ranked characteristics form axes on which the company plans its activities and communications (and monitors their effects), and everything must be subordinated to achieving and expressing those characteristics. The process of searching for those characteristics is not necessarily an exclusive task of top management, however. In order to make employees identify with the selected identity characteristics, it is advisable to involve employees in the process of selecting characteristics. This can be done by repeating the selection on different hierarchical levels, by using focus groups, etc. The process can be upgraded by using the 'laddering' method to collect organizational actions, identity attributes, characteristics and goals, then asking the question, 'Why is that important to you?' This process leads to key identity characteristics that are invisible at first glance. All mentioned methods can be also used on the company's customers or other stakeholders, or we can use their perceptions about the company.

In the search for suitable attributes, we can also **analyse** the communication of **competing companies**. The content of such messages often directly or indirectly reveals the corporate identity of the sender, and almost certainly reveals its attributes and comparative advantages that it emphasizes. It is important to capture and analyse the most complete palette of communication as possible, and to be aware of primary as well as secondary competitors.

Regardless of the method chosen, or the combination of methods, we tend to select such **characteristics or traits** that are:

- central – meaning that they are as much as possible characteristic of the organization and widespread among employees;
- durable – meaning that they bind the present with the past and will remain relevant in the future;
- unique – meaning that they differentiate the company from similar companies in the branch and strengthen its uniqueness.

Selected characteristics or traits are usually divided into seven main dimensions (Lux 1986).

1. *Needs*: internal and external motives are the key aspects of corporate identity and are a basis for organizational behaviour. Examples of identity traits are growth, security, healthy organizational climate etc.
2. *Distinctive competencies*: special knowledge, institution's unique features and competitive advantages of the company.
3. *Attitude*: philosophical and political backgrounds of the company. This dimension shows how the company sees itself and its competitors.
4. *Structure and constitution*: the physical location, structure and legal form of the organization.

5. *Temperament*: the mode of operation of the company. This dimension measures the strength, intensity, speed of organizational behaviour and how the organization achieves its goals.
6. *Origin/heritage*: characteristics that influenced the company in the past. This dimension shows the relationship between the company's present identity and its past.
7. *Goals, expectations and interests*: the vision and middle-to-long-term goals of the company and what the company wants to achieve in the future.

2.6 Communicating corporate identity

The articulation of identity attributes that are real is a necessary but not a sufficient step. The next step includes the much more important phase, that is, the consistent execution and communication of identity attributes in all activities of the organization and its representatives. It is not enough if management creates an optimum plan that does not manifest in the real behaviour of the organization. That is why all employees should be included in the process of executing corporate identity, as well as the marketing and institutional communication departments.

When **communicating corporate identity**, however, we must keep in mind that it is not permanent and unchangeable. Organizations are faced with the paradox that they must be **actual and adaptable** at all times, but at the same time also represent **continuity** that guarantees security. This concept is called adaptive instability (Gioia *et al.* 2000) and demands that the organization must learn to constantly change and nonetheless stay the same. Companies tend to preserve the continuity of their identities, but they must constantly keep paying attention to whether their identity is still actual, relevant and attractive in view of the changes in the environment, perceptions and meanings. In case there are discrepancies between perceptions and preferences of important stakeholders, and the corporate identity, the latter needs to be adjusted, refreshed and re-actualized. This does not, however, call for radical changes and complete discontinuity, except in extreme cases. The **core of identity** must remain as it is and preserved through verbal and visual signs used for communicating identity; however, the meaning of signs themselves can change over time. Identity is therefore not created in the subjects, but it comes from interactions among subjects. Identity is a social signifier which enables it to relate to itself and to others. The function of corporate communication is not only to transmit corporate identity but also to express it, and to continually reinvent it. What we see as stable, unchangeable, coherent and continued is nothing else than the result of the search for sense, meanings and patterns in our minds. One of the principles of corporate communication is to communicate only such messages that can be proven correct at any time. However, we must not forget to communicate visibility, authenticity, diversity, responsiveness, consistency and transparency, which are characteristics that promote the formation of highly favourable perceptions of different stakeholders about corporate identity.

CASE: HIDRIA

Hidria is an international company working in automotive technology and the air conditioning of buildings. The corporation employs over 2,000 people and offers its products under a corporate brand name in 80 countries. Since the 1960s, the company has grown organically and through acquisitions. At the start of the new millennium, the Hidria Group consisted of different independent companies, namely AET, Rotomatika, IMP Klima, Iskra ERO and Tomos. The companies operated independently on the market, each with their own brands and identity system. Because the vision of Hidria was to become a strong, visible and reputable corporation, known for its investment in globalization, human development, high technology, and its innovative environment and synergy approach, in 2001 the management decided to introduce the umbrella corporate brand Hidria. The enterprises of the Hidria Group, however, continued to develop their own brand strategies, which meant that each of the companies of the group used their own brand names for the marketing of their products and services.

In 2005, the corporation decided on a monolithic brand architecture, which meant that all products would be marketed under the Hidria brand. The reasons for such a decision were analysis of the competition, the need for management simplification and cost rationalization, but above all, the desire to be more visible and recognizable in international markets and to make employees more committed to the corporation. The corporate management knew there were other factors much more important than visual identity for being successful in the market, for example, the content symbolized by the brand and practised by the company. For this reason, the management team decided to articulate and fortify the content of the brand. The management team cooperated with a communication and counselling agency which, in a three-month project using seminars, workshops and analysis, helped Hidria to create a strategic document called the 'Identity of the Hidria Brand'. The agency made a thorough overview of information about the company, organized meetings and workshops with top and middle management, and suggested some basic identity elements. During the project, benefits of the corporate brand, distinctive advantages, personality, values, vision and mission were articulated. The functional characteristics and emotional and experiential promises of the corporate brand were also written down in order to create a corporate story.

The corporation took the document as a starting point for further work. Top and middle management involved the employees in the process of defining the Hidria corporate brand. The year 2008 saw a series of internal workshops for departments for HR development of all key companies of the group, and several meetings of the marketing team. The employees were included in a survey which tried to answer three major groups of questions: What do you think of when you hear the name Hidria? What would you like Hidria to bring to the fore? In which area do you think improvements are most needed? After the studies about corporate identity were made and research among employees carried out, one last step was taken to determine the key values of the Hidria brand. The management collected all values that appeared in any of the research reports and presented them in one document. Values that appeared most often were divided in four groups according to their content; those four groups were then defined as the four key values of the Hidria corporation that would be communicated internally and externally. These values are: responsibility (Hidria is responsible. It respects people and the environment. It operates with future generations in mind); knowledge and competence (Hidria brings competent people together. All its employees have the knowledge, experience, personal qualities, motivation, abilities and skills required in their area of work); innovativeness (Hidria is innovative. It is oriented toward the future and creates new opportunities. It appreciates and rewards creativity and originality); excellence (Hidria strives for excellence at all levels of operation. We value neatness, accuracy, harmony and aesthetics).

Hidria justifies each of these values with its mode of operation, while it communicates these same values to its internal and external publics. For communication with its own employees, it uses its printed newsletter *Hidria*, noticeboards, the company's intranet, training programmes for employees, forums, and the organization of events for employees and their families. With external audiences, the company communicates through personal sales, trade fair appearances, presentations, events, advertising, public relations and websites. The company has set up a corporate marketing service and corporate communication service. Hidria believes that a clear system of values will help it to create a desired image and a reputable network of business partners.

Key terms

Corporate identity. Represents a mix of characteristics of a corpus that make the corpus unique – uniform inwards and diverse outwards. Identity characteristics are real, central and relatively constant attributes that distinguish one entity from another. It is a strategically planned, internally and externally implemented representation that relates above all to the entity's distinctive and unique characteristics. Corporate identity relates not only to characteristics that enable recognition of the organization, but configures a system that makes an organization unique and different from others.

Diversity outwards. Means that, besides their separate legal existences, each company develops its own series of characteristics that make the company recognizable. The emphasis is on the identification, articulation and development of unique capabilities of a company; of such attributes that enable the company to develop value on the market, that make the company incomparable and explicitly different from other companies in the branch of industry.

Uniformity inwards. Means that corporate identity provides employees with the possibility of personal and group identification, which functions as a glue that holds together different organizational departments and strategic units, but also individuals and groups in the organization.

Branch or industry identity. A mix of properties or characteristics that can be implicitly or explicitly demanded by customers and other stakeholders, which are common to all companies inside a particular branch, and which a particular company has to have in order to operate competently inside the respective branch or industry. This concerns those identity characteristics that are pivotal, common and distinguishing for all companies in a particular industry.

Branch or industry. This is a group of companies and other institutions that offer interchangeable services or products. An industry is any type of specific marketplace and can be classified in a variety of classes or sectors. Different classification systems commonly divide industries according to similar functions and markets and identify businesses producing related products.

Corporate identity management. This refers to the process of identification, articulation and development of the unique capabilities of the organization in order to make it successful and reputable. It also involves consistent execution and communication of identity attributes in all activities of the organization and its representatives.

Adaptive instability. Organizations are faced with the paradox that they must be actual and adaptable at all times, but at the same time also represent continuity that guarantees security. Organization must learn to constantly change and nonetheless stay the same. They tend to preserve the continuity of their identities, but they must constantly keep paying attention to whether their identity is still actual, relevant and attractive in view of the changes in the environment, perceptions and meanings.

REVIEW QUESTIONS

- Define the concept of corporate identity and explain the meaning of the 'diversity outwards' and 'uniformity inwards'.
- Discuss the aims and tasks of corporate identity management and explain the strategic role of the well-defined corporate identity.
- Examine the main steps in corporate identity management and the usefulness of different tools (ACID test, cobweb) for articulation of corporate identity.
- What are the main concerns when deciding corporate identity traits?

Explore the Hidria group website. Identify the main identity traits which this company uses in its communication. What was its way in articulation of its identity? Choose the organization of your choice which is active in the business to customer sector and with use of the ACID test explore its communicated identity. Discuss the difference between corporate identity management in the business to business sector compared to the business to customer sector.

References

Ackerman, Laurence D. 1988. Identity strategies that make a difference. *The Journal of Business Strategy* 9 (3): 28–32.

Balmer, John M.T. and Guillaume B. Soenen. 1997. *Operationalising the concept of corporate identity: articulating the corporate identity mix and the corporate identity management mix. Working paper.* Glasgow: University of Strathclyde, International Centre for Corporate Identity Studies.

———1999. The acid test of corporate identity management. *Journal of General Management* 24 (4): 53–70.

Downey, Stephen M. 1986/87. The relationship between corporate culture and corporate identity. *Public Relations Quarterly* 31 (4): 7–12.

Gioia, Dennis A., Majken Schultz and Kevin G. Corely. 2000. Organizational identity, image, and adaptive instability. *Academy of Management Review* 25 (1): 63–81.

He, Hong-Wei and John M.T. Balmer. 2005. The saliency and significance of generic identity: an explanatory study of UK building societies. *International Journal of Bank Marketing* 23 (4): 334–348.

Kotler, Philip, Gray M. Armstrong, John A. Saunders and Veronica Wong. 1996. *Principles of Marketing.* European edition. London: Prentice Hall.

Lux, Peter G. C. 1986. Zur Durchführung von Corporate Identity Programmen. In *Corporate Identity, Grundlagen, Funktionen, Fallspielen,* eds. Klaus Birkigt and Marinus M. Stadler. Landsberg, Lech: Moderne Industrie, 515–537.

Marquis, Harold H. 1970. *The Changing Corporate Image.* New York: American Management Association, Inc.

Martineau, Pierre. 1984. Sharper focus for the corporate image. In *Business and its Public,* ed. Douglas N. Dickson. New York: John Wiley & Sons, 159–184.

Newman, William. H. 1953. Basic objectives which shape the character of a company. *The Journal of Business* 26 (4): 211–223.

Olins, Wally. 1979. Corporate identity: the myth and the reality. *Advertising* 60: 16–25.

Podnar, Klement. 2003. *Vprašanje resničnosti korporativne identitete. Raziskovalno delo podiplomskih študentov v Sloveniji – ena znanost.* Ljubljana: Društvo mladih raziskovalcev Slovenije.

———2004. Is it all a question of reputation? The role of branch identity (the case of an oil company). *Corporate Reputation Review* 6 (4): 376–387.

Selame, Elinor. 1975. Tell bank marketer to learn retail merchandising, use common symbols as a part of total marketing system. *Marketing News* 8 (23): 5.

———1984. Guidelines to identity. *The Public Relations Journal* 40 (11): 35–38.

———and Joseph Selame. 1975. *Developing a Corporate Identity. How to Stand Out in the Crowd.* New York: Lebhar-Friedman Books.

Selame, Joseph. 1968. The corporate symbol at work. *The Public Relations Journal* 23 (10): 80–81.

Stone, W. Robert and Donald F. Heany. 1984. Dealing with corporate identity crisis. *Long Range Planning* 17 (1): 10–18.

Topalian, Allan. 1984. Corporate identity: beyond the visual overstatements. *International Journal of Advertising* 3 (1): 55–62.

van Riel, Cees B. M. 1995. *Principles of Corporate Communication.* Hemel Hempstead; London: Prentice Hall.

3

CORPORATE BRAND AND BRANDING

CONTENTS

The following chapter focuses on the corporate brand and its significance. We present the advantages and disadvantages of corporate brands and discuss the basic principles of corporate branding with an emphasis on identity, the positioning of the corporate brand, brand architecture and the organizational structure of corporate brands.

3.1 Definition of corporate brand

A **brand** can be defined as a series of functional and emotional values that promise a certain experience to its stakeholders (de Chernatony and McDonald 2003). Values are encoded in the name and/or in any of the signs of the entity; their function is to give the brand recognition in the market and to distinguish it from the competition.

When dealing with the name and/or logos or symbols of a company as a whole, we are talking about the **corporate brand**, which is also called the face of the organization. It is a consciously and strategically managed representation of the company that unites and represents the collection of products, services, units and business under one name and common identity symbols. It denotes an entity that guarantees recognition and lasting competitive advantage and is something that makes the company recognizable to all audiences. Hence, this is a type of branding that is based on and originates from the organization or the company. But the corporate brand is not limited to a single company; it can designate a subsidiary, a group of companies or a holding company.

A corporate brand involves, in most instances, the conscious decision by senior management to distil, and make known, the attributes of the organization's identity in the form of a clearly defined branding proposition (Balmer 2003, 312). The corporate brand can also be defined as the visual, verbal and behavioural expression of an organization's unique business model (Knox and Bickerton 2003, 1012). It represents the company (or any other organization) and reflects its heritage, values, culture, employees and strategy (Aaker *et al.* 2004, 16).

A study of corporate brands should use similar starting points as a study of brands in general. Such starting points are a basis for understanding the very concept of the brand, especially in relation to the brand's stakeholders. That is why there are three **different approaches to studying brands**: cognitive, relational and experiential (Zarantonello 2008).

- The *cognitive approach* focuses on the mental processes of an individual, such as perceptions, memorization, learning, formation of attitudes and decisions, and explains the corporate brand as a means that triggers a set of associations in the individual.
- The *relational approach* sees the corporate brand as an active subject and not a passive object. The brand has a constructed personality and acts as a pseudo-person in relationships that a company has with its stakeholders, including relationships of trust, emotional attachment, commitment, etc.
- The *experiential approach* treats the corporate brand not only as an actor/performer that has pseudo-human relationships, but also as a subject that has in itself the means for creation of experiences that are beyond merely rational processes. Those experiences are, for example, aesthetic pleasures, emotional experiences, ethical satisfaction, unusual experiences and a sense of belonging to brand communities.

The core of every corporate brand is an explicit commitment or promise that functions as a standard, based on which the organization or a group of organizations operates and interacts with internal and external stakeholders (audiences). Corporate brands with their visual appearance and meanings function as an identifier, reminder, guarantee and stimulation for desired associations, relations and experience. A strong corporate brand exists when the brand's and the company's stakeholders have clear, favourable and unique associations, relationships and experience, in accordance with those that were articulated and constructed by the management.

The fact that the complete company operates and communicates within the market makes corporate brands more complex to manage than product or service brands. In this context, we would like to emphasize the issue of intangibility of brand equity on the one side and the diversity of organizational activities on the other; the number of audiences that an organization has to address; contact points and other means of communication that need to be managed; the role of employee commitment in order to make customers believe in the corporate brand; consistency among different parts of the organization, etc. That is why the primary responsibility for the corporate brand as the most important intangible asset of the organization lies with the management and, above all, with the executive officer, but cannot be realized if employees of the organization are not committed to it. Corporate brands are seen as a means for achieving long-term competitive advantage in the market and, because of that, are often characterized as a company's greatest (intangible) asset.

3.2 Purpose and consequences of corporate brands

Although brands can be traded, this is not their primary purpose. Basically, management will use corporate brands to (van Riel and Fombrun 2007):

- create a sense of internal coherence and simplify internal cooperation;
- demonstrate the strength and size of the organization to outside audiences;
- strengthen control and increase uniformity;
- decrease costs because maintaining a corporate brand is cheaper than having to support a range of different product brands;
- achieve identification of internal and external audiences with the company.

A strong **corporate brand functions** as a focus of attention, interest and activity of stakeholders in their relationship with the corporation. Corporate brands attract and direct different publics, unite them around different values and symbols that make the organization recognizable and different. But not only different; corporate brands can also be seen as planets that use their force of gravity to attract different stakeholders and be a source of commitment and at the same time enable them to, through identification with the corporate brand, express values personified by the specific brand and create their own identities. Three major **benefits of corporate brands** are (Balmer 2001):

- providing a platform to communicate a clear and consistent promise that represents the brand;
- providing differentiation from competitive brands and companies;
- fortifying respect and loyalty of customers and other stakeholders with respect to the organization.

A successful corporate brand, besides the above mentioned benefits, also significantly influences the behaviour of financial markets, including stock price, attracts the best workforce and provides advantage in the battle for talent. It significantly influences relationships in the supply chain, simplifies customers' decision making, supports synergies among the company's product and service brands, strengthens the unity of the company's communication programmes, creates cohesion and enables coordination among different parts of the organization, and fulfils the growing demands of stakeholders for the transparent operation of companies (Einwiller and Will 2002). Corporate brand is the element on which reputation is attached and defines, to a large extent, stakeholders' trust in what the organization does and offers.

The use of the corporate brand is suggested when there is a communication asymmetry between a company and its customers and other stakeholders, meaning that the latter are much less well informed about the company's offer and activities than the company would like. The use of the corporate brand is also reasonable when consumers feel a high degree of risk in purchasing the products and services of the company, and when stakeholders want to know who is behind the specific product and service and what its attitudes and actions are with respect to current social issues. Last but not least, the use of the corporate brand is suggested when the characteristics of the company are relevant for the purchase of products and services if these characteristics can positively influence purchase decisions and business decisions of exchange partners.

However, there are also some **pitfalls in the use of the corporate brand**. Because corporate brands are in close connection with all organizational activities, it is possible that any mistake in any of the organizational parts can have negative overall consequences. Corporations are usually large systems and possible changes on the corporate brand level consequently demand much effort from the organization, which would stretch the time needed for the implementation of changes. When an organization has a strong corporate brand to which clear associations are attached, this could have an inhibitory effect on eventual new programmes that the company would like to put on the market, in case these new programmes do not correspond to the established perceptions about the company and its activities. If the content of the corporate brand is not transferrable to the company's new offer, this could negatively influence the reception of the offer, and the corporate brand could do more damage than good.

Because corporate brands directly influence the relationship and experience of various stakeholders with the company, we must be aware that it is not at all necessary that the relationship and experience would be *a priori* positive. Corporate brands are becoming common targets of criticism, opposition, fears, accusations, protest, mockery, cynicism or even verbal or physical attacks from various audiences. It seems that corporations and their brands have never before been so thoroughly scrutinized by a critical public. Hence, careful management of corporate brands is even more important.

3.3 Corporate branding

Processes in connection with the formation and management of the corporate brand are called **corporate branding**. Corporate branding consists of the systematically planned activities of a company, undertaken to create favourable associations about the company, superior relationships, desired experience, and consequently a positive reputation with internal and external stakeholders by continually sending them appropriate, consistent and relevant implicit and explicit messages and other signals and by fulfilling its own promises and commitments.

The key to a successful corporate brand is employees' readiness to believe in the brand and to realize its essence in their everyday activities. That is why authors

Hatch and Shultz (2003) recognize the close connection of strategic vision, organizational culture and corporate images as key activities of corporate branding that demand integrated and simultaneous management.

- *Strategic vision* relates to the central idea behind the organization that embodies and expresses top management's aspiration for what the company will achieve in the future.
- *Organizational culture* relates to the internal values, beliefs and basic assumptions that embody the heritage of the company and communicate its meanings to its members. It manifests itself in the beliefs and attitudes of employees about the company.
- *Corporate images* relate to the views of the organization developed by its stakeholders.

It is very important to coordinate all three factors in such a way that they support one another in the formation of a relevant corporate brand. At the same time, we must also consider the competitive landscape in the industries in which the company is active or could be active in the future (Knox and Bickerton 2003).

Scholars and practitioners have developed numerous models of corporate branding, which all have some common main tasks that can be classified in the following categories.

1. The first category comprises activities and content that lead to a **clear identity and clear position of the corporate brand**. Here, we define the basic attributes of the brand and desired associations that we would like stakeholders to have about the brand.
2. The second category deals with the **brand architecture**, including the management and branding of the organization's product or service mix.
3. The third set relates directly to the **organizational structure** and processes connected to **management** of the corporate brand. The processes are a basis for executing brand-strengthening programmes, creation and use of the corporate story, its communication through different media, and integrating communicated messages.

3.4 Identity and position of corporate brands

The most important starting points for the definition of the main attributes of the corporate brand are corporate identity characteristics. To define **brand identity**, a company selects such existing characteristics that are the most relevant for the brand and which have the most potential to mobilize various stakeholders. The identity of the corporate brand relates to those articulated key attributes which we want to come to mind when hearing the company's name. The point is in identifying and articulating visually and verbally those characteristics that arouse desired associations in stakeholders and send them a specific guarantee or promise. Because the identity attributes of the corporate brand are a starting point for all future branding activities, they should convey the company's real identity, values and strategy, but at the same time, we must make sure that at least some of them meet the criterion of uniqueness. The content of attributes must be unambiguous, clear and of such a design to be appreciated by their target audiences.

Some authors (Aaker 1996; Aperia and Back 2004) distinguish between **the core** of the corporate brand identity, which includes the key attributes that rarely change in time, and its **extended part**, which includes those elements and content that additionally explain and articulate key ideas of the brand and adapt more easily to market demands. Hence, if the core of the corporate brand provides answers to the questions of who and what the brand is in its essence, its expanded part provides clear answers about what the key attributes and benefits are, what the brand offers in exchange, and what the brand's tonality, iconography and appearance are. Corporate brand identity encompasses company characteristics and attributes, benefits, commitments, promises and basic organizational values that are also its stakeholders' values. It includes intangible (such as values, image and feelings), as well as tangible elements (such as appearance) of the brand.

Corporate brand identity is closely related to the **positioning process** of the company, which can be defined as the art of creating perceptions and values of the company that the company communicates in order to make stakeholders understand and appreciate the company's efforts in comparison to its competitors. Position in this respect means the place that the brand occupies in the mind of a consumer, or any other stakeholder, in relation to the position of competitors. Efficient positioning does not only express a clear image of the corporate brand in the public eye, but also presents a good reason to enter into the exchange process with the company.

The **competitive position** of a company (Hooley 2001) therefore relates to an attempt at creating and communicating the overall competitive advantage of the company in its markets. Mixed into this is the complete mix of offers and perceptions (images) of the company in comparison with the competition, while the product position is basically determined by a very concrete offer (product or service) based on how the offer is accepted and understood compared to the closest competition. It is very important to realize that the product and the corporate positioning are interdependent.

When companies position themselves on the market, they must substitute the classical marketing mix used for brand positioning with the following elements (Knox and Maklan 1998; Knox and Bickerton 2003; Knox 2004, 109):

- organization attributes that include the company's purpose, commitments and values;
- performance of the company and its offer regarding the company's main activities;
- portfolio of products and customers, who are the company's main stakeholders;
- networks of key stakeholders and interactions with them.

These elements enable the positioning of the company either independently or in combination with other elements and are in close connection with the key processes in an organization, such as the company's own practices in relationship with suppliers, marketing planning, market development and resource management (Knox *et al.* 2000).

3.5 Company's brand architecture

Brand architecture is an important part of managing brands, their appearance and relationships among brands. Coherent architecture of the brands that a company owns and develops is an important mechanism for creating and managing relations among brands. In short, we can define **brand architecture** as 'the organizing structure of the brand portfolio that specifies brand roles and the nature of relationships between brands' (Rajagopal and Sanchez 2004, 236). Brand architecture is the management of relationships between the corporate brand and other product and service brands owned by the company. In terms of management, there are five dimensions of brand architecture (Aaker and Joachimstahler 2000):

- number and types of brands;
- relationships among different brands;
- role and importance of different brands;
- width and depth of the product mix within a brand;
- visual identity of brands.

Brand architecture must be clear, easy to understand and should make visible both the internal and external strategies of the company. Architecture shows the outside observer how the company is organized, whether it is centralized (and to what extent) or decentralized, and gives information about its individual departments, subsidiaries, brands and their relationship with the whole company (Olins 1989, 1995). Many **types of brand architecture** (see Figure 3.1) suggested by various authors have as the basic structure an explanation of the role of the corporate brand on the visibility of the company's offer (Olins 1989, 1995), where we can distinguish between corporate domination, product domination and mixed forms (Laforet and Saunders 1994).

1. **Monolithic structure** describes organizations where the corporate brand is the only brand of the company and has one name, a uniform visual identity and is strongly centralized. Such a form is, in most cases, the least expensive one and can be used to create a very recognizable brand with strong symbolism. Such an approach can be used to demonstrate the power and unity of the organization. This is a corporate brand in its purest form with all advantages and weaknesses that have been mentioned earlier in this chapter.

2. **Endorsed or supported structure** describes organizations that make sure that their integral parts and product and service brands have their own identities, but the corporation and its corporate brand stand firmly behind them.

    a. *Strong endorsement* means that the corporate brand clearly and consistently appears beside the product or service brand.

    b. *Shadow endorsement* means that the corporate brand is not explicitly present beside a specific brand, but some other elements imply that the brand is a part of the corporation. Such a form gives the organization an increased level of flexibility and allows for autonomous management of strategic business units without losing focus on the whole. It combines advantages of both extreme forms of brand architecture, because the powerful corporate brand supports specific brands, and vice versa. Possible weaknesses of such a structure include potential stakeholders' confusion in understanding the identity of different organizational units, relatively high costs due to the investment in a number of brands, underestimation of individual parts when compared to stronger brands in the portfolio, or discords in the loyalty of employees who can have problems choosing between loyalty to their local business unit or to the corporation as a whole.

3. **Mono brand structure** describes organizations that manage part of their portfolio and individual product or service brands in such a way that those brands do not seem related to each other, or to the corporate brand, and function as completely independent entities. Stakeholders do not recognize the company behind them because the primary focus is on the identity of the brand and not of the manufacturer. Such a structure allows the organization to do a variety of different, often unrelated activities, perform in various markets and provides security in relation to risks. On the other hand, it is related to high costs and the absence of corporate brand capital that can be a huge support in times of crisis.

In principle, the brand architecture structures are a continuum where, on the one extreme, there are companies that use only their corporate brands, while on the other, there are companies that manage a great number of brands and do not call attention to themselves. In the middle of the two extremes, there are various combinations of the approaches where either a corporate brand or an individual brand dominates (de Chernatony 2001). We are talking of two opposite poles that are called 'a house of brands' and 'a brand of house' (Aaker 1991).

The types of architecture are systematization of what the companies do, either in pure or in mixed forms, in the process of corporate branding. The concrete form depends to a certain extent on external circumstances; that is why architecture often changes along with circumstances. We speak of basic guidelines that companies consider when planning brand architecture and where special forms apply for strategic business units in order to balance the risks connected with corporate brands. The architecture mechanism allows for a clear, transparent and simple

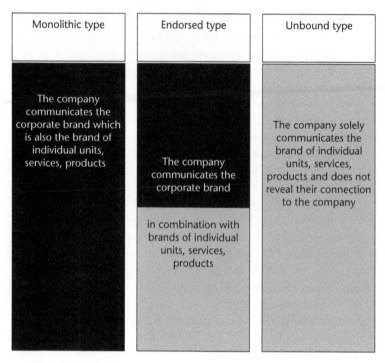

Monolithic type	Endorsed type	Unbound type

The company communicates the corporate brand which is also the brand of individual units, services, products

The company communicates the corporate brand

in combination with brands of individual units, services, products

The company solely communicates the brand of individual units, services, products and does not reveal their connection to the company

FIGURE 3.1 Basic types of brand architecture

perception of brands, thus enhancing brand value and effectiveness. This happens in the process of coordination between opportunities that brands (or services with the potential to become brands) have on the market and market environment in which they develop (Rajagopal and Sanchez 2004). When deciding about the type of architecture, companies can make the selection based on two key criteria: the potential independence of a brand is used to test the specificity or differentiation of a unit and its (potential) value in the eyes of stakeholders, and the financial criterion is used to test the importance of a unit for the company in terms of revenue, profit, market potential, etc.

3.6 Organizational structure of corporate brands

Every organization has to study its identity and brand architecture from the viewpoint of its own organizational structure and processes. Brand architecture not only defines relationships among individual brands but it also sets a framework for future marketing and corporate planning and, most notably, marketing communication. Furthermore, brand architecture also manifests relationships that, in relation to brands, attach to the organizational structure and internal constitution of an organization. This means that brand architecture not only defines the visual identity of individual brands but also expresses relationships and hierarchy among individual strategic units.

In respect of the influence that the corporation exerts on its strategic business units (Kammerer 1988), there are four major strategies.

- *Financial orientation.* Strategic business units are understood exclusively as financial investments that preserve their autonomy and identity. The corporation does not interfere with or influence the unit's strategy and everyday operations.
- *Organization-oriented corporate branding.* The corporation takes over one or more of the management functions in the strategic business unit and tries to simplify the rules of operation. The changes only take place within the unit, while from the outside, changes are not visible, because individual units preserve their brand and apparent autonomy.
- *Communication-oriented corporate branding.* It is clearly expressed through communication that a certain strategic business group is a part of the corporation. This is a possible upgrade from the organization-oriented corporate branding, but not necessarily. There might be only an appearance of attachment, while the unit still preserves independence in strategic decisions and business processes.
- *Branding of the complete corporation (single company identity).* This is the closest form of cooperation between the corporation and its units, with monolithic management and communication, where the most influence is exerted on the units. All actions, messages and symbols are uniform and express the uniformity of the company.

In this context, the **SIDEC model** (van Riel 1997) posits the following.

- The higher the degree of strategic congruity between different activities of individual units of the corporation, the greater the support of a corporate brand to the individual strategic business units and their product brands.
- The higher the degree of centralization of the corporation, the greater the support by the corporate brand.
- A high level of external reputation positively influences the inclination toward the support by the corporate brand.
- The more that managers of strategic business units identify with the organization as a whole, in contrast with lower identification with their own business unit, the more they will support the importance and the role of the corporate brand.

If the company decides to develop its corporate brand, it must guarantee at least the minimum level of integration between the parent company and its strategic business units. The minimum connection that leads to a consistent corporate brand can be guaranteed by implementing the principle of **common starting points** (CSPs). These are central values that function as a basis for any communication by an organization. The CSPs are defined based on the business strategy and can be used as groundwork for concrete communication strategies and tactics (van Riel 1995, 20). CSPs are expressed internally and externally through promises, evidence, communication, knowledge, relations and the behaviour of the organization.

Another useful approach for companies is the common operational system, which can facilitate coordination of communication. It brings uniformity in the mode of operation and activities of identical and complementary functions within the company. Lastly, a cooperative decision-making structure can also help in orchestrating communication. There are several different types of coordination, for example, coordination by one person, coordination by a steering committee, ad hoc meetings, coordination by grouping several communications managers together in one location, and a combination of any of these approaches (van Riel 1995, 163).

3.7 Corporate rebranding

If the existing corporate brand and its contents no longer correspond to the changes and challenges on the market, or if it has lost its relevance in the eyes of key stakeholders and it addresses its target groups with less and less success, if it does not correspond to the actual corporate identity or to some other circumstances, then it is time that the company thinks about adapting, renovating, changing or repositioning the corporate brand. **Corporate rebranding** relates to the disjunction or change of the primary structure of the corporate brand and the process of formulating a new brand. The whole company and all of its strategic units try to move from the existing frame of reference into a different one that is more attractive and actual. In the process, the company must make strategic decisions about how and to what extent the existing structure should change, what the benefits and costs of changes would be, what obstacles in terms of resistance of internal and external audiences can be expected, and how to produce commitment from stakeholders to the new brand (Merrilees and Miller 2008).

The rebranding of a corporate brand demands changes, which can be classified in three clusters.

- *Minor changes*, relating to the aesthetic and designer improvements to corporate imagery.
- *Intermediate level of changes*, which encompasses the repositioning of the brand with the goal of changing the existing image of the brand in the eyes of its different audiences. The changes are implemented by transforming the brand's imagery, tonality or modifying its attributes.
- *Total change* is a process of complete renovation of the corporate brand, often going so far as to completely substitute the existing brand, change of name or redefinition of target groups.

A rebranding of the corporate brand can use the classical steps for marketing planning (Daly and Moloney 2004).

1. The first step is a thorough **situation analysis** that includes classic market analyses, internal and external perception studies, examination of competitive brands, identification of pitfalls and opportunities, etc.
2. The situation analysis is followed by **gaining the support and commitment** of internal audiences for changes. (Internal stakeholders are of key importance for the success of rebranding.) This step includes education and the introduction of programmes that the employees need in order to participate in the rebranding process. Furthermore, a decision must be made about which elements of the current brand will be preserved in the new brand.
3. A very important step is to decide on which parts of the old brand will be **changed** or discarded, and to decide which brand elements will be newly introduced. Such decisions should be made on the basis of a good understanding of the key stakeholders and their preferences. Key elements of a brand are often defined in the corporate brand management manual, which will also include a brand story about the contents of the corporate brand.
4. When all decisions concerning identity attributes, **company position** and new **corporate architecture** have been made, a communication campaign is launched, aimed at internal and external audiences. Very important procedures are those securing a **clear expression** and manifestation of the corporate brand in everyday interactions.
5. The final and ongoing steps are an **evaluation of the programmes** and an analysis of whether the goals of rebranding have been met.

The process of **rebranding** must adhere to the following **principles**: the definition of new brand vision should find balance among existing and lasting attributes, corporate brand values and brand development, in such a way that the brand is adapted to and relevant for the existing situation. In the rebranding process, at least a few of the basic or even marginal elements should be preserved in order to establish continuity between the old and renovated brand. Also, we must keep in mind that the rebranding usually means entering new segments and reaching target audiences that can quickly become more important than old audiences, meaning that the company can lose those old audiences. In general, programmes will be successful if they succeed in using internal marketing, education and communication programmes to create greater involvement from internal stakeholders in the process of corporate rebranding. The renovation process must be done systematically, with all activities carefully integrated and coordinated. A successful rebranding demands intensive communication with all groups of stakeholders through all channels. Awareness of the existence of a new brand can only be raised through intensive communication, but this is still only the first step in making the new brand recognizable and popular (Merrilees and Miller 2008).

CASE: LEGO

In 1932, Ole Kirk Christiansen selected a name for his wooden toys workshop from the combination of two words, *leg godt*, meaning 'to play well' in Danish. Today, Lego® Group is the name of a company with revenue of $1.54 billion and about 7,000 employees worldwide. It is the sixth largest toy manufacturer in the world, only behind such corporations as Mattel, Hasbro, Bandai, Tomy/Takara and MGA Entertainment. The company, still owned by the grandson of the founder, is run by the president of the board, financial director and four executive directors. Those four are responsible for finances and controlling, product development, marketing and sales, supplies and distribution, and direct contact with consumers through retail stores, post and online sales, education of sales representatives, development of new direct sales channels and relations with brand communities. A special department, under jurisdiction of the president of the board, is also the corporate management division, which unites various services, including administrative support, HR management, information services, legal affairs, social responsibility and corporate communications.

The formal mission of the corporation is: 'inspiring and developing the builders of tomorrow', while its goal for the future is to be the leading developer of new games, innovator of new toy materials and to organize modern business models in relation to toys and playing.

The basic philosophy of the company is that playing enriches childhood and strengthens the development and capacities of an individual. The company believes that play is the key process that helps a child to learn and grow their imagination, as well as develop new ideas, thinking and creative expression. The philosophy 'learning and developing through play' is consequently applied by Lego when designing its products (which are sold in 130 countries worldwide). Despite its diversified product line and constant development of new products, the most important product brand is still the classic Lego brick that was patented in 1958. Many other products carry the Lego brand as well, such as Duplo, Lego City, Lego Creator, Lego Star Wars, Lego Power Miners, Lego Games, Legoland, etc. The company is aware of the fact that the Lego brand is its most valuable asset and that it is much more than a logo – it conveys people's expectations toward the company, its products and services and responsibility toward the environment. The company is aware that in such a context, the brand represents a warranty of quality and originality and that the company has to stand up to this responsibility. That is why the message of the corporate brand is 'only the best is good enough'. To avoid false expectations from stakeholders and to give employees a clear knowledge of what is necessary for the fulfilment of Lego brand promises, a framework and core of the Lego brand was articulated in 2008. The framework consists of four key promises that represent the core of the relationships that the company wants to have with its consumers, employees, partners, and society in general. In relation to play, the company promises feelings of joy when building and feelings of pride when the building has been finished. This promise is made to children who discover their potential when playing with products of flawless quality, as well as to parents who are sure that they have given their children the best product for their development. In relation to employees, the company promises pleasure at work through the feeling that work has sense, team spirit, creativity and perfect execution. To partners, the company promises to create value and benefits for all exchange partners, either for users, customers, shareholders, employees, suppliers or for other business partners. Its promise to the planet has environmental and social dimensions, such as care for children's right to childhood, respect for nature, protection of the environment and dialogue with stakeholders. To clearly show what the Lego brand means, its key values were identified: imagination, creativity, fun, learning, quality and care.

Different parts of the corporate brand are reflected through various business policies: Lego products and services, social and environmental initiatives, brand community management, various programs (LEGO Club, LEGO factory, Adult LEGO fans, LEGO Ambassador, etc.), events, and many carefully integrated communication tools, including the corporate website, social responsibility reports and indicators of its progress, education, annual reports, corporate image, consumer publications, etc.

Key terms

Brand. This is defined as a series of functional and emotional values that promise a certain experience to its stakeholders. Values are encoded in the name and/or in any of the signs of the entity; their function is to give the brand recognition in the market and to distinguish it from the competition.

Corporate brand. This is the visual, verbal and behavioural expression of an organization. It is a consciously and strategically managed representation of the company that unites and represents the collection of products, services, units and business under one name and common identity signs. It denotes an entity that guarantees recognition and lasting competitive advantage and is something that makes the company recognizable to all audiences. But the corporate brand is not limited to a single company; it can designate a subsidiary, a group of companies or a holding company. A strong corporate brand exists when the brand's and the company's stakeholders have clear, favourable and unique associations, relationships and experience, in accordance with those that were articulated and constructed by the management.

Corporate branding. Processes of the formation and management of the different aspect related to the corporate brand. Corporate branding consists of the systematically planned activities of a company which involve the identity creation and positioning of corporate brand, brand architecture and portfolio, brand storytelling and communication programmes and organizational structure and processes connected to management of the corporate brand.

Corporate rebranding. This relates to the disjunction or change of the primary structure of the corporate brand and the process of formulating a new brand. The whole company and all of its strategic units try to move from the existing frame of reference into a different one that is more attractive and actual.

Corporate brand identity. This encompasses company characteristics and attributes, benefits, commitments, promises and basic organizational values that are also its stakeholders' values. It includes intangible (such as values, image and feelings), as well as tangible elements (such as appearance) of the brand. It provides clear answers about what the key attributes and benefits of the corporate brand are, what the brand offers in exchange, and what the brand's tonality, iconography and appearance are.

Corporate positioning. This is the art of creating perceptions and values of the company that the company communicates in order to make stakeholders understand and appreciate the company's efforts in comparison to its competitors. Position in this respect means the place that the brand occupies in the mind of a consumer, or any other stakeholder, in relation to the position of competitors.

Brand architecture. This is the organizing structure of the brand portfolio that specifies brand roles and the nature of relationships between. Brand architecture is the management of relationships between the corporate brand and other product and service brands owned by the company. Architecture shows the observer how the company is organized, whether it is centralized (and to what extent) or decentralized, and gives information about its individual departments, subsidiaries, products and services and brands and their relationship with the whole company. There are three main types of corporate architecture: monolithic, endorsed and mono brand structured.

REVIEW QUESTIONS

- Explain the difference between the terms brand and branding. Explore the different approaches to studying the brands.
- What is the core and function of corporate brand? Why is corporate brand important internally and externally?
- Which are the main tasks of corporate branding? When, how and to what extent can a company conduct corporate rebranding?
- Explore the different types of brand architecture and their advances and weaknesses. How, if at all, is the brand architecture related to organization of the company? In this context discuss and use the SIDEC model.

Which corporate brands come first to your mind? Try to understand why. Explore the Lego group website. Look for Lego brand values and discuss their way to fulfil the brand promises. Search for a company that has recently undergone a corporate rebranding process. Explore its brand values, brand architecture and compare it to those of Lego.

References

Aaker, David A. 1991. *Managing Brand Equity: Capitalizing on the Value of a Brand Name*. New York: The Free Press.

——1996. *Building Strong Brands*. New York: Free Press.

Aaker, David A. and Erich Joachimstahler. 2000. *Brand Leadership*. New York: Free Press.

Aaker, Jennifer, Susan Fournier and S. Adam Brasel. 2004. When good brands do bad. *Journal of Consumer Research* 31 (1): 1–26.

Aperia, Tomy and Rolf Back. 2004. *Brand Relations Management: Bridging the Gap Between Brand Promise and Brand Delivery*. Malmo: Liber.

Balmer, John M. T. 2001. Corporate identity, corporate branding and corporate marketing: seeing through the fog. *European Journal of Marketing* 35 (3/4): 248–291.

——2003. The three virtues and seven deadly sins of corporate brand management. In *Revealing the Corporation: Perspectives on Identity, Image, Reputation, Corporate Branding, and Corporate Level Marketing*, eds. John M. T. Balmer and Stephen A. Greyser. London: Routledge, 299–316.

Daly, Aidan and Deirdre Moloney. 2004. Managing corporate rebranding. *Irish Marketing Review* 17 (1/2): 30–36.

de Chernatony, Leslie. 2001. *From Brand Vision to Brand Evaluation: Strategically Building and Sustaining Brands*. Oxford: Butterworth-Heinemann.

de Chernatony, Leslie and Malcolm McDonald. 2003. *Creating Powerful Brands in Consumer, Service and Industrial Markets*. Oxford: Butterworth-Heinemann.

Einwiller, Sabine and Markus Will. 2002. Towards an integrated approach to corporate branding – findings from an empirical study. *Corporate Communications: An International Journal* 7 (2): 100–109.

Hatch, Mary Jo and Majken Schultz. 2003. Bringing the corporation into corporate branding. *European Journal of Marketing* 37 (7/8): 1041–1064.

Hooley, Graham J. 2001. Positioning. In *The IEBM Encyclopedia of Marketing*, ed. Michael John Baker. London: Thomson Learning, 238–250.

Kammerer, Jürgen. 1988. *Beitrag der produktpolitik zur Corporate Identity*. München: GBI-Verlag.

Knox, Simon. 2004. Positioning and branding your organisation. *Journal of Product and Brand Management* 13 (2): 105–115.

Knox, Simon and David Bickerton. 2003. The six conventions of corporate branding. *European Journal of Marketing* 37 (7/8): 998–1016.

Knox, Simon and Stan Maklan. 1998. *Competing on Value: Bridging the Gap Between Brand and Customer Value*. London; Washington, DC: Financial Times Pitman.

Knox, Simon Stan Maklan and Keith E. Thompson. 2000. Building the unique organization value proposition. In *The Expressive Organization: Linking Identity, Reputation, and the Corporate Brand*, eds. Majken Hatch Schultz, Mary Jo Hatch and Holten Larsen Mogens. Oxford; New York: Oxford University Press, 138–156.

Laforet, Sylvie and John Saunders. 1994. Managing brand portfolios: how the leaders do it. *Journal of Advertising Research* 34 (5): 64–76.

Merrilees, Bill and Dale Miller. 2008. Principles of corporate rebranding. *European Journal of Marketing* 42 (5/6): 537–552.

Olins, Wally. 1989. *Corporate Identity: Making Business Strategy Visible through Design.* London: Thames and Hudson.

Olins, Wally 1995. *The New Guide to Identity.* Aldershot: Gower Publishing.

Rajagopal and Romulo Sanchez. 2004. Conceptual analysis of brand architecture and relationships within product categories. *Journal of Brand Management* 11(3): 233–247.

van Riel, Cees B. M. 1995. *Principles of Corporate Communication.* Hemel Hempstead; London: Prentice Hall.

——1997. Research in corporate communication: an overview of an emerging field. *Management Communication Quarterly* 11 (2): 288–309.

van Riel, Cees B. M. and Fombrun, Charles. 2007. *Essentials of Corporate Communication.* London: Routledge.

Zarantonello, Lia. 2008. A literature review of consumer-based brand scales. In *Handbook on Brand and Experience Management*, eds. Bernd H. Schmitt and David L. Rogers. Cheltenham: Edward Elgar Publishing Limited, 188–218.

4

EMPLOYER BRANDING

CONTENTS

This chapter deals with the branding of the employer in relationship with its current and potential employees. It first examines steps in the process of employer branding, a process that is aimed primarily at getting the desired workforce from the labour market. We further explain the different aspects of internal branding, which is aimed at employees. Internal branding is understood as an attempt to raise the attractiveness of the employer, building its organizational identity and competitive organizational culture.

4.1 Corporate brand and employees

Theory stipulates that a strong corporate brand and identity cannot be built without people who believe in these corporate values and manifest them in their everyday interactions with consumers and other stakeholders. The belief that a corporate brand is intended only for external audiences is therefore wrong. A growing number of authors suggest that external and internal activities, in connection with the development of the corporate brand, need to be aligned (Simmons 2009). This means that corporate branding should be directed at external audiences, but it should be based on the manifestation of messages/promises that were directed at employees. Trained employees are the ones who can, to a large extent, recreate the success of the corporate brand with other stakeholders. Employees are more than passive observers who only execute orders of management and present them to consumers; they are active interpreters of instructions and messages, and manifest the corporate brand and its values. That is why employees are an important target group for programmes dealing with corporate brand management.

A company in its role as an employer does not only have an utilitarian contractual relation with its employees, but it needs to develop such relationships that lead to harmony between an individual and an organization and with everything that the corporate brand represents and promises. This calls for a complete management programme aimed at simplifications, focus on priorities, raising productivity, and improving the recruitment, retention and commitment of employees. The company must define its identity as an employer with the same clarity, coherence and commitment that it uses with its corporate branding aimed at consumers (Mosley 2007). Such a management framework includes values, systems, policies and behaviour in relation to attracting, motivating and retaining existing and potential members of the organization, at the same time guiding them to behave in such a way that is coherent with the standards and promises set by the company and its corporate brand. The primary goal of such employer programmes is to make **employees ambassadors of the corporate brand** – every individual who comes to the organization or works for it will internalize identity characteristics of the corporate brand as a part of their own self-image and will live the corporate brand. In the process, the priorities and commitments of the corporate brand become the priorities and commitments of the individual. This also increases the commitment of the employees to the organization, which is, besides the recognizable corporate brand, another element in attracting new co-workers. The literature describes such processes as 'employer branding' or 'internal branding'.

4.2 Employer branding

Employer branding can be defined as a targeted, long-term strategy to manage the awareness and perceptions of employees, potential employees and related stakeholders with regards to a particular firm or company that we try to present as a good place to work (Sullivan 2004). An **employer brand** can be defined as the perception of a company as an employer in the eyes of existing and potential employees, directly connected with the employment experience or a perception of how it is to work in/for the company. It includes tangible (such as salary) as well as intangible elements (e.g. organizational culture) (Bergstrom *et al.* 2002). The employer brand relates to a mix of functional (e.g. development of work-related knowledge), economic (e.g. material and monetary awards) and psychological benefits (e.g. reputation and value of an individual) that are provided by the employer and are connected with it (Ambler and Barrow 1996, 187). In the marketing literature, these elements have been named the **'internal marketing mix'** (Jančič 1990). They constitute a psychological agreement between the company and the individuals working for it. The term **psychological contract**, which is not an explicitly written document, in this context means a relationship between the company and the employee. It involves overall expectations of the employee and the organization, defining what the employment relationship will bring for both sides (Beardwell *et al.* 2004). A distinction should be made between **instrumental**

attributes, relating to objective, **tangible** and physical attributes that an organization either has or does not have, and **symbolic** attributes that are subjective, intangible and accrue from how people perceive the organization and from the fact that they are working for it (Lievens and Highhouse 2003). Interestingly, studies have shown that when judging the attractiveness of an employer, symbolic values are slightly more important than utilitarian values.

The essence of the employer brand is that it emphasizes the unique aspects that the company offers to its employees, such as direct compensation and a good working environment (Backhaus and Tikoo 2004). The basic **objectives of employer branding** are to attract, acquire, develop and retain key human resources (employees) that the organization needs for its successful operation. To meet these objectives, companies use various means and factors that distinguish them from others and influence past, current and future perception of them by potential employees. This should be a carefully planned and managed strategy of how the company wishes to be perceived and recognized on the labour market (Figure 4.1). Strategies are aimed at existing and potential employees and have the objective to make the organization attractive to job seekers. On the operational level, employer branding consists of three steps (Backhaus and Tikoo 2004):

- articulation of the content and key promises of the employment brand;
- communication of the above to job seekers and controlling their suitability;
- internal branding.

In the *first step*, a *company develops a proposal of key values* and attributes that it intends to encode in the employer brand. This process should be based on its organizational culture and identity, managerial style, existing corporate image, capabilities and qualities of current employees, the image of the company's products and services and, above all, the corporate brand. Consideration of these elements guarantees a clear articulation of what the company can offer to its employees in exchange for their work (Sullivan 2002). In this phase, a detailed profile should be made of people that the company wishes to recruit and retain. Next, the company should identify factors and benefits that attract job seekers and motivate them to join the company. It is also important to identify key factors that influence employees' motivation and their affective commitment to the company. We must keep in mind, however, that these factors vary according to different professional and personal profiles. In the next step, the company defines key values that can be found in organizational culture and corporate identity. We must also not forget identifying evidence that supports values that the company stands for, thus making them credible. In the final phase, a clear and unambiguous statement is formulated which should provide reasons why working for the company is a great career opportunity. A good statement is:

- *unique* or different from the statements and reasons given by main competitors;
- *consistent* in terms of content and visual identity and congruent with the corporate brand;

- *relevant and direct*, thus attractive to target groups;
- *real*, meaning that they promise only what the company can, in fact, guarantee.

In the *second step* of the employer branding process, companies find candidates for employment and identify ways to convince and acquire the most capable and desirable human resources (employees) in the labour market for the organization. Communication of the employer brand to external target groups must be congruent with and complementary to all other activities in connection with the corporate brand and its communication to the external environment. The proposal of employer brand key values serves as a central message that is transmitted to the labour market, either directly to potential employees or to agencies that provide services in the human resources market. Using various media, we can focus on different aspects. We can distribute an offer that informs potential candidates that the organization offers more than others in terms of utilitarian and symbolic values. We can emphasize characteristics of corporate and organizational identity, together with an appeal that the company is the perfect place for employment if those characteristics are compatible with the candidate. Instead of articulating the desired personal attributes of the candidate, we can also mention organizational values and what the company stands for. Alternatively, we can simply communicate goals and opportunities that an employee would have if we believe that the realization of such goals and opportunities would be attractive to candidates.

In this phase, it is important to examine whether and to what extent the individual and the organization match. The match of interest is between the characteristics and values of the individual and the identity and values of the organization, as perceived by the individual (Yaniv and Farkas 2005). The concept of congruity between the individual and the organization encompasses:

- the degree to which individual knowledge, skills, competences and abilities match job requirements;
- the degree of congruence between individual needs and organizational structures;
- the match between individuals' values and organizational culture and values;
- the degree of similarity between the individual personality and perceived organizational image.

A number of researches have shown that a higher match between the individual and the organization positively influences the retention rate of employees, personal satisfaction, organizational identification, sense of belonging, productivity, etc. Also, congruity between the individual and the organization directly influences the successful manifestation and operation of the corporate brand, because such individuals are its best ambassadors (Harris and de Chernatony 2001).

The *third step* in the employer branding process relates to activities aimed at the company's internal audience, that is, the company's employees. Company values used to recruit new members should be incorporated in the existing organizational culture.

This process aims to promise a work experience that has similar values and commitments as they are expressed to external audiences through the corporate brand. Processes and tasks that aim to achieve those objectives are called internal branding.

The aim of branding is to develop such human resources (employees) who are committed to the values and objectives of the organization. If we want employees to uniformly express the corporate brand externally, we must first ensure that they understand and accept the brand in a way that is desired by the organization (Gapp and Merrilees 2006, 174).

4.3 Internal branding programmes

Internal branding encompasses the activities of a company that are aimed at getting employees to accept the attributes of the corporate brand on rational and emotional levels. The main objective of such activities is gaining competitive advantage on the market by means of the people who are members of the company and represent its brand (Mahnert and Torres 2007). To achieve that, employees must create behavioural and psychological connections between themselves and the corporate brand. Research shows that companies with consistent, recognizable and strong values are more successful than companies whose values are expressed less strongly (Collins and Porras 2004).

That is why internal branding is focused on achieving congruity between the behaviour and the actions of employees and the corporate brand identity. If the employees understand the attributes and values of the corporate brand and are committed to them (adopt them as their own), then they will, with their daily actions, fully implement the commitments and promises that the corporate brand is making to its external stakeholders, for example, consumers (Punjaisri et al. 2009).

There are many theoretical and practical models of internal branding using a number of programmes, including:

- influencing the employees' association with the company and its achievements;
- implementation of business processes that support successful operation;
- making sure work tasks are attractive;
- articulation and communication of the company's key values to employees;
- balancing career with private and family life;
- issues of remuneration and career management;
- ways to achieve and steer employee participation;
- creating a motivating workplace and employee well-being;
- innovativeness and effectiveness of work tasks.

On the operative level, internal branding consists of (Bergstrom et al. 2002):

- designing such aspects of the corporate brand that are authentic and relevant to employees and articulating the contents of the employer brand;
- communicating the brand effectively to employees;

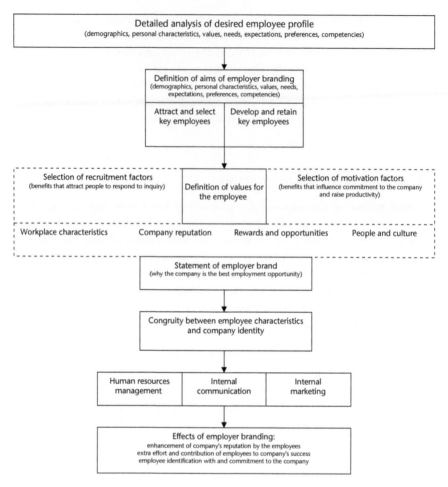

FIGURE 4.1 Steps in formation of the employer brand

- convincing employees of the relevance and worth of the corporate brand;
- successfully linking every job in the organization to support the effective communication of the brand essence so that a simultaneous manifestation of the corporate brand is achieved in all organizational levels.

Companies need to link their departments and employees under a common symbol, so that employees are able to transfer and manifest the core of the brand in their interpersonal relationships and in their interactions with consumers.

In accordance with that, five steps in internal branding of the employer have been established (Berthon *et al.* 2005).

1. The first step is to understand your organization well, including its identity and the corporate brand.

2. Next, the brand promise for customers should be meaningfully adapted to become a compelling brand promise for employees.
3. Standards should be developed to measure the fulfilment of the brand promise.
4. Measures should be designed that will direct all employees' activities into fulfilling the brand promise.
5. Suggested activities are executed and their effects measured.

The success of such activities largely depends on listening carefully to employees, informing, guiding, directing and involving them.

The **positioning of the employer brand** is, similarly to branding for external audiences, especially consumers, a useful step in the internal branding process. Most importantly, a company must create detailed profiles of employees that it wants to recruit and retain. It needs to articulate key attributes that will motivate a quality workforce to join and stay with the company, such attributes that will motivate employees to work devotedly and be committed to the organization. The company must write down its relevant key values, identity characteristics and organizational culture, including the elements that prove those really exist. Finally, the process concludes with a formation of a position statement which, based on those elements, unambiguously declares why the company is the perfect organization to work for. We must find such reasons that attract the best employees and keep them from moving to a competitor.

For internal branding programmes to be successful, we need to pay special attention to the similarity of members or employees, who will represent the corporate brand to the outside, on the homogeneity and strength of values that members of the organization share, and on a sufficient intensity and mutuality of communication between them (Harris and de Chernatony 2001, 447). There are some other pitfalls that can hinder the success **of internal branding programmes**, especially issues connected with the introduction of changes to organizations (and potential opposition to changes), (non)cooperation among departments, rivalry among employees, management style, getting support from different management levels for branding programmes, creating, managing and (non)cooperation in work groups, making sure that all employees are well informed, competent exchange of information and coordination within the organization (including locating and resolving miscommunications), integration of different objectives and strategies, issues of human resource management, getting active support of employees for programmes and, last but not least, the level of awareness and concrete education of employees (Mahnert and Torres 2007).

These factors influence the image of the company in the eyes of its employees. The internal marketing programmes are aimed at raising the appeal and the attractiveness of the company as an employer in the eyes of current employees, which in turn influences the recruitment of potential candidates for employment. The attractiveness of the employer is a perception of benefits that employees or potential employees think they will get if they work in a specific company (Berthon *et al.*

2005). This is achieved by raising positive associations with and feelings about the organization. These associations and feelings are thoughts, ideas and deductions that the brand arouses in the minds of employees, and are a basis on which a lasting image of the company is created in the eyes of employees.

The dimensions involved are the innovativeness of the company and its work processes, good relations between employees and superiors, functional benefits, such as financial and other rewards, promotion and job security, raising employees' self-image, personal and professional growth, and the social and altruistic aspects of business activity. That is why the consistency of the internal branding process and congruity between communications and the concrete situation in the company are of crucial importance.

4.4 Internal branding and organizational identity and culture

Programmes of internal branding are not aimed solely at arousing positive associations and consequently raising the attractiveness of the employer; those programmes also help to construct organizational identity. **Organizational identity** relates to the cognitive and emotional relationship between an individual and a group of co-workers in a company (Zaheer *et al.* 2003). It is defined as the characteristics of an organization that are most central, recognizable and durable for the organization's members (Albert and Whetten 1985; Whetten and Godfrey 1998). Organizational identity is seen as an answer for employees to the question, 'Who are we as an organization?' (Whetten and Godfrey 1998) within a wider social system, of which we are a part (Fiol *et al.* 1998). The central focus is on studying how members of an organization see the organization and themselves, and how they interpret the organization (Hatch and Schultz 1997). It is the feeling of organizational identity that guides an individual's interpretation of the organizational activity and reality and, in this way, influences in the long term the life of the organization and the commitment of its members. The emphasis of internal branding is therefore on how to strengthen such a feeling of identity that is congruent with the company's strategic objectives and is able to unify the identities of various individuals and groups inside the company.

Any discussion on internal branding and organizational identity cannot ignore the concepts of organizational culture and climate. **Organizational culture** is defined as a 'general system of rules that govern meanings in organizations' (Fiol *et al.* 1998, 56). **Organizational climate** is an established way of thinking, communicating and operating within an organization as a community.

Organizational culture is an expression of norms and behavioural patterns that evolve through time in groups inside organizations (Zaheer *et al.* 2003). It can be dealt with on many levels, but there should be basic assumptions at the core of the organizational culture, based on which groups inside organizations function when attempting to adapt externally and integrate internally. Other levels of organizational culture are basic values, behavioural norms, behavioural patterns, artifacts and symbols of the organization (Schein 1985). Organizational culture is all about relations between the visible and invisible levels in the organizational reality. Organizational culture defined in such a way is a context in which the organization's identity and corporate brand form, transform, change and disintegrate (Fiol 1991; Whetten and Godfrey 1998; van Rekom 1998; Hatch and Schultz 2002).

Organizational climate, on the other hand, describes the atmosphere in the organization, as perceived by its members; it is the perception of the situation in the organization by its employees (Tyagi 1985). It relates to the contents, power and state of organizational culture. Both the organizational culture and climate are transferable by nature because organizational culture transfers by learning from one group to another (Mesner-Andolšek 1995, 75), whereas organizational climate transfers through mutual influence and sharing of feelings by individuals when evaluating their attitude toward the organization. Hence, organizational culture and climate have a direct influence on the individual, their socialization and well-being in the organization.

The relationship between organizational identity, culture and climate on the one hand, and corporate brand on the other, is not only one-directional. Organizational identity and culture are undoubtedly among the most important elements of the corporate brand identity because they relate to the subjective reality of values and assumptions of employees and how they conduct their behaviour (Harris and de Chernatony 2001). The contents of the internal brand can be drawn from existing organizational identity, culture and values. In turn, the brand – once articulated – strengthens organizational identity, culture and climate in such a way that suits the objectives of the organization and increases the identification, sense of belonging and productivity of employees. Similarly, we can test the effects of internal branding programmes by measuring the organizational climate and the perceptions of other employees. The atmosphere in the organization is a clear sign of how individuals see themselves and their role in the organization, how they evaluate the exchange between themselves and the organization, and whether a perceived common reality, created through communication of the internal brand, is of such a nature that it creates a feeling of community in the individual and creates a sense that he/she actively helps in shaping the corporate brand and the company's identity. The internal brand is a tool that communicates to individuals and groups within the organization the story about what the organization is, what it stands for, what it offers to its employees in exchange and what it expects of them.

In this way, it directs, in the long term, the actions of employees, influences the company's identity, atmosphere and culture, which in turn brings competitive advantages in the form of employees acting as ambassadors of the corporate brand. The key value of the internal brand is thus hidden in the complex task of coordinating the beliefs of employees with the messages and promises of the corporate brand to its external stakeholders.

The success of such actions can be tested by using various measurements, such as the number of candidates applying for employment, quality of work from employees, costs per employment, retention level, profit per employee, level of work absence, levels of employee identification and commitment, level of employee satisfaction, etc.

CASE: MERCATOR

In 2009, Mercator celebrated its 60th anniversary. Its predecessor, the company Živila Ljubljana, was founded in 1949. In the 1970s and 1980s, with Marjan Goslar as the managing director, Mercator grew to become the largest integrated business system in the former Yugoslavia. In the early 1990s, the company was reorganized and in 1993 privatized through public sales of shares. Pursuing a clear strategy, organic development and smart acquisitions in the past two decades, the company became the biggest Slovenian retailer and one of the largest retailers of textiles, electronics and sports equipment in Southeast Europe. Annual revenue of the Mercator Group is over €2.6 billion. The company has a strong corporate brand and a number of other services (e.g. Intersport, Modiana) and retail brands (Lumpi, Zdravo življenje), and is regularly rated among the most reputable Slovenian companies.

The company has 1.4 million Mercator Pika loyalty card users. In 2010, the company's vision was articulated, according to which Mercator would be the number one choice for purchase of goods for everyday use. Mercator's mission is to guarantee return on investments through growth and efficient operating, and to improve the quality of life in social and natural environments where Mercator is present. The most important goal of Mercator is to offer the best possible services and products for everyday use to its consumers.

By attracting quality and motivated personnel, Mercator wants to offer the best service in a pleasant shopping environment. Mercator addresses over 22,000 employees with key values of responsibility, honesty, respect, cooperation, learning and responsiveness. The department that is primarily concerned with employees is the Executive Sector for Strategic Personnel Management and Corporate Culture, which is a strategic partner of the Board of Directors and advises the Board on questions relating to staff management and implementation of organizational changes. The sector is divided into the HR Department, Department for Education, Department for Communication with Employees, and HR Development Department. One of Mercator's seven strategic aims in relation to staff is its emphasis on internal communication and dialogue with employees. The most extensive parts of dialogue are the annual interviews conducted with all employees regardless of their position within the company. Interpersonal internal communication takes place in meetings, boards, video-conferences, presentations, workshops, forums, consultations, panel discussions, etc. Furthermore, Mercator publicly rewards the best salespersons, managers, internal speakers, partners, while once a year the Chairman of the Board invites the public to his office.

Formal part of internal communications in Mercator also consists of regular meetings with two representative unions and with the Mercator works council. The most common forms of internal communication are e-mails, personal letters of gratitude, reports, plans, minutes, messages on the intranet, messages on notice boards, congratulation cards at birthdays and anniversaries, etc. The department for internal communication also closely cooperates with the PR department, which prepares messages for external communication, because it feels that it is beneficial to inform first the internal audiences about the content of external messages. The most important form of written communication is the internal newspaper (e.g. Časomer, Moj M, Info M, Naš M), which aims to inform employees and to strengthen the desired corporate culture. Mercator issues internal newspapers in five of its international markets, in the respective languages. In the newspapers 20 per cent of the content usually deals with corporate issues while 80 per cent are exclusively local. Mercator runs a special web portal, Kariera, aimed at employees and persons seeking employment, informing them about career opportunities, events for employees, and publishes personal stories and career paths of employees. All new employees receive, upon signing the employment agreement, a Manual for new employees that offers practical information to help an individual to integrate easier into the new work environment. New employees also receive a Codex that defines work standards and values upon which Mercator's organizational culture is based.

Key promises that Mercator makes to its employees are work in a pleasant environment, possibility of further training and education, personal reward, career development, international opportunities and mutual help and solidarity. That is why the company runs its own Humanitarian foundation, its own business academy and other institutions for knowledge transfer, supports associations that bring together employees, organizes sports and cultural events for employees, supports internal mobility of employees, supports a friendly work environment and regularly measures employee satisfaction and organizational climate. Mercator aims to be an arena, where 'everybody can create their own story'.

Key terms

Employer brand. This is the perception of a company as an employer, in the eyes of existing and potential employees, directly connected with the employment experience or a perception of how it is to work in/for the company? It relates to a mix of functional (e.g. development of work-related knowledge), economic (e.g. material and monetary awards) and psychological benefits (e.g. reputation and value of an individual) that are provided by the employer and are connected with it. The essence of the employer brand is that it emphasizes the unique aspects that the company offers to its employees.

Employer branding. A targeted, long-term strategy to manage the awareness and perceptions of employees, potential employees and related stakeholders with regards to a particular firm or company that we try to present as a good place to work. The basic objectives of employer branding are to attract, acquire, develop and retain key human resources (employees) that the organization needs for its successful operation.

Internal branding. This encompasses the activities of a company that are aimed at getting employees to accept the attributes of the corporate brand on rational and emotional levels. The main objective of such activities is gaining competitive advantage on the market by means of the people who are members of the company and represent its brand. It is focused on achieving congruity between the behaviour and the actions of employees and the corporate brand identity.

Psychological contract. This refers to a relationship between the company and the employee. It involves overall expectations of the employee and the organization, defining what the employment relationship will bring for both sides. It is not an explicitly written document, but rather represents the mutual beliefs, perceptions and informal obligations between an employer and an employee.

Organizational identity. This relates to the cognitive and emotional relationship between an individual and a group of co-workers in a company. It is defined as the characteristics of an organization that are most central, recognizable and durable for the organization's members.

Organizational culture. An expression of norms and behavioural patterns that evolve through time in groups inside organizations. Is a context in which the organization's identity and corporate brand form, transform, change and disintegrate.

Organizational climate. Describes the atmosphere in the organization, as perceived by its members; it is the perception of the situation in the organization by its employees. It relates to the contents, power and state of organizational culture.

REVIEW QUESTIONS

- Why are employees important for corporate branding?
- Explain the essence of employer branding and describe the main steps of employer branding.
- Which are the main tasks of internal branding? How and why do companies conduct corporate internal branding?
- Explain the difference between organizational identity, organizational culture and organizational climate. How are these concepts interrelated with internal branding?

Carefully read the Mercator case study. What are Mercator's main communication tools for communicating with employees? Search for a similar retail company (such as Tesco, Whole Foods, Aldi, Wal-Mart) and examine its communication with employees. What does this company promise to its prospective employees?

Collect different employee ads in your local newspaper and compare their contents and in the context of corporate branding make a critical examination. Imagine that you are a job seeker and think of the corporate image of the companies from the ads based on the communicated attributes. Would the company descriptions and offers affect your decision of which company to choose?

References

Albert, Stuart and David Whetten. 1985. Organizational identity. *Research in Organizational Behavior* 7: 263–295.

Ambler, Tim and Simon Barrow. 1996. The employer brand. *Journal of Brand Management* 4 (3): 185–206.

Backhaus, Kristin and Surinder Tikoo. 2004. Conceptualizing and researching employer branding. *Career Development International* 9 (5): 501–517.

Beardwell, Ian, Len Holden and Tim Claydon. 2004. *Human Resource Management: A Contemporary Approach*. Harlow: Financial Times Prentice Hall.

Bergstrom, Alan, Dannielle Blumenthal and Scott Crothers. 2002. Why internal branding matters: the case of Saab. *Corporate Reputation Review* 5 (2/3): 133–142.

Berthon, Pierre, Michael Ewing and Li Lian Hah. 2005. Captivating company: dimensions of attractiveness in employer branding. *International Journal of Advertising* 24 (2): 151–172.

Collins, James Charles and Jerry I. Porras. 2004. *Built to Last: Successful Habits of Visionary Companies*. New York: HarperBusiness.

Fiol, Marlene C. 1991. Managing culture as a competitive resource: an identity-based view of sustainable competitive advantage. *Journal of Management* 17 (1): 191–211.

Fiol, Marlene C., Mary Jo Hatch and Karen Golden-Biddle. 1998. Organizational culture and identity: what's the difference anyway. In *Identity in Organizations: Building Theory Through Conversations*, eds. David A. Whetten and Paul C. Godfrey. Thousand Oaks, CA: Sage, 56–62.

Gapp, Rod and Bill Merrilees. 2006. Important factors to consider when using internal branding as a management strategy: a healthcare case study. *Journal of Brand Management* 14 (1/2): 162–176.

Harris, Fiona and de Chernatony, Leslie. 2001. Corporate branding and corporate brand performance. *European Journal of Marketing* 35 (3/4): 441–456.

Hatch, Mary Jo and Majken Schultz. 1997. Relations between organizational culture, identity and image. *European Journal of Marketing* 31 (5/6): 356–365.

——2002. The dynamics of organizational identity. *Human Relations* 55 (8): 989–1018.

Jančič, Zlatko. 1990. *Marketing: strategija menjave*. Ljubljana: Gospodarsko vestnik: Studio marketing.

Lievens, Filip and Scott Highhouse. 2003. The relation of instrumental and symbolic attributes to a company's attractiveness as an employer. *Personnel Psychology* 56: 75–102.

Mahnert, Kai F. and Ann M. Torres. 2007. The brand inside: the factors of failure and success in internal branding. *Irish Marketing Review* 19 (1): 54–63.

Mesner-Andolšek, Dana. 1995. *Vpliv kulture na organizacijsko strukturo*. Ljubljana: Fakulteta za družbene vede.

Mosley, Richard W. 2007. Customer experience, organisational culture and the employer brand. *Journal of Brand Management* 15 (2): 123–134.

Punjaisri, Khanyapuss, Heiner Evanschitzky and Alan Wilson. 2009. Internal branding: an enabler of employees' brand-supporting behaviours. *Journal of Service Management* 20 (2): 209–226.

Schein, Edgar H. 1985. *Organizational Culture and Leadership*. San Francisco, CA: Jossey-Bass.

Simmons, John Aydon. 2009. Both sides now: aligning external and internal branding for a socially responsible era. *Marketing Intelligence & Planning* 27 (5): 681–697.

Sullivan, John. 2002. Crafting a lofty employment brand: a costly proposition. *Ere-net*, 25. November. Dospono prek: http://www.ere.net/2002/11/25/crafting-a-lofty-employ-ment-brand-a-costly-proposition (9 October 2010).

——2004. The 8 elements of a successful employment brand. *Ere-net*, 23. February. Dospono prek: http://www.ere.net/2004/02/23/the-8-elements-of-a-successful-employment-brand (9 October 2010).

Tyagi, Pradeep K. 1985. Organizational climate, inequities and attractiveness of salesperson rewards. *Journal of Personal Selling and Sales Management* 85 (5): 31–37.

van Rekom, John. 1998. *Corporate Identity, Development of the Concept and a Measurement Method*. Doctoral Dissertation. Rotterdam: Erasmus Universiteit Rotterdam.

Whetten, David Allred and Paul C. Godfrey. 1998. *Identity in Organizations: Building Theory Through Conversations*. California: Sage Publications, Inc.

Yaniv, Eitan and Ferenc Farkas. 2005. The impact of person-organization fit on the corporate brand perception of employees and of customers. *Journal of Change Management* 5 (4): 447–461.

Zaheer, Srilata, Margaret Schomaker and Mehmet Genc. 2003. Identity versus culture in mergers of equals. *European Management Journal* 21 (2): 185–191.

5

ETHICAL BRANDING AND CORPORATE SOCIAL RESPONSIBILITY

CONTENTS

This chapter focuses on the ethics of branding and its pitfalls. We take a closer look at corporate social responsibility, its definitions and the role of society expectations regarding corporate responsibility. Further, we present the features and tools of social responsibility, and what companies should take into account when communicating and reporting their social responsibility.

5.1 Ethical branding and its misuses

In the last 20 years, many companies have started to acknowledge corporate ethics and moral standards and other actions that contribute to the well-being of the local environment in the communication of their attributes and characteristics. For some companies, this is merely a response to growing pressures and demands from various publics, while for others it is a defence strategy to protect themselves from criticism of their corporate decisions. A third group of companies have built their key competitive advantage on emphasizing their responsibility toward society and/ or nature and have set those values as the core attributes of their corporate brand. Such branding emphasizes the ethical commitments of the company and its morally and socially responsible actions taken in the relationship with stakeholders and the society (Fan 2005; Morsing and Schultz 2006; Basu and Palazzo 2008) and can be manifested either on the product/service level or on the corporate level. The ideal is an integrated version of both – moral or ethical brands with their promise that an organization – and with it, all its employees, products and services – will be able to fulfil the set ethical standards and will consistently implement moral decisions to which they have committed. The field of classic external and internal corporate branding involves concepts of morality, ethics and responsibility and offers a different view on the company's operations that is inseparable from society. This kind of (corporate) branding is, needless to say, probably one of the most complex and demanding ones, because a company with such a strategy has to make sure that the brand promise is realized on all levels and forms of the company's operations, while at the same time everyone – employees, business partners, managers, owners as well as consumers – have to believe in these commitments and live by them.

Practical examples show that many companies that have decided in their communications to stress ethical or moral attributes and promises are not able to fully and consistently exercise them or have not even tried to do so. Instead, they resort to fabricating, misleading and even lying. This phenomenon is known by various terms which raise a customer's scepticism and public dislike (CorpWatch 2001). One such example is **'greenwashing'**, the deceptive perception of the environmental behaviour or advantages of products and services a company provides. A similar term is 'deep greenwashing' – companies operate according to the ethical codes, while at the same time they ignore national and international environmental agreements about environmental management or even disregard various laws and regulations. **'Bluewashing'** is a term that refers to corporations that unjustly wrap themselves in the blue flag of the United Nations in order to associate themselves (unjustly) with themes of human rights, labour rights and environmental protection. The term **'sweatwash'** is used to describe companies that try to divert attention from their own factories' practices, ethically questionable relationships toward employees or subcontractors and even child labour.

Such inadequate and highly disputable company practices can refer to disrespecting various forms of responsibilities that companies are obliged to fulfil. TerraChoice Environmental Marketing Inc. (2007) recognized six **false or misleading environmental claims** of greenwashing which have been around the longest.

1. *Hidden trade-off* is based on emphasizing a single environmental attribute and at the same time neglecting all environmental issues caused by the function or production of a certain product. Such claims are not usually false, but are used to paint a more environmentally friendly picture of the product.
2. *Vagueness* refers to claims that are so poorly defined or vague that their real meaning is likely to be misunderstood. Some examples of vagueness are claims such as a product being 'natural', 'eco', etc.
3. *Fibbing* refers to making false environmental claims. Most of these are misuse or misrepresentation of ecological certification.
4. *No proof* is any environmental claim that cannot be substantiated by easily accessible supporting information, or by a reliable third party or 'independent' agency certification.
5. *The principle of the 'lesser of two evils'* describes products harmful to environment or humans with claims that may be true within the category, but no version of these products can eliminate their harmful effects.
6. *Irrelevance* is making an unimportant environmental claim that distracts the consumer from finding environmentally preferable products.

Companies start using transformations and falsifications that are related to ethical branding when they believe that benefits will be greater than the potential costs if such acting is revealed, or when they are not able or simply not willing to fulfil their promises. In most cases, they deny the problems or challenges they are confronted with (Ogorelec Wagner 2007). In such cases, the first phase is usually that, officially, the problem does not exist. The company denies there is a problem by ignoring or even intentionally concealing it. In the second phase, the management faces the problem and tries to find potential solutions. It can either seek alternatives to improve or solve the problem or it just makes apparent corrections to protect or improve its public image. In the third phase, the company realizes that the necessary improvements or even solutions are too expensive. Therefore, it starts seeking to pursue cheaper variations that do not solve the problem completely. The basic problem remains, but not necessarily in its original extent or even field. In the last phase, the alternatives to a full solution of the problem or challenge are possible and feasible – the company offers an alternative product or service, adapts the production process, improves its relationship with the group of stakeholders, alters its business decisions, etc., to resolve the adverse problem and prevents its repetition.

If a company wants to build its brand on ethical attributes, it is clear that this can only be efficient and successful if a very clear response is made to challenges, and the principles of corporate social responsibility are actually implemented. The only warning related to **ethical branding** and based on responsible acting of the company that can be given at this point is that lies can quickly be discovered and that, in the business world, the price to pay for lying is simply too big to even consider it.

5.2 Understanding corporate social responsibility

In the 1950s, discussions on concepts of corporate social responsibility in the framework of management became more intensive (Carroll 1999), and by the 1960s corporate social responsibility was discussed in the context of marketing (Choudhury 1974). Today corporate social responsibility has become an important topic in the business world of first world countries and is increasingly becoming a 'licence' for a company's activities. The notion of corporate social responsibility 'is grounded in the social nature of business and the corporation' (Klonoski 1991, 13), at the same time authors emphasize the role of social expectations toward companies (Zenisek 1979; Mahon and McGowan 1991; Hopkins 2003). The main idea of social responsibility is that 'company and society are closely interwoven and not completely separate entities; the society has certain expectations about suitable companies' behavior and its results' (Wood 1991, 695), and companies have to meet these expectations to ensure undisturbed functioning.

The understanding of social responsibility to some extent depends on the characteristics of individual socio-economic and political systems, based on various cultural orientations. What is considered as social responsibility unavoidably differs from one country to another. In particular, the emphases that stakeholders in various countries give to socially responsible practices are different. Today, the following prevailing **models of understanding corporate social responsibility** can be recognized (Golob 2006).

- *The Anglo-Saxon model* discusses social responsibility in a narrow sense, from the aspect of the company's own interest. The key question arising from this model is whether corporate social responsibility contributes to the company's profitability and competitiveness. Social responsibility is something that needs to be measured in order to ensure the company's transparency in public, reduce negative external impacts on the company and maintain its reputation intact. The Anglo-Saxon model characterizes the system that has long been implemented in the USA and less so in the UK, where the role of the government and the wider community in forming socially responsible policies is becoming more obvious. The USA has also been increasingly following this trend. In addition to the Anglo-Saxon model, there are at least four more equally important models present in the European area that co-shape the 'European' concept of corporate social responsibility: German, Latin, Nordic–Dutch and the post-socialist model (Golob 2006).
- A typical characteristic of the *German model* is the formation of legal frameworks for the operation of companies that are a response to public expectations. These legal frameworks are formed in dialogue among social partners with society representatives (employees) and the public playing an important role. The German tradition is based on the system that gives a vote to every actor/participant in the company and forms a so-called collective discipline that clearly states its responsibilities. Company policies in the German model are acceptable and have a meaning only if a broader consensus is built around them.
- *The Latin model* is partially similar to the German one. It gives priority to formally written structures and rules, but with an idea of a 'higher ideal' of serving public interest behind them, so a company as a cell of the society has to be adequately regulated and controlled. The legal system in the Latin model reflects general public interest, so the most important factor for the company is to respect legal provisions. France is the first state that demanded social responsibility reports by law. Social responsibility in the Latin model is especially expressed in the relationship between the company and employees. The legislation plays a key role in this model.
- *The Nordic–Dutch model* supports the confrontation of opinions, building a consensus and mutual adaptation. This demands the formation of appropriate stakeholder networks, needed for the company's functioning. The company's functioning is not primarily directed toward meeting owners' or shareholders' interests. In Scandinavian countries and the Netherlands, there is a high level of environmental and consumer activism, while at the same time, the spheres of environment and consumer protection are legally regulated.
- *The post-socialist model* is only in its development phase and its characteristic is an emphasizing interest for problems of corporate social responsibility. The

model gives priority to a building of a social state, supporting the role of the civil society in socio-economic questions, encouraging competitiveness and concluding the period of transition. It seems that countries included in this model are seeking the balance between the prevailing Anglo-Saxon model and its tendency toward bigger competitiveness and profitability and establishing social dialogue with various stakeholders, drawing from the 'tradition' when the essence of a company was not its profitability, but its employment possibilities.

The key difference between different understandings of corporate social responsibility lies within their implicit and explicit approach.

Implicit corporate social responsibility is based on formal and informal state institutions that are a tool for attaching the responsibility to companies. Implicit social responsibility is based on values, norms and rules that are expressed through demands toward companies to deal with social questions. These demands are often formalized as policies, regulations or laws.

Explicit social responsibility includes policies led by companies to take over responsibility toward certain social demands. It includes policies that are based on volunteering as well as programmes and strategies led by the company's interests in addressing problems in society that need to be included in the process of corporate social responsibility according to the company and/or its stakeholders. The explicit model does not highlight the power of the institutional framework; it depends only on pressures of the informal public and stakeholders and tries to alter them according to its own interests.

5.3 Societal expectations as the foundation of corporate social responsibility

Corporate social responsibility can be understood as society expectations of corporate behaviour that is socially expected or morally required and is therefore justifiably demanded of a business (Whetten *et al.* 2001). Their expectations, which are the reason and at the same time the foundation of corporate social responsibility, arise from the 'stake' various stakeholders have in a company and who are affected by the company's socially responsible behaviour. The most widely quoted definition of social responsibility states that social responsibility encompasses the economic, legal, ethical and discretionary expectations that society has of organizations at a given point in time (Carroll 1979, 500). These expectations refer to various aspects and obligations of the company to the public. Therefore, companies should make a profit and deliver repayment of shareholders' investments, guarantee fair payment of wages and contributions and also provide good products and services at appropriate prices for consumers. They have to respect the laws and rules of the business game, and act in respect of what is right, just and fair. Most of all, they must not cause harm to stakeholders. Additionally, they should contribute to the community and improve quality of life. Interestingly, the researches stress that in European cultural society, the components concerning non-economic responsibilities (e.g. legal, ethical and philanthropic) are especially important, while economic responsibilities are, in some cases, even negatively linked with non-economic ones (Aupperle *et al.* 1985; Maignan 2001; Golob 2006).

Society expectations represent the minimal level of social responsibility or are respectively defining it (Monsen 1972, 126–127). Each company's action that does not live up to society expectations quickly leads to conflict and makes the company's operation more difficult (Vallentin 2004).

Pressures on corporate social responsibility of companies can be divided into internal and external pressures. Internal pressures are mostly created by employees (Aguilera *et al.* 2007). The other kind of pressure is external pressure, which is more common (Smith 1990; Klein 2001). Companies and big corporations can be placed under such pressure by individuals in various roles, most commonly as active citizens, members of different non-governmental organizations and pressure groups, or as aware consumers. Functioning of individuals is explicitly obvious at the consumer level. Although the majority of consumers are inactive, Dyhr (2003) noted that many at least declaratively favour ethically and socially responsible consumption, even though they do not exert this power in practice. The consumers are aware of the latent power that is a good enough motivator for the companies to respond with more socially responsible practices or products. A well-founded fear of consumers' latent power manifestation by media pressure could persuade some consumer segments to boycott a company. Dyhr (2003) also feels that legislation and the state in general can be powerful motivators of socially responsible consumption. Among other things, this can be product labelling which also encourages ethical consumption. The **socially conscious consumer** is a consumer who takes into account the public consequences of his or her private consumption or who attempts to use his or her purchasing power to bring about social change (Mohr *et al.* 2001, 47).

It would be wrong to assume that the only motive companies have to act socially responsible is in their effort to gain a 'licence to operate' from the public or to handle the risks that all companies are faced with due to increasingly critical and active audiences. Further important motives are gaining a desired position in the eyes of the target public and company differentiation from the competition. For a significant part of the public, linking the company with social responsibility is such an important attribute of the company's offer that consumers are willing to pay more for it, be loyal to it and recommend it to others. The same applies for its employees who reward their company's social responsibility with identification and commitment to the company, but also with higher productivity and functioning in accordance with the promises of the corporate brand (Paine 2003).

We can conclude with Steiner's (1977) findings that at any time and in any society there is a set of generally acceptable relations, obligations and commitments between institutions and people. These relations are based on 'social contracts'. And social responsibility is linked to these social contracts, as it is a set of generally acceptable relations, obligations and commitments affecting companies' influence and power over social well-being and general welfare that rewards everyone in this exchange.

5.4 Implementation of corporate social responsibility

An answer to how companies should implement their social responsibility is offered by Lantos (2001, 601), who says that social responsibility has to be reflected in the balance of a company's activities. The company must balance its economic, ethical and direct social performance, while at the same time balancing the interests of multiple stakeholders. It is a fact that economic as well as non-economic criteria are benchmarks for socially responsible actions, but companies can have multiple objectives (Lantos 2001, 601). Social responsibility is the balance of all dimensions of responsibility and an activity that is balanced by stakeholders' and society's expectations, values and norms (Golob 2006).

Companies have to pay attention to internal as well as external dimensions of their activities. The **internal dimension of socially responsible practices** primarily involves employees and relates to issues such as investing in human capital, health and safety, and managing change, while environmentally responsible practices relate mainly to the management of natural resources used in production and to the production itself (European Commission 2001). Employees participate in the formation of socially responsible policies on two levels. We talk about direct participation where employees participate themselves, or indirect participation where their role is taken over by representatives in the company. In practice, employees most commonly participate in socially responsible practices by cooperating in different internal surveys (e.g. satisfaction surveys) or by co-creating the ethical principles of company functioning (e.g. focus groups). This enhances corporate cultural identity and contributes to the company's development toward social responsibility. Employees can also have a more specific role in the implementation of social responsibility; usually their role affects the internal dimension of social responsibility, for example, work quality, work environment, health and safety at work, but also environmental impact of their working activities. A very important component is also internal communication about employee satisfaction. Employees' roles in the framework of corporate social responsibility can be further defined by participation in these fields:

- setting up ethical principles and standards of operation (employee focus groups);
- corporate governance (employees' representatives participating in supervisory boards);
- socially responsible investment;
- marketing with the support of charities (employees volunteering for non-profit and charitable organizations);
- partnership in the local community (voluntary assistance to local organizations);

- measuring the effects of social responsibility and reporting (independent evaluation of corporate social responsibility by employees).

The **external dimension of social responsibility** refers to mutual relations with stakeholders and the company's integration in its local environment. These are relations and effects on local communities, business partners, suppliers and consumers, as well as policies of consistently respecting basic human rights and environment protection but also active involvement in achieving global environmental and social improvements (European Commission 2001). The study of Bhattacharya and Sen (2004) also distinguishes between internal and external social responsibility and divides various socially responsible activities into six groups according to monetary or non-monetary aid, knowledge and time.

1. *Community support* includes the support of the arts, health and educational programmes in the community.
2. *Diversity* includes assistance in establishing gender and race equality.
3. *Employee support* refers to concern for work safety, job security, profit-sharing and employee involvement.
4. *Environment* includes recycling, environmental protection and environmentally friendly products.
5. *Non-US operations* include operations in countries with major human rights violations and high poverty rates.
6. *Product* refers to product safety, ecological products and their R&D/ innovation, etc.

Kotler and Lee (2005) explore six initiatives that are undertaken by companies to fulfil their social responsibility or to contribute to community well-being.

1. *Cause promotion* are initiatives for which a corporation provides funds, in-kind contributions, or other corporate resources to increase awareness and concern about a social cause or to support fundraising, participation, or volunteer recruitment for a cause.
2. In *cause-related marketing*, a corporation commits to making a contribution or donating a percentage of revenues to a specific cause based on product sales. So, the corporation can attract new consumers, raise funds for the specific cause and strengthen its brand, but also bridge market gaps, increase sales of a particular product, generate close relations and build a strong brand identity.
3. In *corporate social marketing*, a corporation supports the development and/ or implementation of a behaviour change campaign intended to improve a specific social problem (e.g. an anti-smoking campaign or a campaign for encouraging healthy lifestyles). This can raise certain questions, such as does the problem coincide with the company's goals, or can appropriate professional support be guaranteed?
4. *Corporate philanthropy* is when a corporation makes a direct contribution to a charity or cause, most often in the form of cash grants, donations, products

or services. It is important that the corporation chooses a specific cause that is linked with the company's operations and in accordance with its strategic orientation which enables its employees to identify with it. Another important factor is to choose a cause that can benefit from the contributions and that allows the company to communicate about the campaign's success in a modest way.

5. *Community volunteering* is a socially responsible initiative in which a corporation encourages employees, business partners and franchise members to volunteer their time to support local community causes. In this form of social engagement, the authors suggest that a corporation may use it when other forms of socially responsible practices need to be additionally supported by volunteering, when employees or partners express the willingness to help or when technology enables employees to have a simple engagement in social problems.

6. In *socially responsible business practices*, a corporation adopts and conducts discretionary business practices and investments that support social causes (such as, for example, suspension of all marketing activities aimed at schoolchildren). The majority of these practices include internal processes within a company, such as marketing safe or ecological products.

Therefore Kotler and Lee (2005) suggest that a company needs to address such initiatives by developing a programme that includes identification of needs and true problems that are indirectly even beneficial for the company, an integrated approach to implementation, appropriate communication with employees, education, and a definition of goals that will be fulfilled by such an operation.

5.5 Communicating corporate social responsibility

CRS communication is a process of anticipating stakeholders' expectations, articulation of CSR policy and managing of different organization communication tools designed to provide true and transparent information about a company's or a brand's integration of its business operations, social and environmental concerns and interactions with stakeholders (Podnar 2008). We have to distinguish between persuasive and informative communication of corporate social responsibility (McWilliams *et al.* 2006).

While **persuasive communication** attempts to positively influence consumer attitudes toward products or the company itself, **informative communication** merely gives information about the CSR practices of the firm and is not trying to persuade consumers to buy the company's products or services.

When it comes to communicating corporate social responsibility, the saying 'one action speaks louder than a thousand words' is definitely true. Various authors believe that different socially responsible initiatives or programmes communicate enough and any additional tools for communicating CSR are not necessary. Stakeholders' extremely negative reactions (and consequently the high cost of eliminating them) toward companies spending more funds for communicating corporate social responsibility than actually investing in CSR programmes are a sufficient warning to everyone thinking of using communicating CRS to improve their public image. Such actions are visible examples of social irresponsibility that bring more doubts about the true intentions of socially responsible activities and cause stakeholders to respond to such activities with caution. Some authors point out that companies that are already perceived as socially responsible have little to gain from planned communication of this fact (Stuart 2004). While on the contrary, others write that communicating corporate social responsibility brings positive effects, especially in gaining stakeholders' trust and approval, consequently influencing the company's reputation (Morsing and Schultz 2006). However, authors agree that the most effective method of communicating CSR is references and reports prepared by independent stakeholders, be it consumers, non-governmental institutions, other independent organizations, media, internet communities or others. Sponsorship is an important controlled communication tool, while the company's website, public relations and advertising departments are less effective (Stuart 2004).

Golob (2006) writes that the best tool for communicating and evaluating corporate social responsibility is a two-way communication model. Haas (2003) discusses the meaning of establishing actual and simulated dialogues between the company and its environment. With the actual dialogue between a company and its stakeholders, the latter are given the possibility to articulate their expectations and criticism that could change the company's way of operation. Companies should not avoid public discourse or influence it, but rather actively participate and, if necessary, encourage it. However, we cannot forget that the core of communication and its efficiency is not the message itself, but is hidden in the company's motive for such action as seen by stakeholders. The consumers positively react to the company's socially responsible operating and detect it as a well-intentioned, honest, long-term and consistent investment that is related to the company's identity and values, while on the other hand short-term activities are seen as one of the attempts to implement the company's egoistic motives and a trick to enhance sales. In order to effectively communicate corporate social responsibility and achieve maximum impact, it is important that a company communicates a project that is congruent with its identity, activities and with the problem the company is addressing. Personal involvement of employees and the company's consumers in the programme creates good conditions for successful communication.

The presence of the implicit model that demands that companies are extremely socially responsible, but does not allow them to loudly communicate and build their competitive advantage and reputation represents a big challenge for the managers who have to justify their investments in social responsibility. Morsing and Schultz (2006) write that the path should be carved from inside-out. The 'inside-out' approach simply means that employees are the first and most important stakeholders in socially responsible activities. The communication process has to act in the framework of proactive involvement and participation of employees. This is a so-called proactive endorsement, in which employees as important stakeholders

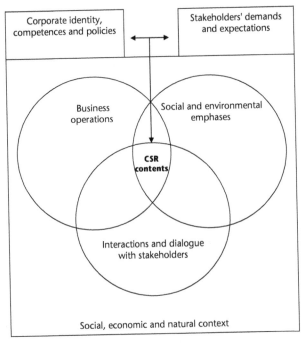

FIGURE 5.1 The framework of communicating corporate social responsibility

express their agreement and support of the company's socially responsible initiatives. Often communication involves activities that affect other groups of stakeholders, such as the local community. The management has to ensure that employees as well are committed to socially responsible policies and practices. The corporate communication or PR department can promote various socially responsible policies, but without employees' active involvement or 'adoption' of the same view, these policies will not be supported in the organization. The policies will not be implemented in practice and trustworthy communication will not evolve. If employees do not perceive their company as a socially responsible one, the company's external communicating social responsibility does not build trust and credibility.

Therefore, the small steps that a company makes in its own environment are of key importance. These may include better work conditions and a stimulating work environment, employees' involvement in decision-making processes, family-friendly policies, etc. If the interest exists, the company can actively engage its employees to act in the community and beyond, but this is not possible unless employees are satisfied with the internal dimension of socially responsible policies. Further, it is important that employees are fully involved in creating socially responsible practices in the company and in the wider environment. This enhances their commitment and support for the socially responsible policy that the company pursues in relation to other stakeholders and society. According to a British survey on human resources, every 'involved' and motivated employee generates about

£2,500 of additional annual profit. In terms of social responsibility communication, it is not enough to merely include the employees in the socially responsible practices of the company; it is wise to include them in the process of communication as well. Besides the media, employees are the most important group of stakeholders to engage in direct dialogue with external stakeholders.

In practice (see Figure 5.1), this means that employees and management representatives are actively involved in the interaction with various interest groups and help create the external dimension of socially responsible practices of the company. While this engagement strengthens their commitment to the company and its CSR practices, it also communicates the commitment of employees to their company, which raises trust in the company among the general public and enhances the company's reputation. In this way, the company can avoid the unfavourable 'bragging' about its CSR practices which can bring negative effects and adverse public responses.

5.6 Reporting corporate social responsibility

An important component of corporate social responsibility communication is also transparency. This is one of the reasons for the emergence of reports on socially responsible activities, and some stakeholders now even explicitly demand such reports, which can be defined as a medium by which information about a company's socially responsible activities and programmes affecting the company's image among stakeholders is voluntarily communicated (Adams and Zutshi 2005). Information on the company's operations is commonly communicated either in a section within its annual reports or as a stand-alone report presenting only the socially responsible practices. Most commonly, these reports are provided in hard copy format as well as being available on the internet (Adams and Zutshi 2005).

Golob (2006) established that **reporting social responsibility** can be divided into three categories which include mandatory, solicited and voluntary disclosure (Woodward *et al.* 1996; van der Laan 2004).

- *Voluntary disclosure* refers to textually mediated discourses about a company's organizational activities, outputs and goals which are not readily observable to stakeholders. The content of such disclosures is unregulated, because they are a result of a voluntary decision of what to report on, usually in the form of standard reports or brochures.
- *Solicited disclosure* refers to disclosing information requested by stakeholders (van der Laan 2004). Most typically it takes the form of a dialogue with the company or interviews, standardized questionnaires, independent reviews, etc. The main idea of solicited disclosure is the diminished control over the extent and nature of the disclosed information, which also diminishes the company's power.
- *Mandatory disclosure* refers to legally prescribed regulations and also other forms of regulation of demanded information that a regulator requests from the company.

In the majority of European Union members, there is an obligation to report on socially responsible practices (Nielsen and Thomsen 2007). In some countries, according to their national legislation, large companies have to disclose information about their environmental policies and work environment. This approach is based on the fact that companies' interests about what and how to report do not necessarily correspond with interests of society and the state and that stakeholders have poor access to information in comparison with companies, therefore legal steps are necessary to ensure that relevant and transparent information is provided to all (Doane 2002).

Adams and Zutshi (2005, 212–213) write that regardless of the communication tool used in communication, reports on corporate social responsibility should be transparent and the company should demonstrate its intent of being responsible toward all stakeholders. A report should include negative and positive effects on the environment and society, demonstrate corporate acceptance of its social, ethical and environmental responsibilities, incorporate details of impact on communities and the environment, and it should be complete. These are also the principles that lead to a successful corporate brand and corporate communication based on corporate social responsibility.

CASE: KRKA

The pharmaceutical laboratory Krka was founded in 1954 under the leadership of Boris Andrijanič and had nine employees. Today, the Krka corporation from Novo Mesto in Slovenia with its subsidiaries and representative offices abroad employs almost 8,000 people. Operating in more than 70 markets worldwide, Krka produces around €1 billion of annual net sales revenue.

The basic activity of the corporation is the production and sale of medicinal products for human and veterinary use, self-medication and cosmetic products, but the group also offers services in tourism and health resorts. Krka's basic aim is to enable people to lead a healthy, good-quality life.

The company's values are 'speed and flexibility' in discovering new needs in the markets, but also in sales, swift acquisition of registration documentation, distribution and in overcoming obstacles. The company communicates its 'creativity and efficiency', whereas 'partnership and trust' in the relationship with all stakeholders of the company are its core values.

Since its beginnings, the company has been closely connected with the local and national environment. The management continually reaffirms its commitment to social responsibility. Krka has among other things committed to preserve economic, social and environmental responsibility of the local environment. Krka demonstrates its social responsibility and related activities by maintaining a caring relationship with its employees, environment protection activities, giving financial support in the form of sponsorships and donations to science, research, culture, sports projects, and by actively supporting some socially beneficial initiatives.

Employee care is demonstrated by the level of benefits and bonuses, which are higher than those set out in the collective agreement for the sector, including remuneration for overtime and standby duty at work or at home, allowances for transport, annual leave bonus, long-service awards, and paying the highest premiums for supplementary pension insurance. Krka also helps its employees resolve housing issues by means of housing loans and the possibility of renting Krka-owned flats. The company systematically employs people with disabilities and adapts their workplaces. It organizes various sport and cultural projects for its employees and rents holiday accommodation, which is also available to retired Krka staff. It organizes 7–10-day preventative health activities and supports the Krka Trim Club.

The company actively supports the Krka Culture and Arts Society, which offers an art gallery, a choir, a drama club and creative workshops, as well as organizing visits to various cultural events. Krka organizes many employee gatherings during the year, including a social and sports event for all employees, the Krka Awards Day, New Year's events held by the various organizational units, and meetings for retired Krka employees, etc.

Environmental protection has been part of Krka's development since the very beginning and is part of all levels of the company's activities. A vital part of this support is the environmental management system, which is in compliance with the requirements of the ISO 14001 standard. The regulations about waste water, waste management, air and noise are also met. The company's Environment Protection Service is responsible for the implementation of environment protection programmes and for informing, consulting and educating employees. Krka is also working with educational establishments and gives students and researchers the chance to work with mentors who are responsible for environment protection.

The company supports various local, national and international projects by giving financial or organizational aid and through employee participation. Krka allocates funds to health institutions for modernization and equipment upgrades by donating medical equipment, it participates in health preventive events and it supports publishing of professional literature. For several years now, Krka has been the major donor to the charity Sožitje Novo Mesto, for people with learning disabilities, and a primary school for children with special needs, OŠ Dragotin Kette in Novo Mesto. Krka also gives donations to the Red Cross and supports the nursing home in Novo Mesto and contributes to its development.

Since the early 1970s, Krka has been giving Krka Awards to encourage young researchers, their mentors, but also institutions, high school students and students. The company is actively supporting graduate studies and is cooperating with universities. In the field of culture, Krka supports the Marjan Kozina music school and the Dolenjsko regional museum, the Krka wind orchestra and the Anton Podbevšek theatre. Krka has also supported the Slovenian Alpine Museum in Dovje and the Lubljana Festival, as well as numerous exhibitions and events in Cankarjev dom. Since 1971, the Krka Culture and Arts Society has been active in the company. The company also helps to mark hiking trails, supports more than 20 sports societies, numerous sport events, teams and the Slovenian Olympic team. All these activities enable Krka to achieve its mission of 'Living a healthy life'.

Key terms

Moral or ethical branding. Emphasizes the ethical commitments of the company and its morally and socially responsible actions taken in the relationship with stakeholders and the society, and can be manifested either on the product/service level or on the corporate level. The ideal is an integrated version of both – moral or ethical brands with their promise that an organization, and with it, all its employees, products and services, will be able to fulfil the set ethical standards and will consistently implement moral decisions to which they have committed.

Corporate social responsibility (CSR). A form of corporate self-regulation and can be understood as society expectations of corporate behaviour that is socially expected or morally required and is therefore justifiably demanded of a business. Social responsibility encompasses the economic, legal, ethical and discretionary expectations that society has of organizations at a given point in time.

Implicit corporate social responsibility. This is based on formal and informal state institutions that are a tool for attaching the responsibility to companies. Implicit social responsibility is based on values, norms and rules that are expressed through demands toward companies to deal with social questions. These demands are often formalized as policies, regulations or laws.

Explicit social responsibility. This includes policies led by companies to take over responsibility toward certain social demands. It includes policies that are based on volunteering as well as programmes and strategies led by the company's interests in addressing problems in society that need to be included in the process of corporate social responsibility according to the company and/or its stakeholders. It depends only on pressures of the informal public and stakeholders and tries to alter them according to its own interests.

The internal dimension of socially responsible practices. Primarily involves employees and relates to issues such as investing in human capital, health and safety, and managing change, while environmentally responsible practices relate mainly to the management of natural resources used in production and to the production itself.

The external dimension of social responsibility. Refers to mutual relations with stakeholders and the company's integration in its local environment. These are relations and effects on local communities, business partners, suppliers and consumers, as well as policies of consistently respecting basic human rights and environment protection but also active involvement in achieving global environmental and social improvements.

CRS communication. A process of anticipating stakeholders' expectations, articulation of CSR policy and managing of different organization communication tools designed to provide true and transparent information about a company's or a brand's integration of its business operations, social and environmental concerns and interactions with stakeholders.

CSR report. A medium by which information about a company's socially responsible activities and programmes affecting the company's image among stakeholders is voluntarily communicated. Reporting social responsibility can be divided into three categories which include mandatory, solicited and voluntary disclosure.

REVIEW QUESTIONS

- What is the basic idea of ethical branding? In this context critically examine the inadequate company practices and find examples of such practices.
- Explain different understandings and models of corporate social responsibility.
- What is the role of customers and other stakeholders in the corporate social responsibilities and what is the role of 'social contract' when determining the role that companies have in a contemporary society?
- How and why do companies implement, communicate and report their corporate social responsibility?

Visit the Krka website and explore what aspects of its socially responsible behaviour it communicates. How does its corporate social responsibility relate to its company mission, vision and values? Name the most socially responsible companies you know, and explain why you think they are the most socially responsible companies. Put yourself in the place of a customer and think whether CSR behaviour and communication of a particular company would affect your buying decision. Would you be willing to pay more for an offer from a socially responsible company compared to a similar offer from a non-responsible company? Discuss whether CSR is a competitive advantage or is it merely a licence to operate in modern society.

References

Adams, Carol and Ambika Zutshi. 2005. Corporate disclosure and auditing. In *The Ethical Consumer*, eds. Rob Harrison, Terry Newholm and Deirdre Shaw. London: Sage Publications Ltd, 207–217.

Aguilera, RuthV., Deborah E. Rupp, Cynthia A.Williams and Jyoti Ganapathi. 2007. Putting the S back in corporate social responsibility: a multi-level theory of social change in organizations. *Academy of Management Review* 32 (3): 836–863.

Aupperle, Kenneth E., Archie B. Carroll and John D. Hatfield. 1985. An empirical examination of the relationship between corporate social responsibility and profitability. *Academy of Management Journal* 28 (2): 446–463.

Basu, Kunal and Guido Palazzo. 2008. Corporate social responsibility: a process model of sensemaking. *Academy of Management Review* 33 (1): 122–136.

Bhattacharya, C. B. and Sankar Sen. 2004. Doing better at doing good: when, why, and how consumers respond to corporate social initiatives. *California Management Review* 47 (1): 9–24.

Carroll, Archie B. 1979. A three-dimensional conceptual model of corporate performance. *Academy of Management Review* 4 (4): 497–505.

——1999. Corporate social responsibility. *Business and Society* 38 (3): 268–295.

Choudhury, Pravat K. 1974. Social responsibility: an alternate strategy of marketing. *Journal of the Academy of Marketing Science* 2 (1/4): 213–222.

CorpWatch. 2001. *Greenwash Fact Sheet*. Available at: http://www.corpwatch.org/article.php?id=242 (29 November 2007).

Doane, Deborah. 2002. Market failure: the case for mandatory social and environmental reporting. *Paper presented to IPPR seminar: the transparent company*, 20 March. Available at: http://www.hapinternational.org/pool/files/doanepaper1.pdf (5 October 2010).

Dyhr,Villy. 2003. CSR as a competitive factor in a consumer perspective. In *Corporate Values and Responsibility – the Case of Denmark*, eds. Mette Morsing and Christina Thyssen. Samfundslitteratur: Frederiksberg. Available at: http://www.fbr.dk/debat/alle/csr-book (5 May 2005).

European Commission. 2001. GREEN PAPER Promoting a European framework for Corporate Social Responsibility. Presented by the Commission. Brussels. Available at: http://eur-lex.europa.eu/LexUriServ/LexUriServ.do?uri=COM:2001:0366:FIN:en:PDF.

Fan, Ying. 2005. Ethical branding and corporate reputation. *Corporate Communications: An International Journal* 10 (4): 341–350.

Golob, Urša. 2006. *Posameznik in družbena odgovornost podjetij v času transformacije slovenske družbe*. Doktorska disertacija. Ljubljana: Fakulteta za družbene vede.

Haas,Tanni. 2003. Toward an 'ethic of futurity'. *Management Communication Quarterly* 16 (4): 612–617.

Hopkins, Michael. 2003. *The Planetary Bargain: Corporate Social Responsibility Matters*. London: Earthscan.

Klein, Naomi. 2001. *No Logo*. London: Flamingo.

Klonoski, Richard J. 1991. Foundational considerations in the corporate social responsibility debate. *Business Horizons* 34 (4): 9–18.

Kotler, Philip and Nancy Lee. 2005. *Corporate Social Responsibility*. Hoboken, NJ: John Wiley and Sons, Inc.

Lantos, Geoffrey P. 2001. The boundaries of strategic corporate social responsibility. *Journal of Consumer Marketing* 18 (7): 595–630.

Mahon, John F. and Richard A. McGowan. 1991. Searching for the common good: a process oriented approach. *Business Horizons* 34 (4): 79–87.

Maignan, Isabelle. 2001. Consumers' perceptions of corporate social responsibilities: a cross-cultural comparison. *Journal of Business Ethics* 30 (1): 57–72.

McWilliams, Abigail, Donald S. Siegel and Patrick M.Wright. 2006. Corporate social responsibility: strategic implications. *Journal of Management Studies* 43 (1): 1–18.

Mohr, Lois A., Deborah J. Webb and Katherine E Harris. 2001. Do consumers expect companies to be socially responsible? The impact of corporate social responsibility on buying behaviour. *Journal of Consumer Affairs* 35 (1): 45–73.

Monsen, Joseph R. 1972. Social responsibility and the corporation: alternatives for the future of capitalism. *Journal of Economic Issues* 6 (1): 125–141.

Morsing, Mette and Majken Schultz. 2006. Stakeholder communication strategies. In *Strategic CSR Communication*, eds. Mette Morsing and Suzanne C. Beckmann. Copenhagen: DJOF Publishing, 135–160.

Nielsen, Ellerup Anne and Christa Thomsen. 2007. Reporting CSR – what and how to say it? *Corporate Communications: An International Journal* 12 (1): 25–40.

Ogorelec Wagner, Vida. 2007. *Climate Change and CSR. Predavanje na mednarodni konferenci o družbeni odgovornosti podjetij, Trendi na področju družbene odgovornosti 2007.* Ljubljana: Gospodarska zbornica Slovenije.

Paine, Lynn Sharp. 2003. *Value Shift: Why Companies Must Merge Social and Financial Imperatives to Achieve Superior Performance.* New York: McGraw-Hill.

Podnar, Klement. 2008. Guest editorial. Communicating corporate social responsibility. *Journal of Marketing Communications* 14 (2): 75–81.

Smith, Craig N. 1990. *Morality and the Market: Consumer Pressure for Corporate Accountability.* London: Routledge.

Steiner, George A. 1977. Social policies for business. In *Managing Corporate Social Responsibility*, ed. Archie B. Carroll. Boston: Little, Brown, 319–326.

Stuart, Helen. 2004. *Risky Business: Communicating Corporate Social Responsibility.* Available at: http://smib.vuw.ac.nz:8081/WWW/ANZMAC2004/CDsite/papers/Stuart1.PDF (12 October 2010).

TerraChoice Environmental Marketing Inc. 2007. *The Six Sins of Greenwashing – A Study of Environmental Claims in North American Consumer Markets.* Available at: http://www.corpwatch.org/article.php?id=14753 (15 January 2008).

Vallentin, Steen. 2004. *Corporate Social Responsibilities and Public Opinion.* EUPERA/DGPuK Conference Public Relations and the Public Sphere, 23–26 September: Leipzig.

van der Laan, Sandra L. 2004. The role of theory in explaining motivation for corporate social disclosures: voluntary disclosures vs. 'solicited' disclosures. *Paper accepted for the Fourth Asia Pacific interdisciplinary research in accounting conference*, 4–6 July. Available at: https://www.commerce.adelaide.edu.au/research/aaaj/apira_2004/Final%20Papers/1193-van%20der%20Laan.pdf (9 October 2010).

Whetten, David Allred, Gordon Rands and Paul Godfrey. 2001. What are the responsibilities of business to society? In *Handbook of Strategy and Management*, eds. Andrew Pettigrew, Howard Thomas and Richard Whittington. London: Sage, 373–408.

Wood, Donna J. 1991. Corporate social performance revisited. *Academy of Management Review* 16 (4): 691–718.

Woodward, David G., Pam Edwards and Frank Birkin. 1996. Organizational legitimacy and stakeholder information provision. *British Journal of Management* 7 (4): 329–347.

Zenisek, Thomas J. 1979. Corporate social responsibility: a conceptualisation based on organizational literature. *Academy of Management Review* 4 (3): 359–368.

6

STAKEHOLDER MANAGEMENT AND COMMUNICATIONS

CONTENTS

This chapter focuses on narrow and broad definitions of the stakeholder concept. It highlights the most common classifications of stakeholders, and factors underlying such classifications. It explains the basic strategies of stakeholder management and deals with possible stakeholder activities in relation to the organization. The chapter concludes with an explanation of objectives, principles and methods of communication with stakeholders.

6.1 Stakeholder paradigm

The stakeholder theory addresses mainly the spectrum of connections, communications, exchanges and relationships of a specific corpus with its environment and subjects in this environment. Important to the concept of stakeholder management is the organization's need to continuously engage and communicate with different individuals, groups and/or institutions and to systematically pay attention to interests and relationships between the organization and its stakeholders, and make sure that these are balanced and acceptable (Cooper 2003, 232). The basic question is: Which of the groups beside shareholders and consumers in accordance with its 'stake' deserve the attention of the management in order to secure benefits for the organization?

There is no unified understanding of stakeholders in the theory. Some authors define as stakeholders only such individuals and groups who have direct relevance to the firm's core economic interests, or who are necessary for the firm's survival, or those who have placed something at risk in relationship with the firm, or are contractors or participants in exchange relationships (Mitchell *et al.* 1997, 857). This includes above all people whose support is essential for the organization to exist (Bowie 1988). Definitions that view stakeholders in a broader context expand relationships based on economy to moral commitments and relations also in the sense of the just distribution of the harmful and positive effects of organizational activities (Donaldson and Preston 1995). In this sense, the stakeholders of an organization are everybody who has or could have any interest to the organization, or the organization has or could have an interest in them, or there could be a potential influence between the two (Gray et al. 1996). This does not only include people, groups and institutions, but also other living beings, the natural environment and even the offspring (Starik 1994). These broad definitions originate in the actual wide complexity of environments in which organizations operate.

On the one hand, if stakeholders are defined in a narrow sense, then an organization enters in relationships and communicates with them in a limited and selective manner, according to available resources. On the other hand, an understanding of the concept in a broad sense puts the links between a company and its stakeholders in a very wide setting, because the company can influence almost anybody and almost anybody can influence the company (Mitchell et al. 1997), which corresponds to the actual complexity of environments in which organizations operate.

It seems that the most common **definition of stakeholders** in the literature, the one that defines stakeholders as 'groups and individuals who can affect, or are affected by, the achievement of an organization's mission' (Freeman 1984, 46) is a compromise between narrow and broad definitions and suitability for application in the corporate communication framework.

6.2 Public and public sphere

It is interesting that in the same year that Freeman (1984) published his prominent stakeholder approach to strategic management within the public relations field, Grunig and Hunt (1984) also published their book Managing Public Relations, in which they established a very similar term **publics** to be used in the communications context. The public is defined as a group of people that face a common problem, recognize the problem and organize themselves in order to solve the problem. The actors are involved in the problem, know the problem and there is nothing that would hinder them from solving the problem. For them, the process of mutuality among the interest parties is of key importance. Although Grunig (1992) later adopted the stakeholder concept, he nonetheless made a distinction between stakeholder and public, which is very important for communication planning. Individuals and groups are stakeholders because they are in a category affected by decisions of an organization or if their decisions affect the organization. When and only after they become more aware and active toward the organization and particular issue can they be described as publics (Grunig and Repper 1992, 125). It is important to note that, from the corporate communication point of view, not all stakeholders are also public; they only become public when they develop an active relationship to the company (Jančič 1999, 75). However, to get the whole picture of representing interests and making opinions, we must also consider the broader definition, which can be found in the **public sphere** concept (Ihlen 2008), and where public is defined as a complex network of people and organizations at which communications of social subjects are directed, where the public opinion is formulated, and where the actions of social actors are legitimized.

If we understand and, more importantly, follow the public sphere, this enables identification of a third group that does not coincide with any of the stakeholder groups, nor do they have the characteristics of the public. Within the public sphere, the social consensus is formulated, with (at least a latent) cooperation of people who do not constitute the public or any of the stakeholder groups. This does not mean, however, that they cannot become one or the other in the future if drawn by a specific public theme. The nature of relationships between stakeholders and an organization is dynamic, changeable in time and space, and inherent to the organization (Podnar and Jančič 2006).

Jančič (1999) ascertains that not all publics are equally important for the organization, as some are active and others passive or latently active. In a model that explains the levels of equivalent exchange between the company and its stakeholders, Jančič defines 24 groups that can act as stakeholders of a company. These 24 groups are divided into three categories, according to the type of exchange or relationship with the company. The first category involves stakeholders, with whom the exchange is inevitable, the second one includes groups, with whom the exchange is necessary for a company to meet its objectives and mission, whereas the third category consists of stakeholders, with whom exchange or relationship is desired, and can, in some cases, be very beneficial (Jančič 1999, 77–78).

6.3 Categories of stakeholders

A study by Podnar and Jančič (2006) established that various groups of stakeholders are not equally important for a company, but can be classified according to their importance. For the management of corporate communication, it is therefore necessary to identify the key stakeholders and publics. The literature offers numerous attempts to define criteria that would help with the classification. A distinction has been made between primary and secondary stakeholders, where **primary stakeholders** are considered as groups or individuals whose lasting support is essential for the existence of the company, while **secondary stakeholders** are all others (Cooper 2003). There is also a distinction between voluntary and involuntary stakeholders (Clarkson 1995), saying that **voluntary stakeholders**, such as investors, shareholders, employees, consumers and suppliers, decide to 'have their stake' in the company and can break off their connection with the company, while **involuntary stakeholders**, such as local communities, environment or future generations, do not have a choice of entering into or terminating their relationships with an organization.

Wheeler and Sillanpää (1997) present four categories of stakeholders based on whether they are primary or secondary, and whether they have social or non-social interests.

- *Primary stakeholders with social interest* (shareholders and investors, managers and employees, consumers, local community, suppliers and other business partners).
- *Secondary stakeholders with social interest* (state, regulatory bodies, social pressure groups, civil society, media, opinion leaders, competition).
- *Primary stakeholders with non-social interest* (environment, future generations, animals).
- *Secondary stakeholders with non-social interest* (environmental pressure groups, animal welfare organizations).

Friedman and Miles (2002) constructed a model that presents possible relations between an organization and its stakeholders, in which they claim that relations can be necessary and contingent, while the organization and its stakeholders can be either compatible or incompatible. A necessary and compatible relationship is a defensive relationship. In case it is compatible but only contingent, the relationship is opportunistic. If the sides are incompatible, the relationship between them is a compromise if the relationship is necessary and elimination of the relationship is contingent (Friedman and Miles 2002, 7). The authors stress that their model takes into consideration that relationships between companies and stakeholders can change. Stakeholders move from one group to another if they are influenced by different external and unforeseeable factors (Friedman and Miles 2002, 11).

6.4 Distribution of power among stakeholders

Manktelow (2003) suggests dividing different stakeholders according to their power and interest they have in relation to an organization. This is also the key factor in the literature, according to which stakeholders should be classified. The **power** is defined as a relationship between social actors, where one actor causes an activity of the other that would otherwise not have taken place. Thus, according to the criterion of power, we can distinguish four groups of stakeholders, with which companies communicate in different ways: stakeholders with great power and great interest, stakeholders with great power and small interest, stakeholders with small power and great interest, and stakeholders with small power and small interest.

When discussing the power of individuals and groups, it is necessary from the management point of view to know the source of power. Yukl (1998) suggests the following sources.

- Power that comes with a certain formal position. This is formal authority that draws its power from the control over rewards and penalties, control over information and control over the political, social, technological or organizational environment.

- Personal power that is based on personality and interpersonal relationships. This is an authority that draws its power from expert knowledge, friendship, commitment, charisma, etc.
- Political power that is based on a formal distribution of power or on a temporary cooperation agreement in order to pursue common interests. This type of authority draws its power from control over decisions and decision-making processes, choices and institutionalization.

In close connections to the sources of power are the types of power, as classified by Greene and Elfers (1999, 178).

- Coercive power is a formal power based on the fear of punishment.
- Acquaintances bring power based on the inclusion in social networks of influential individuals and groups; this is a combination of personal and political powers.
- Reward power is a formal power in which someone is expected to cooperate and take up suggestions from the other party in return for rewards.
- Legitimate power is based on an organizational or hierarchical scale and is a combination of formal and political powers.
- Referent power is an individual's power to attract others and is based on personal attributes.
- Information power is derived from possession, access to or control over information, and is a combination of formal, personal and political powers.
- Expert power is an individual's power deriving from their skills, expertise and knowledge.

Being aware of the source and type of power exercised is important for the identification of stakeholders, above all for predicting their actions and planning responses to them (Bourne and Walker 2005). The type, source and the mode of exercise of power enables classification of publics, stakeholders and other actors within the public sphere, and reveals connections among them.

The analysis must also consider the distribution of power between an organization and its stakeholders to find an answer to the question, which side is more dependent on the other in the given circumstances, or in other words, who needs the other side more to achieve its goals? Organizations can take four stances in relation to their stakeholders and distribution of power (Frooman 1999): low mutual dependence, stakeholder power or domination, company power or domination, and high mutual dependence.

6.5 Criteria for classification of stakeholders

When discussing the criteria for the classification of stakeholders (see Figure 6.1), we must mention the study by Mitchell *et al.* (1997) who, beside the criterion of power, use the concepts of legitimacy and importance of stakeholders' demands or interests (urgency). **Legitimacy** is defined as a perceived congruity between outcomes of actions of social actors with value patterns of the relevant system – of those who are influenced by the outcomes. Legitimacy means that psychological traits are being ascribed to a person, institution or social procedure that make stakeholders believe that the entity is appropriate, faultless and just (DeCremer and Tyler 2005). **Urgency** is related to the level of responsiveness that a demand from stakeholders deserves. According to the mentioned criteria, we distinguish among seven categories of stakeholders that are of varying importance for the organization (Mitchell *et al.* 1997).

- The first group is called *dormant stakeholders*, whose relevant attribute is power. They possess power to impose their will on a firm, but they do not have a legitimate relationship or an urgent claim, so their power remains unused. They have little or no relationship with the organization, which nonetheless must keep an eye on them due to their dynamic nature.
- *Discretionary stakeholders* have legitimate interests in the relationship with the organization, but they have no power to influence the organization and no urgent claims. Although there is no pressure on the organization to engage in a relationship with such stakeholders, they can be important recipients of activities with which organizations express their responsibility.
- The sole relevant attribute of *demanding stakeholders* is urgency, with which their interests are expressed, but they have neither legitimacy nor power to justify their claims. This group of stakeholders does not require a response from the management.
- Stakeholders who are powerful and have legitimate claims to the organization are called *dominant stakeholders*, because they are the key partners of the organization. Often, dominant stakeholders will have a formal mechanism in place to achieve their objectives that are not characterized as necessary, thus they are not always expressed.
- We characterize stakeholders who lack power but who have urgent legitimate claims as *dependent stakeholders*. These stakeholders depend either on the organization or on the support of other stakeholders who have the power necessary to carry out their will.
- *Dangerous stakeholders* are those who have urgent claims and power but lack legitimacy. Such individuals and groups do not shy away from any means to reach their goals, including acts of violence. Such stakeholders can be very dangerous for the organization, its existence, prosperity and members.
- *Definitive stakeholders* exhibit power and legitimacy and have an urgent claim, therefore they are the most important group of stakeholders demanding immediate attention of the management.

If an individual and a group have only one of the criteria presented in this classification in common, its importance in terms of a need for active communication based on this criterion is low. If there are two common criteria, the need

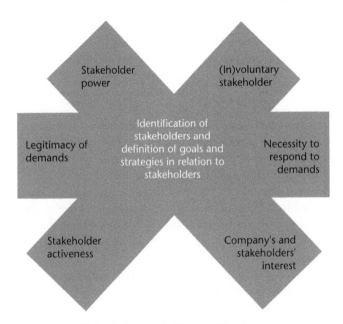

FIGURE 6.1 Criteria for stakeholder classification

for communication is moderate, but if an individual and a group have common necessary and legitimate interests and the power to exercise the interests, then an organization must communicate with them intensively. Such a public must be a priority for managers in order to operate to the benefit of the organization. Thus, organizations can communicate with different groups with varying intensity (Fill 2002), and this intensity should be constantly tuned or managed by the organization according to the importance and influence of specific stakeholders, their situation and the company's long-term strategic objectives, because stakeholders are not constants, but dynamic subjects that traverse from one group to another and change their interests and goals.

6.6 Stakeholder management

The **first step** in the management of stakeholders is to identify groups and to carefully monitor their behaviour, including potential threats they pose to the organization, and advantages that close cooperation might bring. A good knowledge of stakeholders enables the organization to interpret relevantly stakeholders' actions that are based on their objectives, interests, perceived insecurities or threats and other perceptions that individuals and groups within the public sphere have. We should not overlook that individuals and groups, although having different roles, bond with one another; that is why the management's task should be to identify similar interests, responses and other links and anticipate potential coalitions, either among the stakeholders or between stakeholders and the organization.

A useful tool for the visual presentation of such information are **stakeholder maps**, which graphically illustrate stakeholders, relationships with them, coalitions among stakeholders, their interests and powers, and the key publics. Maps can also include potential topics that are characteristic of specific stakeholders, based on which we can prepare communications and coordinate different, often conflicting, interests.

The **next step** is to consider to what extent stakeholders and their interests would be included in the decision-making processes, to what extent the current behaviour of an organization would be adjusted to demands and expectations of stakeholders, and how the organization would communicate with them.

Regardless of the level of stakeholders' involvement in an organization, they can never be completely overlooked; in any case, an organization must define the objectives that it wants to achieve in a relationship with each stakeholder, and must know how to act in order to meet those objectives. There are four **generic strategies** that define these dealings with stakeholders (Freeman 1984; Savage *et al.* 1991) according to the attitude toward a threat that specific stakeholders pose to an organization, and according to the possibilities for cooperation.

- *Offensive strategy* is suitable in cases where there is a great potential for cooperation and a low degree of risk that stakeholders pose to an organization. The strategy concerns stakeholders who are supportive of the organization and can help the organization in reaching its goals, either through changing their perceptions, involving them in organizational activities or even influencing their interests. Involvement in relevant corporate processes uses their cooperation potential and strengthens alliances. Stakeholder groups that could be involved include managers, employees, subsidiaries and connected companies, suppliers, NGOs.
- *Offensive strategy* is suitable in cases where stakeholders have low potential for cooperation, but they can be a danger to an organization. The strategy includes strengthening existing perceptions of the organization, maintenance of existing programmes and giving the initiative to the stakeholders. The strategy comes into question in relationships with the competition, unions, media and state organizations; in such situations, companies are often forced to defend their position.
- *Strategy of change* is suitable in cases where stakeholders have a great potential for cooperation but can also be very dangerous for the organization. In such instances (relations with employees, customers), the best advice is to change rules, decision-making processes and decisions, or to cooperate closely with stakeholders, which reduces the possibility of conflicts and raises the level of mutual dependence.
- *Inactivity* is a suitable approach when dealing with marginal and latent stakeholders that pose no threat to the organization and also have no potential for cooperation. In such cases, it is enough to monitor their activity, and if the level of their activity is raised, the organization can strengthen its position.

In terms of its activeness, the organizations can either be proactive if they antici-pate their responsibilities and do more than is demanded from them, or they can only adapt, meaning that they accept their responsibility and do everything that is demanded from them. They can act defensively, meaning that they accept responsi-bilities, but they defend in such a way that they only meet the minimum expecta-tions, which is just enough to be socially acceptable. They can also choose a reactive way, meaning that they deny their responsibilities and do less than is demanded of them (Clarkson 1995).

6.7 Stakeholder behaviour

Corporate communication not only studies stakeholders from an organizational point of view; it also tries to anticipate activities, and suggest responses to activities, of multiple stakeholders and publics, who can, while pursuing their own inter-ests, actively influence the organization and its decision making. Whether these interests are concrete or symbolic, social or economic, local or global, is irrelevant (Frooman 1999).

Strategies of stakeholders in relation to an organization (Frooman 1999) should, similarly to relationships of organizations toward stakeholders, be viewed in the context of power distribution and (inter)dependence of exchange partners. Again, this is the question of which of the partners is (more) dependent on the other. In the case where stakeholders possess certain resources or other valuables that are important for the organization, they can directly or indirectly refuse to share those resources and make the organization change its behaviour. Examples of such actions are boycotts, strikes and other forms of labour protests, black lists and expulsion from stock exchanges. This can be named **'withholding strategy'** (Frooman 1999, 198).

The other option that stakeholders have is to continue to supply directly or indirectly the organization with desired valuables, but do this only if the organiza-tion meets some clearly set conditions. This is called **'usage strategy'** (Frooman 1999, 199). Such examples include stock exchange lists of socially responsible com-panies, green indexes, lobbying of stakeholders' groups, public commitments, reso-lutions, strategic alliances among competitive companies or between companies and NGOs, and National Competition Regulator Office's requests and decrees, etc.

There are further strategies beside 'withholding' and 'usage' strategy that stake-holders can employ (Friedman and Miles 2006). For example, they can use a variety of informative, educative or persuasive campaigns, realized by sending open or pri-vate letters, signing petitions, involvement in public debates and dialogues, publica-tion of independent research, creation of black lists, etc. (**'voice strategy'**). Also, they can try to damage the organization without gaining any substantial benefits. A milder form of such a strategy is indirect activism and organization of pressure groups, while the extreme forms include boycotts, excess activities against organizations, sabotages or even terrorist acts (**'damage strategy'**) (Friedman and Miles 2006).

6.8 Communication with stakeholders

There are different phases in how the organization handles stakeholders, and how it responds to their initiatives and activities, and different forms of involvement of stakeholders in organizational processes and objectives; these influence the techniques of communication with stakeholders (Friedman and Miles 2006).

In the **first phase**, stakeholders are involved in the organization's processes only after all key issues have already been settled, and the organization decides only to inform stakeholders about the settlement, without granting them the right to participate in decision making. The extreme forms are manipulation, which is aimed at deceiving stakeholders to influence their expectations, and campaigns aimed at changing stakeholders' perceptions and beliefs. Less controversial is giving information and explanations about actual decisions in order to educate stakeholders.

In the **second phase**, stakeholders have an opportunity to participate in the process of decision making, because they received the required information and can present their views, but they have no guarantee that they will actually be taken into account. Stakeholders have the right to give advice, but the power of decision making remains with the organization. The objective in this phase is to reconcile with the stakeholder, not to truly take into account their suggestions. The concrete forms of actions in this phase are reconciliation, consultation and negotiation. Organizations can use various questionnaires, interviews, advisory bodies, workgroups and negotiation teams.

In the **third phase**, stakeholders influence the decision making of organizations and are involved in their activities. Often, stakeholders set basic conditions for their support, and failure to meet those conditions can cause withdrawal of their support. A concrete example of this phase is participation in the decision-making processes. An upgraded form is collaboration, in which stakeholders have the right to co-decide in specific projects. The third form is partnership where decisions concerning certain projects are made jointly on an equal rights basis. Communication tools in this phase are constructive dialogue, strategic alliances, common projects, etc.

In the extreme form of stakeholder involvement in organizational processes, stakeholders create and confirm an organization's decisions in a kind of co-management. One such form is a delegate system, where stakeholders are represented in the decision-making bodies, and even though they do not have the majority of voices, they *are represented*, and have the power of veto in some cases. Stakeholder supervision is a decision-making system in which stakeholders have the majority of voices and a casting vote in decision-making processes.

One of the key **tasks of corporate communications** (van Woerkum and Aarts 2008) in the context of stakeholder management is conducting research that gives us understanding of views and images that multiple stakeholders have of our organization. We would like to know how they think and act about topics and interests that concern the organization. This is the first step in the process of reducing complexity and uncertainty in the organization's environment. It is important not only to identify our stakeholders, but also to recognize topics that concern them and to evaluate and interpret the findings. It is also important to give information, either on own initiative or as a response to stakeholders' activities. The purpose is to present views, activities and images, and to balance stakeholders' expectations with the organization's possibilities. The third task is to create and strengthen relationships with stakeholders and social networks. This is a process of gaining control through interaction and is, at the same time, a process of adjustment. The fourth task is negotiation, which is a part of everyday reality, especially when dealing with a variety of interests and interdependent subjects. Another task is persuasion, an integral part of interaction with stakeholders, to whom we try to present our views, reasons for such views and arguments for our decisions. An important form (and task) of communication with stakeholders is their involvement in organizational processes and decision making. Of course, in real-life situations, the mentioned tasks appear individually or in combination.

We shall conclude this chapter with a concept originating from stakeholder theory (Strong *et al.* 2001) that the satisfaction of stakeholders depends on the following factors: timely communication, honest and complete information, empathy, and just treatment by the organization's management. Of the many principles that different authors have proposed on stakeholder management and communication, only three are really important: transparency, transparency and transparency (Szwajkowski 2000).

CASE: BARILLA

The family corporation Barilla Group was founded in 1877 as a small pastry shop run by Pietro Barilla in Parma. The corporate brand Barilla was officially registered in 1910. At the same time, a mascot was also registered – an illustration of a small baker's boy in red trousers and blue shirt who pours a giant egg into a wooden bucket full of flour, whilst on a green background there is a group of men, women and children watching him. Today, this Italian company is one of the world's largest and most renowned producers of pasta, pastry and sauces. The group consists of more than 40 companies and factories that produce, distribute and sell food products in Italy and globally. Under the brand names of Mulino Bianco, Voiello, Pavesi, Wasa, Harry's, Lieken Urkorn and Golden Toast, Alixir, Academia Barilla, Misko, Filiz, Yemina and Vesta, the company sells over 3 million tons of food products.

The company operates in 20 countries, it produces food in 10 of them, and exports its products to 150 countries around the globe. The group has around 15,000 employees and has an annual revenue of over €4 billion. Although the scope of business long ago surpassed an authentic relationship between a customer and a known local baker, the company continues to maintain a clear and recognizable identity and leads a genuine dialogue with its customers, thus making the buying experience close to visiting a small local shop. Basic values, accompanying the company's business, are passion, trust, curiosity, integrity and courage. The company's vision says that 'we help people live better by bringing well-being and the joy of eating into their everyday lives'. It stresses the importance of enjoying the food with all five senses, promotes healthy Italian cuisine with superb ingredients and simple recipes, and supports food quality and safety.

The company believes that it is impossible to talk about social responsibility if you don't exchange information, communicate and cooperate with all your stakeholders first. That is why the Barilla Group in 2008 identified and grouped its stakeholders and described the nature of interests it had in relationship with them. In the first step, the company asked the heads of departments and subsidiaries to classify their stakeholders, and the mode of communication with them, into three categories: very important stakeholders and continuous communication, important stakeholders and frequent communication, and important stakeholders and occasional communication. As a result, 116 different, very concrete, groups of stakeholders were identified and then classified according to the relevance of their relationship with the company. Thereby the company established foundations for future policy, communication and reporting.

In order to draw a final map of stakeholders and communication policies with them, the next steps included an organization of two events, to which representatives of different categories of stakeholders were invited. At the first event, held in the Pedrignano factory in Parma, the company presented the stakeholder map to stakeholders, such as consumers, scientific community, suppliers and employees, and asked them to evaluate the map. Next, they jointly defined the frame of responsibility the company had to show toward different groups. The next event, four months afterward, was organized for representatives of other stakeholder groups, unions, distributers, media, trade associations and local communities. At this forum, stakeholders evaluated the challenges, identified at the earlier event, in relation to each individual responsibility of the company toward stakeholder groups. Further, key commitments arising from those responsibilities were defined, and an agreement has been made upon indicators used for measuring to what extent goals and commitments have been fulfilled. The company also decided to maintain such dialogue with all stakeholders on various organizational levels, and to keep a unified system of reporting about its business and commitments.

The company regularly uses annual reports to inform stakeholders how commitments relating to social responsibility are fulfilled. Besides various forums, conferences and other traditional media, the company provides a direct access to all information about the company through the corporate website. The Barilla company included 66 per cent of mapped stakeholders in communication and cooperation activities. One-quarter of stakeholder groups were involved in the definition of the company's plans and activities, 32 per cent participated in organized discussions, while 66 per cent of the stakeholder groups received direct information about the company's business activities.

Key terms

Stakeholder management. A business process and philosophy that supports an organization's objectives by creating positive relationships with stakeholders. It involves stakeholder identification and analysis, stakeholder mapping, stakeholder engagement strategy and communication.

Stakeholders. Refers to organizations, groups and individuals who can affect, or are affected by, the achievement of an organization's mission and behaviour and actions. Individuals and groups are stakeholders because they are in a category affected by decisions of an organization or if their decisions affect the organization, but only after they become more aware and active can they be described as publics.

Public. A group of people that face a common problem, recognize the problem and organize themselves in order to solve the problem. The actors are involved in the problem, know the problem and there is nothing that would hinder them from solving the problem.

Public sphere. A complex network of people and organizations at which communications of social subjects are directed, where the public opinion is formulated, and where the actions of social actors are legitimized. It is a forum where individuals can come together to freely discuss and identify societal problems, debate matters of mutual interest and, where possible, to reach a common (dis)agreement on public issue.

Primary and secondary stakeholders. These are considered as organizations, groups or individuals whose lasting support is essential for the existence of the company, while secondary stakeholders are all others.

Voluntary stakeholders. Groups such as investors, shareholders, employees, consumers and suppliers decide to 'have their stake' in the company and can break off their connection with the company.

Involuntary stakeholders. Groups such as local communities, environment or future generations, do not have a choice of entering into or terminating their relationships with an organization.

Stakeholder power. Defined as a relationship between social actors, where one actor causes an activity of the other that would otherwise not have taken place.

Stakeholder legitimacy. A perceived congruity between outcomes of actions of social actors with value patterns of the relevant system – of those who are influenced by the outcomes. Legitimacy means that psychological traits are being ascribed to a person, institution or social procedure that make stakeholders believe that the entity is appropriate, faultless and just.

Stakeholder urgency. Refers to the importance of stakeholders' demands or interests and it is related to the level of responsiveness that a demand from stakeholders deserves.

REVIEW QUESTIONS

- Describe the stakeholder paradigm, define stakeholders and explain how they differ from the public and public sphere.
- Explain why all stakeholders are not equally important for a company and define different categories of stakeholders. Can you think of alternative ways of classifying the stakeholders?
- What are the criteria for stakeholders' segmentation? Why does a company need a stakeholder map?
- Which are the generic strategies that companies can use for engaging with stakeholders? What kind of actions can stakeholders use when they relate to companies? Critically evaluate each phase of stakeholder involvement in the organization processes.

Discuss Barilla stakeholder identification, involvement and communication process. Think about the necessity of corporate transparency. Imagine that you are a director of corporate communication in the company by your choice. Prepare a stakeholder map for the company, what is 'at stake' for each stakeholder and think about communication strategies for each of the stakeholder groups.

References

Bourne, Lynda and Derek H. T. Walker. 2005. Visualising and mapping stakeholder influence. *Management Decision* 43 (5): 649–660.

Bowie, Norman E. 1988. The moral obligations of multinational corporations. In *Problems of International Justice*, ed. Steven Luper-Foy. Boulder, CO: Westview Press, 97–113.

Cooper, Stuart Martin. 2003. Stakeholder communication and the Internet in UK electricity companies. *Managerial Auditing Journal* 18 (3): 232–243.

Clarkson, Max B. E. 1995. A stakeholder framework for analyzing and evaluating corporate social performance. *Academy of Management Review* 20 (1): 92–117.

De Cremer, David and Tom R. Tyler. 2005. Am I respected or not? Inclusion and reputation as issues in group membership. *Social Justice Research* 18 (2): 121–153.

Donaldson, Thomas and Lee E. Preston. 1995. The stakeholder theory of the corporation: concepts, evidence, and implications. *Academy of Management Review* 20 (1): 65–91.

Fill, Chris. 2002. *Marketing Communications: Contexts, Strategies and Applications*, 3rd edition. Englewood Cliffs, NJ: Prentice Hall.

Freeman, Edward R. 1984. *Strategic Management: A Stakeholder Approach*. Boston: Pitman.

Friedman, Andrew L. and Samantha Miles. 2002. Developing stakeholder theory. *Journal of Management Studies* 39 (1): 1–21.

——2006. *Stakeholders: Theory and Practice*. Oxford: Oxford University Press.

Frooman, Jeff. 1999. Stakeholder influence strategies. *Academy of Management Review* 24 (2): 191–205.

Gray, Rob, Dave Owen and Carol Adams. 1996. *Accounting & Accountability: Changes and Challenges in Corporate Social and Environmental Reporting*. London: Prentice Hall.

Greene, Robert and Joost Elffers. 1999. *Power: the 48 Laws*. London: Profile Books.

Grunig, James E. 1992. *Excellence in Public Relations and Communication Management*. Hillsdale, NJ: Lawrence Erlbaum Associates, Inc.

Grunig, James E. and Todd Hunt. 1984. *Managing Public Relations*. Philadelphia: Harcourt Brace Jovanovich College.

Grunig, James E. and Fred C. Repper. 1992. Strategic management, publics, and issues. In *Excellence in Public Relations and Communication Management*, eds. James E. Grunig and David M. Dozier. Hillsdale, NJ: Lawrence Erlbaum Associates, 117–157.

Ihlen, Øyvind. 2008. Mapping the environment for corporate social responsibility: stakeholders, publics and the public sphere. *Corporate Communications: An International Journal* 13 (2): 135–146.

Jančič, Zlatko. 1999. *Celostni marketing. 2., razširjena izdaja.* Ljubljana: Fakulteta za družbene vede.

Manktelow, R. 2003. *Stakeholder Management – Winning Support for your Projects*. Available at: http://www.mindtools.com/pages/article/newPPM_07.htm (9 October 2010).

Mitchell, Ronald K., Bradley R. Agle and Donna J. Wood. 1997. Towards a theory of stakeholder identification: defining the principle of who and what really counts. *Academy of Management Review* 22 (4): 853–886.

Podnar, Klement and Zlatko Jančič. 2006. Towards a categorization of stakeholder groups: an empirical verification of a three-level model. *Journal of Marketing Communications* 12 (4): 297–308.

Savage, Grant T., Timothy W. Nix, Carlton W. Whitehead and John D. Blair. 1991. Strategies for assessing and managing organizational stakeholders. *Academy of Management Executive* 5 (2): 61–75.

Starik, M. 1994. Essay. The Toronto conference: reflections on stakeholder theory. *Business and Society* 33 (1): 82–131.

Strong, Kelly C., Richard C. Ringer and Steven A. Taylor. 2001. THE* rules of stakeholder satisfaction (* timeliness, honesty, empathy). *Journal of Business Ethics* 32 (3): 219–230.

Szwajkowski, Eugene. 2000. Simplifying the principles of stakeholder management: the three most important principles. *Business & Society* 39 (4): 379–396.

van Woerkum, C. M. J. and M. N. C. Aarts. 2008. The orientation of organizations to their environments: functions of the unconscious mind. *Journal of Public Relations Research* 20 (2): 180–206.

Wheeler, David and Maria Sillanpää. 1997. *The Stakeholder Corporation. A Blueprint for Maximizing Stakeholder Value*. London: Pitman Publishing.

Yukl, Gary A. 1998. *Leadership in Organizations*. Sydney: Prentice Hall.

7

STORYTELLING AND ISSUE MANAGEMENT IN TIMES OF CHANGE AND CRISES

CONTENTS

The first part of this chapter looks at the meaning of stories and the definition of corporate storytelling. Next, we present the practical framework and structure of storytelling. Further, we emphasize the importance of managing and communicating changes in an organization and explain approaches to communication in times of crises, when corporate stories and storytelling play an important role.

7.1 Definition of corporate story

Stories are an integral part of human life. From our first fairytales to reminiscing in old age, stories connect people and, through interaction, help to form and give meaning to our environment, as well as help us to understand other people and also our own identity. Stories determine each individual person. They help us, and others, understand who we are, and why we are who we are. We say that to know someone is to know his or her story. Stories help us to organize and structure bits of information; they are tangible, memorable and enthusiastic, and people believe in them more. A good story and its narrative increase our attention, and can include, overwhelm and motivate a person to act. They appeal to our reason and our emotions. A story is a very successful way of constructing meanings and reality, establishing and developing relations, and determining aims and purposes. It is a way of structuring and comprehending information that an individual gains in primary socialization and maintains throughout his or her life.

Companies cannot avoid stories. We could even say that companies as social entities exist through stories. The organizational reality is determined by stories, and the organizational community can be brought together or separated by stories.

Everything that the public relates to a company is in some way expressed through stories. Following and analysing company-related stories is an excellent method of marketing and organizational research, a focal point of corporate communication efforts, and also of establishing a desired internal reality of the company, transferring knowledge, reacting to the challenges of the outer environment and interacting with stakeholders. Further, following and analysing a company's stories is an everyday activity for managers and employees in explaining daily events, motivating and introducing new members to the organizational community, etc. Companies use stories to explain who they are, create and present their corporate and group identity, convey their goals, explain their actions and ground their decisions. Stories also help companies to gain and keep their interactions with various stakeholders on different levels. Stories do not only convey information, but also offer interpretation and understanding of this information.

Stories can be complex or simple and can have different topics. A story could describe events related to stakeholders, such as consumers or company founders, it could describe norms that apply to the company, explain right or wrong decisions by the company, or even describe the company itself. Further, stories can be formal or informal, true or fictional, expressed through hearsay, jokes, metaphors, anecdotes, myths or legends. In some stories, companies have a major role, in others they play only a supporting role, while in some cases there may be a number of equivalent roles for several companies. Some stories are directed by a company, others are forced upon it.

None of the stories referring to the company should be left to its random end, in other words, stories should not run without the company actively following them. Many authors stress the strategic meaning of stories and their management. The narrative approach serves many purposes in an organization and includes various activities or phases from story gathering, story sharing, story making and storytelling (McLellan 2006). Story gathering entails getting feedback from various stakeholders. The company has to form a system that systematically collects stories that circulate in various publics about the company, its activities and offer, as well as about its key stakeholders, such as consumers, suppliers, management and owners. The sharing refers to mutual knowledge and experience transfer, but also stakeholders' (e.g. employees') transfer of memories. Story making refers to envisioning, sense-making, and creating such narratives that appeal and direct those spoken to. Storytelling refers to framing and conveying information so that it is understandable, meaningful and memorable (McLellan 2006, 18–19).

We could say that **storytelling** is defined as an active story management and transmission with selected addressees, a defined context and a carefully chosen code, a central process of planning, implementation and control conducted by those responsible for a company's communication. A company-transmitted story is seen as the company's explanation about the company's behaviour, processes and relations with numerous stakeholders (Berry 2001). A **corporate story** is a comprehensive narrative about the whole organization, its origins, its vision and its mission (Holten Larsen 2000). Van Riel (2000) says the story is a realistic and relevant description of the company, created in an open dialogue with all stakeholders that the company depends on. He sees the story as a tool or means to achieving mutual understanding, which overcomes the problem of achieving uniqueness arising from the fact that many companies articulate identical attributes when defining their own corporate identity. It is the story and its narrative that can prevent the company's attributes from being identical to some other company's attributes and make them unique, which is the desired aim for most companies.

Companies and the individuals connected to them are involved in **linear** as well as **non-linear stories**. The key difference between the two is evident not only in the final product, but also in the production process. If the exact course of the story is known, then the story is a linear one. The course of such a story is fully determined and transmitted by the sender or the company itself. A non-linear story consists of different sub-stories with no fixed order, but still conveying a consistent message. These stories adapt to the recipients and their responses.

To make a successful corporate story, we must take into account many factors. Martin *et al.* (1983) draw attention to the meaning of a story's uniqueness. Van Riel (2000) similarly stresses the importance of uniqueness of corporate stories, while at the same time suggesting that a story has to be as relevant for stakeholders, realistic, sustainable and open for dialogue with stakeholders. Morgan and Dennehy (1997) support the approach of Wilkins (1984) and Zemke (1990), postulating that stories should revolve about real people, events and actions, should be concrete and set in time and space known to their publics so they can relate to it, but they also should be linked to the organization's philosophy and/or culture. In a company or its subsidiaries, stories have to be a matter of common knowledge. Not only should individuals know the stories, they should also be aware of the fact that they know them, and that all members act in accordance with these stories. Further, the story has to be credible, which means that all stakeholders have to believe the story. It should incorporate the message of how the organization and individuals in the organization are or are not operating.

7.2 Framework and structure of the corporate story

When we have in mind strategic corporate story and storytelling, we need to find answers to the questions: What, to whom, why and how do we want to communicate? We need to find and articulate a key message that we want to transmit through a story, because a corporate story has to have a clear purpose. Where we want to convey several messages, we need to decide which one is the central one, or the story could simply fall flat or be unclear and uninteresting. The story has to relate to a 'conflict', a problem, an opportunity or a topic, because these are the elements that entangle different characters into a story and into mutual relationships, and call for a solution. The main characters and their roles have to be carefully defined, but we also need to clearly establish their characteristics. All this leads to the **plot** of the story, which is the structure (time and causal): the sequence of events in the story and its causal relations (Fog *et al.* 2005). The plot refers to the relationship of three key contents that a company can transmit about itself and its operating in the story. These are the company's abilities, mysteries and its accomplishments (van Riel and Fombrun 2007).

Understanding the story and its key messages depends on the addressee and even more so on the context which should not be left to chance by those responsible for corporate communication. In storytelling, we have to think about the context because it is a very important feature. Only after it has been explained where, when and how something happened, can an explanation of why it happened be given. An understanding of reality is not only provided by stories, but also by a frame given by the context. The **frame** is understood as a pattern of interpretation that determines context (Goffman 1974). These are simplified concepts, which can be accessed through existing and known symbols, images, metaphors and meanings. A frame is a reference point for all future decisions and judgements. Through the presenting of a general context around the information presented we can influence how people think about that information. Information within a context, within a frame is altered by that context and frame. The process of **framing** or conveying the point of view refers to choosing certain aspects and their emphasis within the message, in such a way as to encourage a certain view on the topic, causal interpretation, moral evaluation and necessary measures of conduct. In the words of Entman (1993), set frames promote a particular problem definition, causal interpretation, moral evaluation and/or treatment recommendation for the item described. They provide background, add missing information, and tell us what is important and what addressees can ignore, and in that way influence his or her response. Framing defines individual cognitive processing and which of his or her cognitive schemata will be activated in an interpretation of a certain message. Companies with their corporate story and communication want to frame certain situations, attributes, choices, actions, issues, responsibility and news (Hallahan 1999), and they want to frame them better than other publics do. Defining a common frame of reference is a necessary condition for an efficient dialogue, and whoever sets it has an advantage in communication.

When managing, planning, analysing, forming and conveying company-related stories, companies can use an adapted **Propp model** (1928 [1968]) that enables them to conduct accurate analysis and suggest possible endings for the story. In his morphology of the folktale, the Russian scientist identified typical, almost archetypical patterns and derivations of events among various protagonists in folktales. He identified the aforementioned set of folktale protagonists who supposedly have a universal character. In our context and for the purpose of corporate storytelling, we can name them as follows (Fog *et al.* 2005):

- the company as the main **protagonist**;
- **assistants**, stakeholders and other groups helping with the efforts of the company;
- the **company's adversaries** who oppose and limit the company's behaviour;

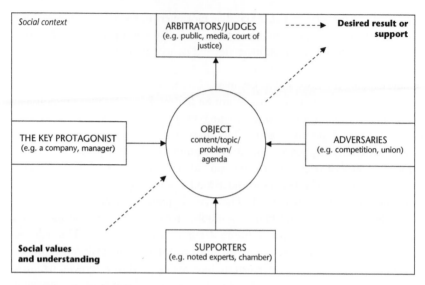

FIGURE 7.1 Key protagonists and factors of a corporate story
Adapted from Fog *et al.* (2005)

- an **object** that could be a business goal or some other kind of company agenda;
- donor or **giver**, a group of stakeholders or a regulatory organ that gives the wanted goal;
- **beneficiary** or the one who achieved what was wanted and the corresponding consequences.

With this model (Figure 7.1), we can analyse virtually any acute issue or topic that involves the company, and its aspirations and activities. Further, based on this model and with thoughtful interpretation of relations between protagonists, we can not only create a convincing corporate story, but can also analyse stories that are circulating among stakeholders. With a universal structure that starts with the anticipation of future events by the protagonist, followed by identifying obstacles and adversaries in pursuit of the goal, finding help along the way through others and finally achieving the goal, we can present the company's past, present and future (Papadatos 2006). Initially, a protagonist (a company, an individual or a group of companies), with which an individual can identify has to be introduced to the story. Changes that lead the main protagonist into action, or are the reason for the story, have to be indicated as well. In the central part of the story, there are tests and trials for the protagonist, and obstacles that cause frustrations, conflicts and drama. The central part concludes with a turning point, a point of no return, where the story turns into the final part involving a famous success or tragic failure of the main hero. However, corporate stories as a tool of management do not finish here, claim Morgan and Dennehy (1997). The moral of the story has to follow, together with the consequences of actions unravelled in the story.

7.3 Plurality of corporate stories and their role in times of organizational changes

Although the strategic management of corporate communication talks about one story, which is often formally written in the corporate identity or/and corporate brand manual (such a manual is a guide that provides guidance and assistance when commissioning or producing (visual) materials for a company across all media), the reality of the company is **plurivocity** – the fact that in a certain moment, various authorized and unauthorized corporate stories exist, all of which try to be dominant and valid in the eyes of key stakeholders (Heugens 2002). We talk about the simultaneous co-existence of many stories or their varieties, which we need to have in mind, to control and, as far as possible, manage. From the management's point of view, it is crucial that the consistency of transmitted messages is achieved, including an appropriate integration of elements on the level of form, complementarity, variation of contents and messages. We talk about a plurality of stories, consisting of one core story, which in different narratives and various emphases creates a mosaic that reveals continuity and order of the company's presentation. The aim of a corporate story is to orchestrate and integrate all communication, where the story functions as a magnifying glass through which seemingly independent and unrelated elements come together as a whole (Polkinghorne 1988). The stories need to be passed on over and over again and they have to adapt to the time, circumstances and publics to which they are told. Although we have to deal with a mosaic of numerous stories, and each separate story offers its own interpretation of events, we must keep in mind that there is a continuous rivalry among the stories for a dominant role in the interpretation of the existing reality (Buchanan and Dawson 2007).

Storytelling does not involve mere descriptions, but also tries to provoke an emotional reaction and involvement from the public, and to create and maintain sense, as well as to discredit competitors' views on reality (Buchanan and Dawson 2007). This is apparent when a company implements changes in the organization and its operations.

Organizational changes occur when the company restructures its resources (human, financial, technological and process) to enhance its abilities to create value and raise effectiveness. In theory, authors distinguish between two main forms of changes, known as **first class changes**, or evolution changes, and **second class changes**, or revolution changes (Cheney *et al.* 2004), which can be represented as a continuum. First class changes are progressive and hidden. These changes are small and occur as a result of everyday reaction to the environment. They can be seen in the constant improvement and adaptation of known approaches to operation and in growing knowledge. They are necessary to avoid bigger changes, both on the level of an individual, as well as on the level of the whole organization. The advantage of such changes is that an individual does not feel anything is actually changing. Another type of change within an organization are **radical changes**, which occur due to insufficient reactions to the changing environment. Revolutionary changes occur abruptly, their scope is large and they include a thorough transformation of the current organizational operations and individuals in the organization, and the outcome is not completely predictable. Corporate stories can play an important role in both types of changes. While an individual can be the main subject of gradual changes, corporate stories can achieve his or her motivation for the implementation of changes in the way of improving work processes and achieving appropriate context to activate his or her creativity. On the other hand, communication in second class changes is more demanding. In the case of great changes, corporate stories help us achieve mutual understanding among participants in this process, support the institutionalization of changes, and help participants to accept needs, measures, processes and results of changes.

In each case, regardless of the type of changes, a gradual approach to communication support is suggested (Armenakis and Harris 2002).

1. In the first phase, we try to achieve *readiness* of participants to the change and persuade them to become advocates of change.
2. The second phase is *appropriating* – the changes are implemented and participants acknowledge the new way of operating.
3. The third phase is *institutionalization*, typically characterized by maintaining changes and enabling their rejection up to the phase when established changes become a predominant operating norm.

Corporate stories can help us carry out information and messages that are the key to reaching successfully implemented changes. We have to address the sentiment that refers to the question whether the changes were necessary. A corporate story has to point at the mistakes in the current operation and at dramatic consequences that may occur if the changes are not implemented. It has to convince individuals and groups related to an organization that the changes are necessary and unavoidable. Further, it has to communicate to the participants that they are able to carry out the changes and that they will succeed in this. The stories should also prove the adequacy and benefits of suggested measures. If communication is unable to do this, we need to rethink the adequacy of such measures. Corporate stories need to offer evidence that measures taken and implemented changes are functioning and in this way give an effective answer to any potential scepticism from the participants. Furthermore, the stories have to demonstrate clearly a personal benefit that an individual will gain or has already gained with the internalization of changes (Armenakis and Harris 2002). Corporate stories give meaning to the work of an individual and his/her role in the organization, add required energy to interactions and conversations, and are also informative (what, how, why), they explain the processes and results of changes, and help to achieve an organizational cohesion of members which is necessary for implementing changes (Elving 2005).

As a communication tool within an organization, stories are powerful tools for communicating changes and constructing reality and social changes (Johansson and Heide 2008), while at the same time, they are a tool for limiting opposite views, preventing misinterpretations, rejecting rumours and hearsay and eliminating communication failures (van Vuuren and Elving 2008). In the words of Bacharach and Lawler (1998), the history of organizational changes is nothing but a history of conflicting interests and negotiations, and related stories are a means to legitimize particular interests and actions (Currie and Brown 2003). However, van Vuuren and Elving (2008) warn that storytelling should not be used to forcibly orchestrate all voices to one singular story, usually the one told by top management. Such monaural communication often results in negative feelings of uncertainty, trust issues, and can create negative rumours, with very high costs in the long term.

Thus, a complete override of alternative stories in the organization will result in conflicts between participants and misunderstanding of the purposes, goals and benefits of the planned changes. At the same time, ignorance of alternative voices results in incorrect informal communication, usually in the form of rumours, which will most likely lead toward rejection of changes by the participants.

The key role of communication in managing changes should not be the enforcing of the one and only corporate story at any cost, but rather the opposite. Participants and their various stories that exist in a system need to be guided and used to create conditions in which every individual will contribute to the introduction and implementation of needed and understandable changes. It is important that every voice is heard and that people get an opportunity to show what they are capable of, and of what their contribution could be. Hence, the successful management of a corporate story in the time of change should not be aimed at standardization and discipline, but be focused on offering an opportunity to each participant to be involved in the changes and to become an active performer (Langer and Thorup 2006). Changes without the participation of those who are affected by them have no chance of being successful.

Organizational changes usually mean stress for the participants, because in general, people are usually against them and find it difficult to accept their implementation. Furthermore, there is often uncertainty about the results of implemented changes and their consequences on individuals. Those responsible for communication in an organization, including managers who lead the process of implementation of changes, have to be able to create an adequate communication climate in which a change is seen as an opportunity and not a threat. A failure to do so leads to rumours that are usually full of negative information, thereby increasing stress levels for participants. It is through storytelling and corporate stories that the management has to achieve the following goals (Bordia *et al.* 2006).

- *Offer answers* to questions related to job security and work conditions, such as issues of redundancy, promotion and work conditions.
- *Advise* about desired goals that will be achieved through organizational changes.

- *React* to poorly implemented changes and build up trust in management, but also draw attention to the negative attitude toward changes and potential consequences of such conduct.
- *Draw attention* to the influence of changes (or lack of changes) to the current functioning of the company.
- *React* to unconstructive stories in the organization.

If the management is not able to offer convincing stories related to the above areas, the participants will make up their own stories, and their goal will not be to support the implementation of needed changes, as the management expects, but rather the opposite, to obstruct the predicted changes.

7.4 Communication in crisis

Just as we cannot implement changes without communication, the mere absence of communication in times of crisis can itself create a new crisis. **Crisis** can be understood as a certain division that physically influences the system as a whole and questions its foundations, subjective sense and existential core (Burnett 1998). Crises are unexpected events or circumstances that bring a company into disrepute and imperil its future profitability, growth and, possibly, its very survival (Lerbinger 1997). From the communication point of view, the key dimension of a crisis that affects its perception is the rate of (collective) social stress it causes. Crises affect an organization as well as its services, products, stakeholders and good name (Fearn-Banks 2001). Due to the large co-dependence of social participants, they affect other environments related to the organization (Boin and Lagadec 2000), and their relationships with the organization (Heath and Millar 2004). Although they usually come as a surprise, crises are the most normal phenomenon for an organization and society in general and, as such, offer us opportunities for changes and improvements.

Due to their suddenness, scale of consequences, and other factors, crises attract public attention, therefore they need to be immediately taken into consideration by the management, but at the same time they include elements of surprise. Although an organization, threatened by a crisis, cannot completely control the crisis, it should nonetheless be able to respond accordingly (Stephens *et al.* 2005). Crisis communication is therefore very important, and unresponsiveness or silence from the organization will appear as a silent confession of guilt (Maynard 1993). At the same time, any unresponsiveness from the organization will trigger a new (information) crisis with an information-hungry public. The company has to undertake both **crisis management** as well as crisis communication prior to, during and after the negative occurrence (Fearn-Banks 2001), where **crisis communication** is understood as an interactive process of exchange of information and opinions about the crisis, its circumstances, possible solutions and responses among different social actors (Lerbinger 1997).

A **rhetorical approach to crisis communication** has to be adopted (Heath and Millar 2004). The core of this approach refers to the fact that next to its technical and management aspect, we also see a crisis as a rhetorical problem, and that the causes of the crisis, its power and duration are objects of public debate. As established by Malešič (2006), the point of this approach is that each and every crisis has its actual and perceived dimensions that are not necessarily in accordance; some crises are perceived as smaller than they actually are and vice versa. The perception of the crisis is influenced by various stories that fight for dominance in the interpretation of actual events. In order to react to them, we can analyse crises according to the following criteria (Burnett 1998):

- severity of the threat;
- threat-demanded time response;
- level of control over what is happening;
- available options for response.

Then we need to analyse each story, the relationships between the key factors and protagonists that play a role in the story, and then prepare a plan of how to react to them and the crisis-related activities. It is important that the company collects and analyses information on time and reacts to actions and messages that are coming from different environments appropriately. Here, credibility and the transparency of the company's activities and its spokespeople play a crucial role. The rule is that a company has to communicate the whole story sincerely. If the company does not communicate the whole story, others will do that instead, but with all the missing parts that journalists will gladly fill with information from various other sources (Cutlip *et al.* 2000). Moreover, it is the media that largely determine what the crisis is, therefore, they often create crises but also end them (Newlove *et al.* 2000). At the same time, the media determine the social frame of how an organization's responses to crisis are judged, and the media determine the norms through which a crisis and its related actions are evaluated, and propose relevant questions and seek those responsible for the crisis. Johansson and Skoglund (1996) point out two roles of the media:

- *functional* (warning about the crisis, seeking and presenting information, seeking causes and those responsible for it);
- *political* (media schematization, competitiveness for exclusivity and media 'condemnation' of those responsible).

When communicating with the media and other publics in times of crisis, a company is torn between full transparency and coordination of various interests that emerge in time of crisis, including the consequences of acknowledging full responsibility.

> On the one side there are interests and needs of various publics to gain information, while on the other there is the interest of the subject, to which the

crisis refers to, meaning that crisis communication is usually torn between the subject's credibility and its potential legal responsibility for the crisis situation.

(Malešič 2006, 298)

In crises, **monoural communication** is applied, meaning that one corporate story is told by a single spokesperson or the company's PR representative, and this story can be carefully and thoughtfully validated by other members of the organization (such as a carefully chosen employee or outside supporters). Communication has to be integrated on the level of goals, content and tools. Storytelling in the time of crisis is actually an intensive battle for dominance over design, content and transmission of information between internal and external publics. The company's story for the media must include exact and unambiguous information about what happened, why it happened and what the company is planning to do about it.

To leave aside the technical and managerial dimensions of the crisis, there is, from a communication point of view, always a crisis-related threat of diminishing corporate image and the company's reputation (Coombs 1995). The affected public and/or media usually bring this about in two ways: the company is accused of executing a certain action and this action is perceived as unpleasant or even insulting.

Both conditions need to be met to talk about the crisis from the company's point of view. Perceptions can be truer than reality itself, therefore for the existence of crisis it is not so important whether the company has actually caused the crisis, but whether it was accused of causing it (Benoit 1997).

According to the sources of the crisis (internal or external) and the intention of the crisis, Coombs (1995) presents the most important **types of crises** that he calls lapse, accident, error and terrorism. Companies can, according to the evidence of responsibility for the crisis (true, untrue), its consequences (great, little), status of the company in crisis (victim, guilty party) and past actions (positive and negative) develop strategies and use different types of **response to crisis**.

Benoit (1997) proposes a theory for improving public image, in which he determines five key categories of communicating strategies that a company has at its disposal to respond to a perceived crisis and to maintain its present corporate image.

- *Denial.* In this category, there are two possibilities. The first one is to simply deny the existence of the crisis. The second one is to place the blame for the crisis on someone else and persisting that, from the company's point of view, there is no crisis.
- *Evasion of responsibility.* The first possibility within this category is that the company presents its functioning as a logical and appropriate response to some other action, event or provocation. The company and its representatives also have the possibility of cancelling a certain key event, related with the emergence of the crisis or referring to the fact that they were not informed about it. The third possibility is that the company refers to unlucky circumstances

or bad luck as causing the crisis. It can also explain the crisis by saying that everything that was done and led to the crisis was done in good faith and with good intentions.

- *Reduce offensiveness.* Companies can decide to emphasize and affirm the positive aspects related to their functioning to reduce the meaning of negative perceptions related to the crisis. This is the support of positive associations with the hope that they will overpower the negative ones. However, companies can decide to reduce the negative impact of associations by making some details or aspect of the crisis marginal and obscure. Another approach is to identify an event that is similar to the company's own actions, but is far more critical for the occurrence of the crisis. One of the possibilities is to set a specific action in a different context, which changes its connotation. A company can also carry out an attack against those who are accusing it. If a company assumes responsibility for the crisis, it can offer compensation to the victims, if they do not find it offensive.
- *Corrective action.* The company announces that it will restore the state of affairs existing before the offensive action, and/or promises to prevent the recurrence of the offensive action. It solves the current problem and prevents future problems.
- *Mortification.* The company decides to assume responsibility for the crisis and begs the public for forgiveness. At the same time, the company apologizes to everyone directly or indirectly affected by the crisis.

Coombs (1995) proposed a similar categorization of various communication responses, arraying possible communication responses on a continuum. On the one side of the continuum, there are measures that present a company as not at all, or only partially, connected to the crisis. On the other side, there are measures with which the company assumes full responsibility for the crisis and its consequences. Companies can adopt various crisis-response strategies (Coombs 1995).

- They can distance themselves from direct responsibility for the crisis.
- They can divert attention from negative to positive aspects of the organization.
- They can use statements that evoke public sympathy and portray the belief that the company itself is the biggest victim of the crisis.
- They can assume responsibility and beg for forgiveness.
- They can also focus on mending the consequences of the crisis and even promise to do everything they can to avoid future crises.

As Dowling (2001) says, there are four categories of strategy.

- *The strategy of denial and hiding.* This strategy does not explain or justify the crisis, but lies low and hires lawyers to solve the crisis.
- *Attack strategies.* The characteristics of these strategies are blaming, threatening, concealing crises and denying them, devolving responsibilities down to others and in public presenting the arguments against the crisis.

- *Fatalistic strategies.* These strategies explain the crisis by referring to the risks of the industry within which the crisis-affected company operates, to accidents that can happen to anyone or preventive operating (referring to the risks of the industry, accident, preventive operating).
- *Eye-for-an-eye strategy.* According to this strategy, the company that is in the crisis accepts the blame, withdraws from the market and asks for a second chance.

The golden rule for crisis communication and crisis management is to **do everything we can to prevent the crisis from happening in the first place**. Therefore, early identification and appropriate responses to potential public themes and events that (could) influence an organization are very important (Ansoff 1980; Chase 1984; Dutton and Ottensmeyer 1987; Mahon and Waddock 1992). By public themes and events, we refer to potential and existing conflicting opinions, debates and judgements that affect an organization or its functioning. If a crisis still occurs, we have to do everything possible to make it the last crisis. According to Belasen (2008), organization and exchange of information in the time of crisis calls for four key steps of action.

1. Giving transparent and responsible information to the public.
2. Reforming or activating employees to overcome disadvantages.
3. Holding promises and creating rules and ethical codes for future functioning.
4. Operating according to the new needs and expectations of stakeholders.

CASE: DOMINO'S PIZZA

In 1960, Tom and James Monaghan purchased DomiNick's, a small pizza store in Ypsilanti, Michigan. One year later, James traded his share in the pizzeria to Tom for a VW Beetle. In 1965, the sole owner renamed the company Domino's Pizza, Inc. and set a goal to make the company the best pizza delivery company in the world with a guaranteed 30-minute delivery time. After two years, the company opened its first franchise store. In the next decades, the company grew rapidly. Store after store was opened in the USA, and in 1983 Domino's Pizza opened its first international store in Canada. In 1993, the company introduced a full guarantee on its pizzas, saying that if a customer is for any reason unhappy with their pizza, they will get another one, or get their money back. In 1996, the company had over 1,500 international stores on all five continents. It also launched its website at that time. Even after the founder of the company had retired and sold his share in 1998, and after the company had begun trading at the NYSE, Domino's Pizza continued to grow intensively. The company now operates in over 60 markets worldwide, and has more than 9,200 stores – half of them international – either owned or franchised. In 2007, Domino's Pizza was included for the tenth time on the list of the best franchise opportunities, and the *Advertising Age* magazine named Domino's Pizza a megabrand. The company is now one of the largest global companies that produce and deliver pizzas and other foods, with an annual revenue of $5.5 billion and employing over 125,000 people. Franchise stores are still the driving force of the company's development. However, Domino's Pizza makes sure that contractors consistently comply with the brand's rules and standards by providing them with manuals and courses. But at the same time, franchisers have a large autonomy in price formation and employment policy.

The company is aware that due to the speciality of its service, consumers value above all quality of products, price, service and convenience – but because the success of the company depends solely on the number of customers and their loyalty, trust in the corporate brand is the key asset of the corporation. Company values, presenting itself under a monolith corporate brand, are 'putting people first, demanding integrity, striving for customer loyalty, delivering with smart hustle and positive energy, winning by improving results every day'.

On Easter Monday, 13 April 2009, at 16:30 the Head of Communications in Domino's Pizza headquarters received a warning from a NGO that recently five vulgar video clips exposing food contamination in one of the restaurants had been uploaded to YouTube. In the clips, two employees sneezed in pizzas, topped pizzas with mucus, and carried out other similar atrocities, and the videos concluded with a message that the lucky buyer would get a pizza with special ingredients.

Soon thereafter two respectable blogs, one of them the most visited blog worldwide at that time, published the videos in order to warn consumers and demanded that two employees be identified. Tim McIntyre, Vice President of Communications at Domino's Pizza, was shocked, and his first reaction was a promise that perpetrators would be found immediately. Two readers, using special tools, successfully located the restaurant in the video. The perpetrators, Kristi Hammond and Michael Setzer, both employees of the Domino's branch in Conover, North Carolina, were identified the same day. The next morning Kristi Hammond sent an e-mail to the President of Communications, saying she was sorry for the videos, that it was all a bad joke and that none of the contaminated food was ever delivered to any of the customers. But the company immediately closed off and sterilized the restaurant. Both employees were immediately arrested, fired and sued. The video was seen by 250,000 people by the afternoon of the following day. The company published a written response at both blog sites, informed the customers in real time of its actions and published an official statement on its corporate website. The next day, the company created a Twitter account to inform its worried customers directly. An official apology by the company's President Patrick Doyle was published on YouTube. In the video, he thanked the online community that warned Domino's of the videos, emphasized that this was an isolated incident and that everything had been done that was necessary to regain customers' trust. He promised that quality standards and hiring practices would be re-examined to make sure something like this would never happen again. He showed awareness that two irresponsible individuals could severely injure the reputation of the entire company and of all its employees. The number of views of the five videos rose from 500,000 to one million within a few hours. At 21:30, the company succeeded in convincing YouTube to remove the controversial videos. On 16 April, a reporter from BBC contacted the company and published the news of the videos outside the online community. Local branches of Domino's Pizza recorded a decrease of 50 per cent in the number of orders. Also the stock price fell due to the scandal. But after 18 April, the crisis started to calm down. The media published reports from the trial and speculated who was responsible for the damage. Also some parodies of the videos appeared online.

Key terms

Storytelling. A means for sharing and interpreting experiences and messages. It can be defined as an active story management and transmission with selected address-ees, a defined context and a carefully chosen code, a central process of planning, implementation and control conducted by those responsible for an organization's communication.

Corporate story. A comprehensive narration about the organization, its origins, its vision and its mission, and its relations with numerous stakeholders. It must be a realistic and relevant description of the company, created in an open dialogue with all stakeholders that the company depends on.

Framing. A schema of interpretation or conveying the point of view refers to choos-ing certain aspects and their emphasis within the message, in such a way as to encourage a certain view on the topic, causal interpretation, moral evaluation and necessary measures of conduct. The frame is understood as a pattern of interpret-ation that determines context. It is a reference point for all future decisions and judgements. Through the presenting of a general context around the information presented we can influence how people think about that information. Information within a context, within a frame is altered by that context and frame.

Plurivocity. A fact that in a certain moment, various authorized and unauthorized corporate stories exist and that all of them try to be dominant and valid in the eyes of key stakeholders. Simultaneous co-existence of many stories or their var-ieties, which organizations need to have in mind, to control and, as far as possible, manage.

Organizational change. Occurs when the company restructures its resources (human, financial, technological and process) to enhance its abilities to create value and raise effectiveness. In theory, authors distinguish between two main forms of changes, known as first class changes, or evolution changes, and second class changes, or revolution changes which can be represented as a continuum. Organizational change is a structured approach in an organization for ensuring that changes are smoothly and successfully implemented to achieve lasting benefits.

Crisis. A certain division that physically influences the system as a whole and questions its foundations, subjective sense and existential core. These are unexpected events or circumstances that bring a company into disrepute and imperil its future profitability, growth and, possibly, its very survival.

Crisis communication. An interactive process of exchange of information and opinions about the crisis, its circumstances, possible solutions and responses among different social actors.

REVIEW QUESTIONS

- Why are stories important in the life of an individual and what is storytelling in an organizational context?
- Why is context important in corporate storytelling? How do frames define the meaning of narrative and how can framing be used by corporate communicators? Who are the key protagonists in the stories?
- How can be storytelling be used for achieving change within an organization? What are the goals and stages in achieving organizational change?
- What is the rhetorical approach to crisis communication? What are the main communication responses to crisis that companies can use?

How should Domino's have responded to the crisis? What kind of strategy would you use if you were a corporate communication manager at Domino's at the time of crisis? How would you react? Identify a corporate crisis/issue in the news. With the help of the key protagonist model analyse the issue and suggest the most effective ways of issue management.

References

Ansoff, Igor H. 1980. Strategic issue management. *Strategic Management Journal* 1 (2): 131–148.

Armenakis, Achilles A. and Stanley G. Harris. 2002. Crafting a change message to create transformational readiness. *Journal of Organizational Change Management* 15 (2): 169–183.

Bacharach, Samuel B. and Edward J. Lawler. 1998. Political alignments in organizations: contextualization, mobilization and coordination. In *Power and Influence in Organizations*, eds. Roderick M. Kramer and Margaret A. Neale. Thousand Oaks, CA: Sage Publications.

Belasen, Alan T. 2008. *The Theory and Practice of Corporate Communication: A Competing Values Perspective*. Los Angeles: Sage Publications, Inc.

Benoit, William L. 1997. Image repair discourse and crisis communication. *Public Relations Review* 23 (2): 177–186.

Berry, Gregory R. 2001. Making sense of the environmental behavior of chemical firms. *Journal of Management Inquiry* 10 (1): 58–73.

Boin, Arjen and Patrick Lagadec. 2000. Preparing for the future: critical challenges in crisis management. *Journal of Contingencies and Crisis Management* 8 (4): 185–191.

Bordia, Prashant, Elizabeth Jones, Cindy Gallois, Victor J. Callan and Nicholas DiFonzo. 2006. Management are aliens! Rumors and stress during organizational change. *Group Organization Management* 31 (5): 601–621.

Buchanan, David and Patrick Dawson. 2007. Discourse and audience: organizational change as multi-story process. *Journal of Management Studies* 44 (5): 669–686.

Burnett, John J. 1998. A strategic approach to managing crises. *Public Relations Review* 24 (4): 475–488.

Chase, Howard W. 1984. *Issue Management: Origins of the Future*. Stamford, CT: Issue Action Publications.

Cheney, George, Christensen Lars Thoger, Theodore E. Zorn and Shiv Ganesh. 2004. *Organisational Communication in an Age of Globalization. Issues, Reflections, Practices*. Long Grove, IL: Waveland Press.

Coombs, Timothy W. 1995. Choosing the right words: the development of guidelines for the selection of the 'appropriate' crisis response strategies. *Management Communication Quarterly* 8 (4): 447–476.

Currie, Graeme and Andrew D. Brown. 2003. A narratological approach to understanding processes of organizing in a UK hospital. *Human Relations* 56 (5): 563–586.

Cutlip, Scott M., Allen H. Center and Glen M. Broom. 2000. *Effective Public Relations*. London: Prentice Hall International.

Dowling, Grahame. 2001. *Creating Corporate Reputations*. New York: Oxford University Press.

Dutton, Jane E. and Edward Ottensmeyer. 1987. Strategic issue management systems: forms, functions, and contexts. *Academy of Management Review* 12 (2): 355–365.

Elving, Wim J. L. 2005. The role of communication in organizational change. *Corporate Communications: An International Journal* 10 (2): 129–138.

Entman, Robert M. 1993. Framing: toward clarification of a fractured paradigm. *Journal of Communication* 43 (4): 51–58.

Fearn-Banks, Kathleen. 2001. Crisis communication: a review of some best practices. In *Handbook of Public Relations*, eds. Robert Lawrence Heath and Gabriel M. Vasquez. Thousand Oaks, CA: Sage Publications, 479–486.

Fog, Klaus, Christian Budtz and Baris Yakaboylu. 2005. *Storytelling: Branding in Practice*. Berlin, Heidelberg: Springer.

Goffman, Erving. 1974. *Frame Analysis: An Essay on the Organization of Experience*. New York: Harper & Row.

Hallahan, Kirk. 1999. Seven models of framing: implications for public relations. *Journal of Public Relations Research* 11 (3): 205–242.

Heath, Robert Lawrence and Dan Pyle Millar. 2004. A rhetorical approach to crisis communication: management, communication processes, and strategic responses. In *Responding to Crisis: A Rhetorical Approach to Crisis Communication*, eds. Dan Pyle Millar and Robert Lawrence Heath. Mahwah, NJ: Lawrence Erlbaum Associates, 1–18.

Heugens, Pursey P. M. A. R. 2002. Strategic issues management: implications for corporate performance. *Business Society* 41 (4): 456–468.

Holten Larsen, Morgens. 2000. Managing the corporate story. In *The Expressive Organisation: Linking Identity, Reputation, and the Corporate Brand*, eds. Majken Schultz, Mary Jo Hatch and Morgens Holten Larsen. Oxford: Oxford University Press, 196–207.

Johansson, Catrin and Mats Heide. 2008. Speaking of change: three communication approaches in studies of organizational change. *Corporate Communications* 13 (3): 288–305.

Johansson, Ingrid and Per Skoglund. 1996. *Crisis Management at the National Level*. Stockholm: OCB.

Langer, Roy and Signe Thorup. 2006. Building trust in times of crisis: storytelling and change communication in an airline company. *Corporate Communications: An International Journal* 11 (4): 371–390.

Lerbinger, Otto. 1997. *The Crisis Manager: Facing Risk and Responsibility*. Mahwah, NJ: Lawrence Erlbaum Associates.

Mahon, John F. and Sandra A. Waddock. 1992. Strategic issues management: an integration of issue lifecycle perspectives. *Business Society* 31 (1): 19–32.

Malešič, Marjan. 2006. Teorija kriznega komuniciranja. *Ujma* 20. Available at: http://www.sos112.si/slo/tdocs/ujma/2006/malesic_2.pdf (18 October 2010).

Martin, Joanne, Martha S. Feldman, Mary Jo Hatch and Sim B. Sitkin. 1983. The uniqueness paradox in organizational stories. *Administrative Science Quarterly* 28 (3): 438–453.

Maynard, Roberta. 1993. Handling a crisis effectively. *Nation's Business* 81 (12): 54–55.

McLellan, Hilary. 2006. Corporate storytelling perspectives. *The Journal for Quality and Participation* 29 (1): 17–20.

Morgan, Sandra and Robert F. Dennehy. 1997. The power of organizational storytelling: a management development perspective. *Journal of Management Development* 16 (7): 494–501.

Newlove, Lindy, Eric K. Stern and Lina Svedin. 2000. *Auckland Unplugged*. Stockholm: ÖCB/The Swedish Agency for Civil Emergency Planning.

Papadatos, Caroline. 2006. The art of storytelling: how loyalty marketers can build emotional connections to their brands. *Journal of Consumer Marketing* 23 (7): 382–384.

Polkinghorne, Donald E. 1988. *Narrative Knowing and the Human Sciences*. Albany: State University of New York Press.

Propp, Vladimir Jakovlevič. 1928 [1968]. *Morphology of the Folktale*. United States of America: American Folklore Society and Indiana University.

Stephens, Keri K., Patty Callish Malone and Christine M. Bailey. 2005. Communicating with stakeholders during a crisis: evaluating message strategies. *Journal of Business Communication* 42 (4): 390–419.

van Riel, Cees B. M. 2000. Corporate communication orchestrated by a sustainable corporate story. In *The Expressive Organization: Linking Identity, Reputation, and the Corporate Brand*, eds. Majken Schultz, Mary Jo Hatch and Morgens Holten Larsen. New York: Oxford University Press, Inc., 157–181.

van Riel, Cees B. M. and Charles J. Fombrun. 2007. *Essentials of Corporate Communication: Implementing Practices for Effective Reputation Management*. London; New York: Routledge.

van Vuuren, Mark and Wim J. L. Elving. 2008. Communication, sensemaking and change as a chord of three strands: practical implications and a research agenda for communicating organizational change. *Corporate Communications: An International Journal* 13 (3): 349–359.

Wilkins, Alan L. 1984. The creation of company cultures: the role of stories and human resource system. *Human Resource Management* 23 (3): 41–60.

Zemke, Ron. 1990. Storytelling: back to basics. *Training Magazine* 27 (3): 44–50.

8

CORPORATE COMMUNICATIONS

CONTENTS

This chapter highlights some aspects of corporate communication that play an important role in transmitting corporate stories. It discusses the role of the company's spokesperson and top management, examines how celebrity endorsers are used by companies and presents elements of the company's visual image, corporate advertising and informal communications among stakeholders.

8.1 Purpose of corporate communications

An important part of storytelling is narration that refers to transmitting the corporate story with a clear purpose of convincing the receivers about the reality and rightness of the company's actions. The stories come to life when they are transmitted through various media, making the target publics accept the stories as their own. The stories have their beginning, climax and decline, and need to be revitalized repeatedly. This must be seen in terms of McLuhan's law that the medium, the means through which the corporate story is transmitted, is itself a message (McLuhan 1964). Due to the symbiotic relationship between the medium and the message, and depending on the characteristics of the medium, and the level of involvement of the respondents, the medium strongly influences how the message is perceived and understood. This results in a need to orchestrate and integrate all communications of a company in the framework of integrated (market) communication and public relations. Corporate communication as an organizational function has to be responsible for the integration of the internal and external communications of the company. It acts as a support for the company's principal activities and tasks, but also helps with the socialization of members in the company. It makes sure

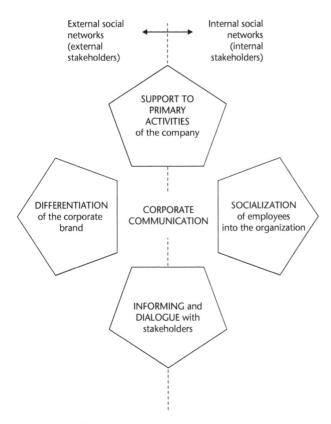

FIGURE 8.1 Key tasks of corporate communication

that internal and external stakeholders are suitably informed, and it orchestrates the appearance of the company in such a way that it ensures differentiation of the corporate brand on various markets (see Figure 8.1).

Even though we do not want to list and describe all **types of communication** that exist in social sciences, we still need to point out those that have an especially important role in the dissemination of the corporate story, namely communication by CEOs and the company's highest management, celebrity or media personalities, such as company endorsers, corporate visual identity, corporate marketing, and rumours.

8.2 Management as the company's spokesperson

The narrator has to master the principles of classic rhetoric. They have to have performing skills, persuasive power and characteristics that raise confidence; they must be able to clearly define the context of the story, know how to transmit the story in an interesting way, and need to explain the meaning of events in the story, as well as any consequences arising from the events. Companies often use special, well-trained spokespeople for transmitting corporate stories and attitudes, and special public relations experts for relations with the media. Although the two roles differ, they both need a communication specialist to do the job. **Spokespeople** have to master the techniques, but should also have strategic knowledge.

Because companies have to be in dialogue with their stakeholders and communicate strategic decisions to them, the Chair or Vice-Chair of the Board very often takes on the formal role of company spokesperson. We say that the **Chair of the Board** is a symbolic representation of the company's values and beliefs or that he/she is the first person to personify the company. The actions of the Chair, board members and of supervisory board members serve as an example – they build organizational culture, and at the same time, encourage other employees to act in the same way.

The people who have the highest place in the organizational hierarchy in their presentations usually draw from the referential reputation and formal power they get from their position in the organization. However, the formal function is not enough for a successful dissemination of the corporate story. The narrator's reputation that significantly contributes to the acceptance and efficiency of his/her message rests on three main foundations: the abilities, activities and achievements of the person who is being evaluated. Therefore, we speak of the **three 'Cs'** that make up the reputation of CEOs and board members: credibility, code of personal and professional ethics, and communication of the corporate vision to internal and external environments. Similar findings were made by the firm Burson-Marsteller, which posits that half of the company's overall reputation is based on the reputation of the management. The main elements that contribute to the reputation of managers are credibility, high ethical standards, successful internal communication, successful employment policy, ability to motivate employees, customer care, efficient crisis management, successful communication with external publics, measures to increase the company's market value and successful management in accordance with the company's strategic vision.

However, there is a distinction between a manager's reputation and their popularity or celebrity status in the media (Rindova *et al.* 2006; Treadway *et al.* 2009). **Popularity** can arise from a manager's or spokesperson's actions and personal reputation, and as such directly refers to their abilities and achievements (Rindova *et al.* 2006). **Personal reputation** refers to collectively perceived identity that reflects a complex combination of distinguishing personal characteristics and achievements, actions and projected images presented in the specified time frame that are observed directly and/or reported about by secondary sources (Ferris *et al.* 2003, 215). However, it is not necessarily so. The company's spokespeople can earn celebrity status simply by being a frequent guest of the media. Here, their real abilities or achievements do not play an important role or are even misrepresented or wrongly credited to them by reporters or the public. In this case, the single characteristic of the manager's popularity is the fact that they are famous (Boorstin 1961).

A combination of both is also possible. This happens when journalists praise a certain manager due to real attributes, decisions and achievements, and at the same time – in accordance with attribution theory (Kelley 1972) – ascribe other attributes or exaggerate in actual descriptions. This can, on the one hand, influence the actual characteristics and decisions of an individual, while on the other, it can raise the public expectations about the company's performance (Hayward et al. 2004).

If a manager wants to step out of mediocrity and be popular or even achieve celebrity status, the theory suggests using a combination of differentiation and consistency. They should break norms to some small extent, but do so in a consistent manner (Hayward et al. 2004). Managers need to know how to use decision and behaviour patterns that are different from regular ones, but need to do that consistently, regardless of the circumstances, time and place. This is what journalists recognize as the main reason for a company's success, and by exposing such a person and attributing to them additional characteristics, journalists enable them to appear frequently in the media, which results in celebrity status.

In the context of the relationship between reputation and fame, we must mention an American survey that divided managers into four groups. The first group are called the *icons*. It includes managers who have both reputation and fame. These managers combine style and smart choices in their work, and enjoy celebrity status in public. Famous managers who lack reputation are the *hound-dogs*. This group has gained many new members after major financial scandals in the USA, when the term manager became almost a synonym for fraud and scams. The *hidden gems* are managers who are not famous, but have a reputation. These are usually very competent managers enjoying a great reputation with the professional public and with the competition; their work is very successful. The last group of managers who are (almost) unknown, and have no reputation, are known as the *silent killers*. These managers have successfully avoided public attention or have covered up their unsuccessful actions. They are often even worse than the *hound-dogs* because their harmful actions remain undiscovered and uncondemned.

The reputation and communication skills of managers are a result of their innovative strategic handling and creating values for the company, while their celebrity status is created by the media. It is a fact that CEOs are becoming celebrities, and though there is no need for them to be one, it doesn't do any harm. Research shows that personal recognition, reputation or even celebrity status actually contribute to a company's reputation and therefore to its success. However, this connection is not clear and one-dimensional, since reputable or celebrity management itself cannot prevent the potential failure of the company. Either way, there is a positive connection between reputation and celebrity status and bonuses for such managers; however, this does not give them employment security (Edwards 2006; Treadway et al. 2009). Although the presence of managers in the media should at least be a minor goal of management, we should warn that managers should devote more attention to improving the company's business than to their own promotion (Edwards 2006).

8.3 Company's celebrity endorsers

Celebrity support in the promotion of the company and its products is a decades-old technique. Primarily concerned are celebrity and media personalities who appear as company supporters and use their visibility to support and promote a certain product, service or company, or to communicate and personify a corporate story. **Celebrity** is defined as the degree to which a social actor is documented by the media and viewed as being well known, powerful, prestigious and admired by media audiences (Perryman 2008). This category includes not only film, television and pop stars, but also sports stars, politicians, writers, businesspeople and people from other professions who directly support a company, publicly announce their support for a company, its products or services, or call on others for support (McCracken 1989). Although much attention is given to celebrities, there are other characters that marketing departments can engage in order to personalize a company or its products, such as cartoon characters, fantasy heroes (Belk 1989), minor celebrities, experts and general consumers (Daneshvary and Schwer 2000). Celebrity endorsements often involve four types of schema: scripts, role schema, individual person schema and object schema (Speck *et al.* 1988). **Scripts** are event schema that describe the prototypic structure of commonplace actions, such as, 'Drinking in a bar'. **Roles** are relational schema used to explain the intention and behaviour of people in specific situations. **Individual person schema** and **object schema** are trait-based impressions of specific people and things (Speck *et al.* 1988, 70). **Famous events** (e.g. the Olympic Games) can be used for endorsement as well (Gwinner 1997).

Early studies of celebrity endorsement (Friedman and Friedman 1979; Atkin and Block 1983; Kamins *et al.* 1989), as well as some newer ones (Farell *et al.* 2000; Byrne *et al.* 2003), show that celebrity support leads to higher efficiency of communication. The effects of celebrity endorsement include higher attentiveness to advertisements, higher recall, better likeability of adverts and brands, higher brand awareness and better brand image. Other studies established a positive correlation to purchase intent (Kahle and Homer 1985; Ho *et al.* 1997; Daneshvary and Schwer 2000), higher sales (Longman 1997), and to greater market value of the company (Farell *et al.* 2000). Celebrities also appear as promoters of positive social values and desired behaviours, such as AIDS prevention (Brown and Basil 1995; Basil 1996; Fraser and Brown 2002), teenage sexual behaviour, equal rights for women (Fraser and Brown 2002), rights of the child (e.g. UNICEF Goodwill Ambassadors), etc. Celebrities play an important role in political marketing, especially in the promotion of political programmes, candidates and parties (Smith 2001), because celebrity endorsement can increase the credibility and attractiveness of political candidates and political parties. The beneficial effects are even greater if endorsers do not present only positive information, but try to report in a balanced manner (Kamins *et al.* 1989).

The key **advantages of using celebrity** endorsement are the increased attention of stakeholders, increased awareness of the company and its offer, and a positive influence on the behavioural and purchase decisions of target audiences (Swerdlow and Swerdlow 2003). Celebrities can be a factor that influences identification of key stakeholders, above all consumers, with a company (Podnar 2004). However, **celebrity endorsement** has its disadvantages, too (Swerdlow and Swerdlow 2003):

- high cost related to celebrity support;
- issues arising from the impossibility of controlling the celebrity's public image;
- the extent of the credibility and effectiveness of celebrity support;
- possible support of other companies from a celebrity;
- vampirism, a phenomenon where a supporter becomes more interesting and important to the public than the cause or business they are supporting.

The successful use of celebrity endorsement focuses on the meanings that a supporter can bring in the process of perception of messages. A **meaning transfer** has, according to McCracken (1989), three stages. In the first, a strategic communication plan defines meanings that are intended for an entity such as product, service or company. Such definitions should be made based on the target audience and its cultural framework. After the meanings have been defined, suitable people, contexts and objects are identified that represent selected meanings and make them tangible. This stage is actually a search for some kind of cultural prototypes or representations of selected meanings that are present in an environment. It is important that the selected entities are trustworthy, credible, homely, likable and similar to the target group. These are the key factors that have the largest influence on identification. Celebrities must be able to make target consumers identify with them. According to Byrne *et al.* (2003), a chosen celebrity should be able to make a consumer identify with them (Byrne *et al.* 2003, 290) and be congruent with the entity they endorse. In the second stage, the meaning is transferred from the celebrity to a product, service or company. This is done by the consumer who realizes that meanings related to objects, context or people in a message are shared by a product or company that appears together with the former. 'The consumer suddenly "sees" the similarity between the celebrity and the product, and is prepared to accept that the meanings in the celebrity are in the product' (McCracken 1989, 316). In the third stage, the meanings from the company and the product are transferred to consumers. They use and take advantage of the meanings related to the company, product or service to create their own identity.

The meaning transfer can occur either based on mere ownership of a product or service, or of their incorporation in one's own identity, or of the acceptance of meanings, or their manipulation in the process of creating a unique identity. Received and adopted meanings help individuals to create their own identity and meanings that construct their lives. Consumers turn to their goods not only as bundles of utility with which to serve functions and satisfy needs, but also as bundles of meaning with which to fashion who they are and the world in which they live (Belk 1989). When this is done, the movement of meaning is complete.

The meaning that began in the culturally constituted world has finally come to rest in the life and experience of the consumer. 'The cultural circuit is complete' (McCracken 1989, 314).

When using celebrity endorsers in support of a company and its offer, it is important to make the right selection. The key criterion for the selection is, according to early studies, the credibility of the endorser, consisting of his/her expertise, trustworthiness and attractiveness (Ohanian 1991). In addition, when selecting suitable endorsers, companies should make sure that they are (Swerdlow and Swerdlow 2003):

- easy to recognize and inoffensive to the target market;
- relevant in terms that they fit the endorsed product;
- appreciated and valued by the target audience;
- distinct enough from other advertising to catch the eye of the target market;
- reliable, meaning that the person's past behaviour indicates he/she would be an ongoing asset to the product campaign.

8.4 Corporate visual identity (CVI)

The visual identity of a company makes a company visible, tangible and recognizable, and also defines a contextual framework for the contents that a company communicates. It can be defined as the 'sum of all the ways a company chooses to identify itself to all its publics' (Margulies 1977, 66). **Visual identity** is a visible part of corporate identity (Baker and Balmer 1997; Melewar 2001), expressed through some key elements, such as the name and logo of a company, its signature colours, typography, tagline and other company descriptors. Carefully planned and designed visual elements are applied to various media, such as banners, clothing, signposts, stamps, stationery, presentation templates, vehicle fleets, and the internal and external architecture of the company's property (van den Bosch *et al.* 2006). Visual identity of a company includes elements that are not only visual, but can also be perceived with other senses, such as a typical sound, smell or feel, which a company uses to communicate its story or to promote its offer. Visual identity is usually standardized and simplifies the manner in which a company presents itself to the public (Marquis 1970, 3).

The process of designing visual identity and communications includes the creation of the structure and form of visual information, from its conception, planning, drafting, to final implementation. Visual identity, as a clear and accurate representation system, not only tries to express the existing corporate identity, but moreover tries to organize, and influence, an individual's perception, understanding and feeling about the company (Sturken and Cartwright 2001). The **visual identity system** as a whole, as well as its individual parts, functions as a symbol that stands in place of something, or in place of its object, either independently or in combination as an icon, indication or symbol (Peirce 1935). As a sign or sign system, visual identity functions both within the symbol, aesthetic and fantasy systems, as well as within the convention system, and plays different communication roles, from identification, explanation to convincing.

Visual identity is thus a visual statement from a company to its environment about who and what the company is and how it sees itself, and has much to do with how the company is seen by the environment. According to Selame and Selame (1975), a successful identity system visually distinguishes a company from its competitors. Visual identity has **four major functions** in corporate communication (van den Bosch *et al.* 2006).

1. It provides a company with *visibility* and *recognition*. If a company stands out with its characteristic elements, it makes it easier for external stakeholders and other observers to recognize and organize the perceived signals. For companies, it is of vital importance that people know that the company exists and remember its name.
2. In addition, visual identity plays an important role in *reminding* individuals that the company exists and operates. Visual identity elements, such as choice of colours, logo or font can affect people's judgement and behaviour.
3. Visual identity is very important in forming a *first impression*, when an individual is only getting to know the company. Visual identity expresses the company's coherence, the structure of the company's organization and the relationships between divisions and units.
4. Through visual identity, a company achieves uniformity of its units, while the symbolic level of visual identity relates to employees' *identification* with co-workers or the organization as a whole.

When creating corporate visual identity, we must, as far as possible, consider the following rules to design a CVI that is:

*   *simple*, in order to be easily remembered;
*   *unique*, to be different from others;
*   *aesthetically durable*, to be attractive over a long period of time.

Although there is a rule that visual identity elements should not be modified often, let alone completely changed, over long years of a company's activities, there appears a need to revitalize its visual appearance. This is most often the case in mergers or the break-up of companies or their units. In addition, changes of visual identity elements are often when a company is in the process of repositioning, or when a company is widening its product range, entering new markets, or when a new management takes over, because the new heads want to mark this new period with changes in specific CVI elements. However, any such measures must be carefully and critically examined and implemented only after there has been a positive answer to the question of whether such measures are indeed needed, and what the consequences will be. It is important to examine the responses of employees and consumers, and to consider what the costs of designing and implementing a new CVI will be. A thoughtless change or modification of the CVI as a whole or in part can have more negative effects, and higher costs, than benefits. However, a good motivation for the renovation of visual identity is, when due to various reasons (e.g. changes in product range, organizational structure, corporate philosophy, scandals) a company is unable to achieve a consistent visual identity; when there is discord or disharmony among different elements of its CVI; or when the existing CVI's aesthetics are out-of-date.

When we decide to create a new or modify the old corporate visual identity, we must do so in a carefully planned, step-by-step manner. In the *first stage*, we set goals for the modification of the CVI based on the strategic aims of the company and its existing and optimal corporate identity. A detailed analysis of the situation must follow, examining both competition as well as the internal situation. In the *next stage*, we prepare an overview of communication tools and create suggestions for new individual communication elements. These suggestions should be tested if possible, and the most appropriate selected and protected. The results are most commonly presented in a visual identity manual, a copy of which must go to everyone who is involved in the application of visual elements to different media. The *last stage* is a sudden or a gradual replacement of the old system with a new one. It is beneficial to support the new solutions with a communication campaign aimed at internal and external audiences.

The management of the corporate visual identity must make sure that the rules of use of visual elements are strictly observed and that visual identity is consistently implemented, as defined in the manual and other instructions. Consistency should apply to every use and appearance with different stakeholders and in different media and campaigns (Fombrun and van Riel 2004). A company can encourage consistent use by making employees understand the strategy of the organization, the socialization processes in the organization and the concrete instruction for the use of visual elements, which facilitates managing the visual elements of the CVI (van den Bosch *et al.* 2006).

As the results of neuroscientific research show, learned and used symbols are imprinted in one's brain and have a direct influence on our decisions and behaviour, while also the recall of known elements is much more effective and cheaper than the constant learning of new elements (Repovš 1995). That is why visual elements of the CVI function as a constant or a signature of a company in all its communications.

8.5 Corporate and institutional advertising

Corporate advertising is, according to Patti and McDonald (1985), a special, paid and impersonal form of communication by organizations that is very often used to transmit key attributes and values of corporate identity in order to achieve, through communication about itself and its own corporate brand, a desired corporate image with the chosen target group. It is about advertising a company and its attitudes as opposed to advertising concrete products and services. This is a tool that helps us to articulate clearly a corporate story and transfer it in a focused way. By transmitting appropriate messages through this communication channel, we try to strengthen the company's reputation, endorse the company's products and services, provide information about the company's field of activity, describe its main achievements, promote its business interests, give important information about the institution (e.g. information on investment policy, new management, the company's goals and standards, etc.), present and defend the company's position and inform stakeholders about the socially responsible practices of the company (Schumman *et al.* 1991). Corporate advertising is also able to meet some other goals, such as influencing the buying of a company's shares, attracting the best employees, unifying organizational culture, updating information about a company's activities on the market, explaining a company's philosophy and values, announcing important anniversaries, promoting company-friendly legislation, or making a company visible, especially in industries where the advertising of products is strictly regulated or even prohibited.

Research shows (see Schumman *et al.* 1991 for an overview) that corporate and institutional advertising are efficient at raising awareness, knowledge and likeability, and it has also been established that companies spending more money on such advertising tend to be regarded more highly in many fields, including the quality of offer, innovativeness, management competence, and honest responsiveness to stakeholders and employees. There is also a correlation between corporate advertising and perception of a company's success, related to the fact that such advertising positively influences the company's public image. This communication not only influences the creation of the corporate image in the eyes of consumers, but also changes consumers' attitudes and behaviour toward the company. Research has also established the influence of corporate advertising on potential investors and shareholders, especially in the form of an impulse that made them examine the possibility of investing in the company more thoroughly. It also makes important and relevant stakeholders have a positive attitude toward the company (Schumann *et al.* 1991). A study also confirmed the influence of corporate advertising on the number and quality of applications for available work placements (Collins and Han 2004). Furthermore, it directly influences the perception of the products and brands that a company markets (Biehal and Sheinin 1998). According to Schumann *et al.* (1991), the effects of corporate advertising coincide perfectly with the typology suggested by Rothschild (1987) that divides corporate advertising into four categories: image, finance, special occasion and defence or public matters.

We use the terms *corporate advertising*, *institutional advertising*, *advocacy* and *issue advertising* (Sethi 1979) to describe advertising that is paid for by an organization, and whose main intention is to communicate the organization's position or attitude toward social, economic, ethical and ecological issues or other topics of public debate, or to respond to negative attitudes of the public toward the company. This special form of advertising serves an organization as a tool for presenting itself as an important social subject that is not only achieving its basic aim by offering products and services, but presenting itself as an organization that helps shape society, the relationships within and conditions in society. Such advertising is not passive, but plays a very active role. Its goal is to help the company to clearly demonstrate its attitude toward certain issues and debates and to influence public attitudes or even formal policies in these contexts (Waltzer 1988). With an appropriate use of corporate advertising, a company can not only present its corporate story or offer its interpretation, but can guide a public discussion into those directions that are beneficial for the company and its stakeholders, and can even reverse negative public opinions about and attitudes toward the company.

Depending on the story a company wants to tell and the communication goals it wants to achieve, corporate and/or institutional advertising can primarily be aimed at the general public in a specific business environment or to specific publics, such as current and potential employees, current and potential shareholders, business and financial publics, different consumer segments, local communities, state institutions, regulatory agencies and special interest groups. These are the groups of stakeholders who can, in specific circumstances, influence the environment in which the company is operating and can, most importantly, influence people who do not yet have an opinion about a matter that is important for a company, and whose opinion is also important (Woolward 1982). Among all groups, shareholders and consumers are the two most important (Schumann *et al.* 1991). However, very often companies want to address different publics and achieve a suitable response with a single content, which makes this tool very challenging to use. For that reason, Ogilvy (1983) highlights the importance of a long-term strategy in planning corporate advertising and points out many corporate advertising campaigns that have failed. According to him, reasons for failure lie mostly in the ignorance and insincerity of intentions and messages. Therefore, we still need to use corporate advertising with great care (Sethi 1979).

Although we usually think of corporate advertising triggers in terms of advertisements in classical media, such as TV, radio and print, this view is narrow-minded because it ignores new media and its potential as a place for the communication of corporate stories. Beside classical media, other media can carry out the goals and functions of corporate advertising, for example, an annual report, which can provide all information required by law, and is besides a perfect medium to convey the corporate story. The same is true for various print materials presenting the company's profile, and other presentations, including the organization of events. Other important media are the intranet and the internet with communication tools such as websites (Hwang *et al.* 2003), presentation and active content management with applications for social networks, forums, etc. (Lee and Song 2010). Independently, but even more so in combination with other accessible media and information channels, an increasingly important role is played by corporate internal and external newsletters, which are media that can have either a print, electronic or interactive form. The advantage of the afore-mentioned media is that a company can disseminate extensive information about itself, its management, employees and offer, and more importantly, it can, through corporate stories for a relatively low cost, establish an interaction with its stakeholders. These media help to form, transmit, modify, unite and monitor corporate stories, which can then become part of stakeholders' lives. Thus, companies thoughtfully supply their stakeholders with corporate stories, and they systematically monitor any mentions of the company's name and its spheres of interest.

8.6 Informal communications

Rumour, gossip and urban legends are seen as informal communication that spreads from person to person, regardless of how (un)authenticated and (un)verified this information may be (Michelson and Mouly 2002). We define corporate rumour as narratives, either in writing or in spoken word, that enable transmission of emotions, opinions, beliefs and positions about an organization and its actors, where its circulation is not paid for but rather happens on a voluntary basis within social interactions (Michelson et al. 2010). We are talking about informal communication among people about ownership, use or attributes of specific products and/or services and their sellers (Westbrook 1987). Word of mouth is an exchange of short, spoken messages between a source and a receiver, which is spontaneous, informal, not paid for and not prepared in advance (Gilly et al. 1998).

According to DiFonzo and Bordia (2007), there are **three forms of informal communications** between individuals.

- **Rumours** are defined as unauthenticated but, for the receiver, potentially useful and relevant information or statements that circulate among people about different social actors, exist in the context of uncertainty, danger or potential threats, and help people understand circumstances and manage risks.
- **Gossip** relates to a form of social interaction, in which evaluated statements and information accompanied with a judgement are transmitted in a conversation or chat about other individuals. The context for the chat is creating, changing and maintaining a social network with the goal to inform, fortify, eliminate and strengthen a member's status in a group, and to transfer norms within the group.
- **Urban legends** relate to unusual, humorous or horrible events in the present time and therefore involve modern topics. They are conveyed as information about something that did happen, or could have happened, and include a moral, although their basic goal is entertainment and amusement.

While rumours address the need for understanding of uncertain circumstances, gossiping and belonging, urban legends address only the need for meaning and purpose (DiFonzo and Bordia 2007). In the context of corporate story management, all three forms of information transfer are very important. Business science holds all three as media that have the most influence on individuals, their perceptions, preferences, choices and behaviours (see Butlle 1998 for an overview). The key to their efficiency lies in the fact that in terms of perception, this is the most vividly presented information (Herr *et al.* 1991), while transmitters of such information are most often perceived as credible, trustworthy and as having no hidden commercial interest. That is why a very difficult situation for a company is if gossip becomes undesirable corporate stories; rather, companies should make sure that their corporate stories are circulating as a controlled positive rumour. A major problem is that in terms of circulation speed, negative information travels much faster than positive (Hart *et al.* 1990; Söderlund 1998).

Although such forms of interpersonal communication are virtually beyond a company's control, this does not mean that companies should take a passive stance. Theoretical and research work provided in recent years gives a thorough knowledge of the character, working and efficiency of such word of mouth information, both in the classical as well as in interactive environments. This knowledge can help companies to actively apply these phenomena to their own benefit. Informal communication is something that an organization cannot avoid when engaged in internal or external communication. It is even better if a company sees this communication form as a medium for conveying its corporate stories and achieving other company goals. According to its source of informal communications, we must distinguish between organic and stimulated information. Companies can influence organic information indirectly by means of their own programmes and by meeting their promises, while stimulated information is in any case a result of a company's active informal efforts to circulate information.

A company's management should actively monitor internal and external information related to the company. Besides the well-established classical media monitoring and careful examination of conditions within a company, in recent times a new professional role has developed within the organization for people whose task is to monitor all mentions of the company on the internet and to make sure that this information reaches those responsible in the company as quickly as possible. Those in positions of responsibility must then be able to detect, monitor and respond to this information (van Laer and Ruyter 2010). To analyse the numerous and heterogeneous interpersonal and private company-related information that a company has to monitor, there are several helpful criteria.

- *Valence*: from an organization's point of view, rumours can be positive or negative.
- *Thematic focus*: different stakeholders emphasize different themes that can relate to employment policy, internal relations, business circumstances, investments, the company's product line and purchase decisions.
- *Time factor*: a distinction is made according to whether rumours were started before or after an interaction with the company took place.
- *Stimulation*: rumours sometimes start at the initiative of stakeholders who actively seek information, but sometimes are provided by the source without stimulation.

- *Intervention*: a distinction is made between rumours that are actually spontaneous and rumours that are stimulated by a company, opinion leaders or competition with a particular agenda.

Allport and Postman (1965) were the first to explain the intensity of interpersonally transmitted rumour. They established that the intensity of rumour (R) depends on two factors: importance of the topic (i) and ambiguity (a). The formula is as follows: $R = i \times a$.

The circulation intensity of a rumour depends on how important the topic is for everyone involved in the communication process, multiplied by the sense of ambiguity of the facts related to the rumour. The fact that both factors are multiplied means that if the circumstances of the topic are certain (e.g. reliable official information), there will be no ambiguity and consequently less chance for rumours. The same happens if the information is not of interest to the people involved. Hence, it has been proposed that the less reliable official information there is, the stronger and more intense rumours and other informal forms of communication are. If we add to the formula fear and (dis)trust in the source (DiFonzo and Bordia 2002) and, according to Dichter (1966), characteristics and motives of the source and the receiver, the link between them, the influence of reference persons (e.g. opinion leaders, experts, innovators, reference groups) and actual attributes of the object that the information is about, we get a real picture of the circumstances in which such communication is created.

A majority of such informal information begins as a report on the actual reality, or on the subjective perception of an individual, which he/she is sure would be interesting for others. We must keep in mind, however, that there is a tendency to reduce, modify and even distort information, provided that this makes the core of the message consistent. Rumours serve namely to convince the audience and not to provide accurate information (Kapferer 1990). There are **three phases in the reduction of information** (Allport and Postman 1965).

1. *Levelling*: in the first phase, the story is abridged to key information, details are left out.
2. *Sharpening*: specific details are perceived, recalled and reported while others are ignored, which makes this a selective preservation of certain information.
3. *Assimilation*: in the last phase, the initial information is supplemented with forms and meanings that are in accordance with cognitive schemes – habits, desires and expectations – of people transmitting this information.

In addition, distortion occurs also through condensation, where the message is reduced to a few easily remembered details; conventionalization, where unfamiliar elements from the message are removed; and exaggeration, which is a representation of something in an excessive manner (Forston 1975).

Buckner (1965) provided an explanation of the accuracy of information transfer. According to him, accuracy depends firstly on the importance of the content:

the more important a piece of information, the stronger the tendency to transmit the information accurately. Accuracy of information also depends on the level of suspiciousness of the receiver: if a receiver is sceptical about the information, they will check the authenticity of the information, which raises the level of its accuracy. Further, an established communication channel means that the reliability of the source will be examined more easily. The last factor influencing accuracy is the intensity of a rumour: the more intensely a rumour is distorted, the smaller effect it has, because it becomes unbelievable.

Companies can encourage individuals and groups to disseminate information about them by forming corporate communities or organized forms of interactions with stakeholders, by offering tools that enable expression and exchange of opinions, motivating the company's advocates, identifying and influencing important opinion leaders, by actively involving stakeholders in organizational processes, honestly responding to their needs, and by actively dealing with the complaints and initiatives of stakeholders. Research shows that even when receivers are aware of the possibility that it is the company itself which disseminates information through informal channels, this can be beneficial for the company (Mayzlin 2006). It was also established that it is suitable and profitable if a company offers formal awards for the dissemination of news and the corporate story. Contrary to the popular belief, however, that the most efficient (paid) disseminators of such news are loyal consumers, it has been established that disloyal or independent consumers do even better. The literature identifies three key factors that influence effective dissemination of such information (Oetting 2009):

- the personal experience of the receiver;
- the role of opinion leaders as disseminators of information;
- the solidness of links within the social network of receivers.

Although opinion leaders play an important role in the transmission of information, we see that networks of which a person is a member are most often even more important (Godes and Mayzlin 2004). It has also been observed that a group of independent people has a greater influence on the forming of opinions as a homogeneous group, even though the latter has more members (Antonides and van Raaij 1998). This also means that a number of small groups can do more damage to a company than one large group.

People responsible for corporate communication should use formal channels to inform the company's stakeholders in a timely, thorough and consistent manner about major events, processes and other important matters. The management should prevent information from being stockpiled by a small group of chosen individuals, but has to rather make sure that information is sent simultaneously to different groups (DiFonzo and Bordia 2002). When a company is faced with rumours, it must respond as quickly as possible and reveal the facts to the public, while at the same time continue to keep its promises and communicate in a transparent way.

CASE: GORENJE

The company Gorenje was founded in 1950 on a site where an old black-smith's workshop, nationalized after WWII, once stood in the village of Gorenje. In the beginning, it was a small workshop for production of agricultural machinery. However, the legendary director Ivan Atelšek soon moved the company to the town of Velenje and transformed it into a competitive enterprise on the European markets. Today, this more-than-60-year-old company, now a stock corporation, sells its products in over 70 countries worldwide. It employs around 11,000 people in different divisions (home appliances, interior design, ecology, energy and services), in a network of connected companies in Slovenia and abroad. Its annual income is over €1.2 billion. More than 90 per cent of Gorenje products are exported, 90 per cent of which are the company's own brands: Gorenje, Atag, Mora, Pelgrim, Etna, Körting, Sidex, Asko in Upo. Gorenje's mission is 'to create innovative, design-driven products and services that bring simplicity to our users'. The greatest concerns of the company are to satisfy the consumers and to create value for every stakeholder in a socially responsible way.

Gorenje strives to become the world's best design-driven innovator of home products, sticking to the principles of sustainable development and adapting to changing consumer needs. This strategy is consistent with company history since Gorenje employed its first industrial designer in 1963, and a few years later a design centre was formed that still exists today as Gorenje Design Studio. The company's devotion to top design is encoded also in its identity sign – 'Gorenje' uses Helvetica typeface, which appears as a symbol of modernism, especially in the post-WWII international style. The typeface uses simple and clear lines, is easy to read, is timeless and easily transferable.

In the 1990s, Gorenje furthered its own programmes of design and development, but it also started to cooperate with some world-famous designers and brands. By the end of the twentieth century, the company's devotion to design resulted in many product series, such as Gorenje Pininfarina, Gorenje appliances made with Swarovski elements, Gorenje Ora-Ïto, Gorenje appliances for iPod and Gorenje designed by Karim Rashid.

Even though there is a product line from Gorenje for each price segment of consumer, the company's communications always emphasize first class design, innovation and technological competence as its key competitive advantages. Products created in cooperation with other quality designer brands were not merely best selling products but also very important elements of the corporate story on which Gorenje based its visibility and market position.

One such strategic move was to launch a special line of refrigerator-freezers with hand-set crystals of respected Austrian manufacturer Swarovski in Europe in 2005. Besides silver or shiny black appliances with 3,500 crystals that were available in stores, there were also five unique black refrigerators with 7,000 crystals each that were sold at a charity auction. The first charity auction event was organized at the famous Opera Ball in Bucharest in 2006. The next auction took place in Ljubljana and the money raised went to Unicef Slovenija. At the Moscow auction, the refrigerator was bought by a Russian millionaire, Rustam Tariko, for US$110,000, which was given to the Sun Circle movement helping homeless Russian children. In September 2006, another successful auction took place in Glasgow. A television broadcast on Channel 5 was hosted by design gurus Justin Ryan and Colin McAllister. The last auction was organized as part of one of the most visible British charity events, Children in Need, in 2006. It was broadcast on Radio 2 in a 'Money Can't Buy' show hosted by Terry Wogan. A Gorenje refrigerator was sold for £33,000 on a radio channel that reaches 13 million listeners per week. Also in 2006, a Gorenje-Swarovski refrigerator was also exhibited at Harrods department store, which was at that time decorated in line with the new James Bond film, Casino Royale, and named Christmas Royale 2007.

Although the campaign's budget was fairly low (about €30,000), the results were great. Instead of the planned 300 refrigerators sold by the end of 2006, Gorenje sold a few thousand of them, whilst its website recorded five times more visitors than planned. Most importantly, media reports in various countries (in Great Britain alone there were 80 unpaid articles) secured Gorenje an immense media presence. To buy such advertising space would have cost millions of Euros. The campaign also opened doors to some distributors that previously have been closed.

Key terms

Corporate spokesperson. Special, well-trained person engaged or elected to speak on behalf of an organization. His role is to ensure that public announcements are made in the most effective way and through the most appropriate channels.

Celebrity. Defined as the degree to which a social actor is documented by the media and viewed as being well known, powerful, prestigious and admired by media audiences. This category includes not only film, television and pop stars, but also sports stars, politicians, writers, business people and people from other professions who directly support a company, publicly announce their support for a company, its products or services, or call on others for support.

Corporate visual identity. The sum of all visual cues standardizes and simplifies the manner a company chooses to identify itself to all its publics. The visual part of corporate identity expressed through some key elements, such as the name and logo of a company, its signature colours, typography, tagline and other company descriptors. The visual identity of a company includes elements that are not only visual, but can also be perceived with other senses, such as a typical sound, smell or feel, which a company uses to communicate its story or to promote its offer.

Corporate advertising. A special form of advertising that is paid for by an organization, and whose main intention is to communicate the organization's position or attitude toward social, economic, ethical and ecological issues or other topics of public debate, or to respond to negative attitudes of the public toward the company. This special form of advertising serves an organization as a tool for presenting itself as an important social subject that is not only achieving its basic aim by offering products and services, but presenting itself as an organization that helps shape society, the relationships within and conditions in society.

Informal communications. Rumour, gossip and urban legends are seen as word of mouth communication that spreads from person to person, regardless of how (un)authenticated and (un)verified this information may be. They are narratives, either in writing or in spoken word, that enable transmission of emotions, opinions, beliefs and positions about an organization and its actors, where its circulation is not paid for but rather happens on a voluntary basis within social interactions.

REVIEW QUESTIONS

- Explain the key tasks of the corporate communication department and its relation to other departments in an organization.
- What is the role of the CEO in corporate communications? How does the CEO's reputation relate to the company's reputation (and vice versa)?
- What are the advantages and disadvantages of using celebrities as means for corporate communications? Why and how can word of mouth be monitored and stimulated by companies?
- What is the strategic role of corporate visual identity and what is important when it comes to its revitalization? How is visual identity related to corporate advertising? How can be a corporate advertisement be placed in the new media?

Discuss how Gorenje overcame the obstacles of a low budget campaign. What was the essence of its success? Think about alternative and new media and their use for corporate communication purposes. How can different communication tools be used to build effective campaigns (think about the different uses of visual identity, publicity, social media, etc.)?

References

Allport, Gordon Willard and Leo Postman. 1965. *The Psychology of Rumor.* New York: Russell & Russell.

Antonides, Gerrit and Fred W. van Raaij. 1998. *Consumer Behaviour: A European Perspective.* Chichester: John Wiley.

Atkin, Charles and Martin Block. 1983. Effectiveness of celebrity endorsers. *Journal of Advertising Research* 23 (1): 57–61.

Baker, Michael J. and John M.T. Balmer. 1997. Visual identity: trappings or substance. *European Journal of Marketing* 31 (5/6): 366–375.

Basil, D. Michael. 1996. Identification as a mediator of celebrity effects. *Journal of Broadcasting & Electronic Media* 40 (4): 478–495.

Belk, Russell W. 1989. Effects of identification with comic book heroes and villains of consumption on materialism among former comic book readers. *Advances in Consumer Research* 16: 414–419.

Biehal, Gabriel J. and Daniel A. Sheinin. 1998. Managing the brand in a corporate advertising environment. *Journal of Advertising* 27 (2): 99–110.

Boorstin, Daniel J. 1961. *The Image: A Guide to Pseudo-events in America*. New York: Harper & Row.

Brown, William J. and Michael D. Basil. 1995. Media celebrities and public health: responses to 'Magic' Johnson's HIV disclosure and its impact on AIDS risk and high-risk behaviors. *Health Communication* 7 (4): 345–371.

Buckner, Taylor H. 1965. A theory of rumor transmission. *The Public Opinion Quarterly* 29 (1): 54–70.

Butlle, Francis A. 1998. Word of mouth: understanding and managing referral marketing. *Journal of Strategic Marketing* 6 (3): 241–254.

Byrne, Angela, Maureen Whitehead and Steven Breen. 2003. The naked truth of celebrity endorsement. *British Food Journal* 105 (4/5): 288–296.

Collins, Christopher J. and Jian Han. 2004. Exploring applicant pool quantity and quality: the effects of early recruitment practice strategies, corporate advertising, and firm reputation. *Personnel Psychology* 57 (3): 685–717.

Daneshvary, Rennae and Keith R. Schwer. 2000. The association endorsement and consumers' intention to purchase. *Journal of Consumer Marketing* 17 (3): 203–213.

Dichter, Ernest. 1966. How word-of-mouth advertising works. *Harvard Business Review* 44 (6): 147–166.

DiFonzo, Nicholas and Prashant Bordia. 2002. Rumors and stable-cause attribution in prediction and behavior. *Organizational Behavior and Human Decision Processes* 88 (2): 785–800.

——2007. *Rumor Psychology: Social and Organizational Approaches*. Washington, DC: American Psychological Association.

Edwards, Lee. 2006. Rethinking power in public relations. *Public Relations Review* 32 (3): 229–231.

Farrell, Kathleen A., Gordon V. Karels, Kenneth W. Montfort and Christine A. McClatchey. 2000. Celebrity performance and endorsement value: the case of Tiger Woods. *Managerial Finance* 26 (7): 1–15.

Ferris, Gerald R., Fred R. Blass, Ceasar Douglas, Robert W. Kolodinsky and Darren C. Treadway. 2003. Personal reputation in organizations. In *Organizational Behavior: The State of the Science*, ed. Jerald Greenberg. Mahwah, NJ: Lawrence Erlbaum Associates, Inc., 211–246.

Fombrun, Charles J. and Cees B. M. van Riel. 2004. *Fame and Fortune: How Successful Companies Build Winning Reputations*. Upper Saddle River, NJ: Financial Times Prentice Hall.

Forston, Robert F. 1975. Sense and non-sense: jury trial communication. *Brigham Young University Law Review* 3: 601–637.

Fraser, Benson P. and William J. Brown. 2002. Media, celebrities, and social influence: identification with Elvis Presley. *Mass Communication and Society* 5 (2): 183–206.

Friedman, Hershey H. and Linda Friedman. 1979. Endorser effectiveness by product type. *Journal of Advertising Research* 19 (5): 67–71.

Gilly, Mary C., John L. Graham, Mary Finley Wolfinbarger and Laura J. Yale. 1998. A dyadic study of interpersonal information search. *Journal of the Academy of Marketing Science* 26 (2): 83–100.

Godes, David and Dina Mayzlin. 2004. Using online conversations to study word of mouth communication. *Marketing Science* 23 (4): 545–560.

Gwinner, Kevin. 1997. A model of image creation and image transfer in event sponsorship. *International Marketing Review* 14 (3): 145–158.

Hart, Christopher W. L., James L. Heskett and Earl W. Sasser, Jr. 1990. The profitable art of recovery. *Harvard Business Review* 68 (4): 148–156.

Hayward, Mathew L. A., Violina P. Rindova and Timothy G. Pollock. 2004. Believing one's own press: the causes and consequences of CEO celebrity. *Strategic Management Journal* 25: 637–653.

Herr, Paul M., Frank R. Kardes and John Kim. 1991. Effects of word-of-mouth and product-attribute information on persuasion: an accessibility-diagnositicity perspective. *Journal of Consumer Research* 17 (4): 454–462.

Ho, Foo Nin, Scott J. Vitell, James H. Barnes and Rene Desborde. 1997. Ethical correlates of role conflict and ambiguity in marketing: the mediating role of cognitive moral development. *Journal of the Academy of Marketing Science* 25 (2): 117–126.

Hwang, Jang-Sun, Sally J. McMillan and Guiohk Lee. 2003. Corporate web sites as advertising: an analysis of function, audience, and message strategy. *Journal of Interactive Advertising* 3 (2): 10–23.

Kahle, Lynn R. and Pamela M. Homer. 1985. Physical attractiveness of the celebrity endorser: a social adaptation perspective. *Journal of Consumer Research* 11 (4): 954–961.

Kamins, Michael A., Meredith J. Brand, Stuart A. Hoeke and John C. Moe. 1989. Two-sided versus one-sided celebrity endorsement: the impact on advertising effectiveness and celebrity. *Journal of Advertising* 18 (2): 4–10.

Kapferer, Jean-Noel. 1990. *Rumours: Users, Interpretations and Users*. New Brunswick, NJ: Transaction Publishers.

Kelley, Harold H. 1972. Attribution in social interaction. In *Perceiving the Causes of Behavior*, eds. Edward E. Jones, David E. Kanouse, Harold H. Kelley, Richard E. Nisbett, Stuart Valins and Bernard Weiner. Morristown, NJ: General Learning Press, 1–26.

Lee, Young Lyoul and Seokwoo Song. 2010. An empirical investigation of electronic word-of-mouth: informational motive and corporate response strategy. *Computers in Human Behavior* 26 (5): 1073–1080.

Longman, John P. 1997. Endorsements for sale. *US News and World Report* 123 (8): 11.

Margulies, Walter P. 1977. Make the most of your corporate identity. *Harvard Business Review* 55 (4): 66–72.

Marquis, Harold H. 1970. *The Changing Corporate Image*. New York: American Management Association, Inc.

Mayzlin, Dina. 2006. Promotional chat on the internet. *Marketing Science* 25 (2): 155–163.

McCracken, Grant. 1989. Who is the celebrity endorser? Cultural foundations of the endorsement process. *Journal of Consumer Research* 16 (3): 310–321.

McLuhan, Marshall. 1964. *Understanding Media: The Extensions of Man*. London; New York; Toronto: McGraw-Hill.

Melewar, T. C. 2001. Measuring visual identity: a multi-construct study. *Corporate Communications: An International Journal* 6 (1): 36–41.

Michelson, Grant, Ad van Iterson and Kathryn Waddington. 2010. Gossip in organizations: contexts, consequences, and controversies group. *Organization Management* 35 (4): 371–390.

Michelson, Grant and Suchitra V. Mouly. 2002. 'You didn't hear it from us but…': towards an understanding of rumour and gossip in organisations. *Australian Journal of Management* 27 (1): 57–65.

Oetting, Martin. 2009. *Ripple Effect: How Empowered Involvement Drives Word of Mouth.* Wiesbaden: Gabler.

Ogilvy, David. 1983. *Confessions of an Advertising Man.* New York: Dell.

Ohanian, Roobina. 1991. The impact of celebrity spokespersons' perceived image on consumers' intention to purchase. *Journal of Advertising Research* 31 (1): 46–52.

Patti, Charles H. and John P. McDonald. 1985. Corporate advertising: process, practices, and perspectives. *Journal of Advertising* 14 (1): 42–49.

Peirce, Charles Sanders. 1935. *Collected Papers of Charles Sanders Peirce,* Volume III. Cambridge, MA: Harvard University Press.

Perryman, Alexa A. 2008. *Linking celebrity to firm performance: A multi-level analysis. A Dissertation submitted to the Department of Management in partial fulfillment of the requirements for the degree of Doctor of Philosophy.* Available at: http://etd.lib.fsu.edu/theses/available/etd-04032008-091454/unrestricted/PerrymanASpring2008.pdf (20 October 2010).

Podnar, Klement. 2004. *Ugled, organizacijska identifikacija in zavezanost zaposlenih.* Doktorska disertacija. Ljubljana: Fakulteta za družbene vede.

Repovš, Jernej. 1995. *Kako nastaja in deluje učinkovita, tržno usmerjena celostna grafična podoba kot del simbolnega identitetnega sistema organizacij.* Ljubljana: Studio Marketing.

Rindova, Violina P., Timothy G. Pollack and Mathew L. A. Hayward. 2006. Celebrity firms: the social construct of market popularity. *The Academy of Management Review* 31 (1): 50–71.

Rothschild, Michael L. 1987. *Advertising: From Fundamentals to Strategies.* Lexington, MA: D. C. Heath and Company.

Schumman, David W., Jan M. Hathcote and Susan West. 1991. Corporate advertising in America: a review of published studies on use, measurement, and effectiveness. *Journal of Advertising* 20 (3): 35–56.

Selame, Elinor and Joseph Selame. 1975. *Developing a Corporate Identity. How to Stand Out in the Crowd.* New York: Lebhar-Friedman Books.

Sethi, Prakash S. 1979. Institutional/image advertising and idea/issue advertising as marketing tools: some public policy issues. *Journal of Marketing* 43 (1): 68–78.

Smith, Gareth. 2001. The 2001 general election: factors influencing the brand image of political parties and their leaders. *Journal of Marketing Management* 17 (9/10): 989–1006.

Söderlund, Magnus. 1998. Customer satisfaction and its consequences on customer behaviour revisited: the impact of different levels of satisfaction on word-of-mouth, feedback to the supplier and loyalty. *International Journal of Service Industry Management* 9 (2): 169–188.

Speck, Paul Surgi, David W. Schumann and Craig Thompson. 1988. Celebrity endorsement – scripts, schemas and roles: theoretical framework and preliminary tests. *Advances in Consumer Research* 15 (1): 69–76.

Sturken, Marita and Lisa Cartwright. 2001. *Practices of Looking: An Introduction to Visual Culture.* Oxford; New York: Oxford University Press.

Swerdlow, Robert A. and Marleen R. Swerdlow 2003. Celebrity endorsers: spokesperson selection criteria and case examples of FREDD. *Academy of Marketing Studies Journal* 7 (2): 13–26.

Treadway, Darren C., Garry L. Adams, Annette L. Ranft and Gerald R. Ferris. 2009. A meso-level conceptualization of CEO celebrity effectiveness. *Leadership Quarterly* 20 (4): 554–570.

van den Bosch, Annette L. M., Wim J. L. Elving and Menno D. T. de Jong. 2006. The impact of organisational characteristics on corporate visual identity. *European Journal of Marketing* 40 (7/8): 870–885.

van Laer, Tom and Ko de Ruyter. 2010. In stories we trust: how narrative apologies provide cover for competitive vulnerability after integrity-violating blog posts. *International Journal of Research in Marketing* 27 (2): 164–174.

Waltzer, Herbert. 1988. Corporate advocacy advertising and political influence. *Public Relations Review* 14 (1): 41–55.

Westbrook, Robert A. 1987. Product/consumption-based affective responses and postpurchase processes. *Journal of Marketing Research* 24 (3): 258–270.

Woolward, Iain. 1982. Rethinking corporate advocacy media strategy. *Industrial Marketing* 67 (5): 74–78.

9

CORPORATE ASSOCIATIONS

Identity traits and corporate image

CONTENTS

Chapter 9 deals with corporate associations and focuses on company identity traits and company image. This chapter presents how companies are perceived by individuals, and discusses the dimensions of perceived identity traits and the process of anthropomorphization. The components of corporate image and several instruments for its measurement are presented. The chapter also presents some critical views of corporate image and concludes with several implications as to what companies should pay attention to in order to achieve a desired positive perception in the minds of individuals.

9.1 Corporate associations

Companies undertake many marketing and communication efforts to influence stakeholders' perception and achieve desired associations in the minds of individuals. Because people today are faced with information overload, companies have growing difficulties building recognition and can no longer expect that their target groups of consumers will have an opinion about them. It is becoming a challenge for companies to communicate clear-cut messages that will positively influence the company image in the minds of stakeholders. If companies want individuals to perceive and interpret information, especially information that is not recognized as relevant or involving, they need to invest a lot of effort – which is, however, necessary because companies and their success are to a large extent directly and indirectly dependent on positive stakeholder perception. Furthermore, people who have an opinion about a company no longer think of a company only in narrow terms of good and bad. People do not hold associations by simply judging a company's products or services (though these are not to be neglected either) but make complex associations relating to different aspects of the visibility and activities of companies, reaching far beyond the narrowly defined stakeholder interests. That is why the term **corporate associations** denotes all information that an individual has about a company. This comprises heterogeneous perceptions relating to different aspects of a company and can be mostly divided into two groups: associations about products and services and associations about the company as a whole (Brown and Dacin 1997).

Brown and Cox (1997) use the term corporate associations as a generic label for all the information about a company that a person holds. According to Brown and Cox (1997, 35),

> corporate associations for a particular company or organization include cognitions, affects, evaluations attaching to specific cognitions or affects and/or patterns of associations with respect to a particular company which are based on a set of memory inputs and/or current sensory perceptions.

Corporate associations are taking place at an individual level; associations consist of the widest sets of perceptions and ascribed meanings that can be – but not necessarily – connected one to another. Brown and Cox (1997, 36) classified corporate associations into six categories:

- corporate abilities and success;
- interaction with exchange partners;
- interaction with employees;
- social responsibility and contributions;
- marketing considerations;
- product considerations.

The key source of corporate associations are the products and services of a company, its communications, media, third parties and generalized prototypes (Brown and Cox 1997, 37). Corporate associations comprise the general perception of a company and its identity traits, as well as its image, reputation and trustworthiness (Berens 2004).

9.2 Perception of a company

The term **perception** denotes a sensory comprehension of the material world or in other words a selection, organization and interpretation of sensory impulses by an individual in order to make sense of his/her environment. It is a process of combining, integrating and interpreting information about the other in order to be able to understand it. Important factors in the process of perception are cognitive

schemes, which are abstract knowledge structures saved in memory, or neural networks in the brain that enable organization and interpretation of information about a perceived entity. A scheme is an organized set of information about an object, phenomenon or event. A related concept is a **script**, which is, from a psychological point of view, the organization of information about an action. Schemes and scripts are results of past experience and knowledge from various sources. Schemes and scripts determine which information is perceived and which is not, and how the information is interpreted. Once the schemes have been constructed they are unlikely to change. They are functional because they structure the world around us, but can be dysfunctional if based on wrong information. Another factor influencing an individual's perception is his/her motivational state, which includes **needs, values and desires**. Of course, some other circumstances must be considered as well, such as physical and emotional conditions, and the mood of the perceiving person. However, we must pay attention to **bias** and mistakes which are very typical of the perception process. One such bias is the *first impression effect*, meaning that the first information that a person gets about the object of perception has the greatest influence on the overall perception and evaluation of that object. Another possible bias is the *selective perception*, meaning that an individual by default pays attention only to one part of the information. Also important are the *contrast effect*, which means that the way that others perceive an object influences an individual's perception of that object; and the so-called *halo effect*, which explains how general perception influences the perception of specific characteristics. The *effects of strictness, lenience and averageness* call attention to the fact that people have different criteria of perception and evaluation. On the other hand, the *similarity effect* shows that the people that are perceived as similar to ourselves are evaluated better than the ones that are perceived as different from us. Further, it has been established that the knowledge of the entity and its attitudes influences an individual's perception of the entity, meaning that *knowledge leads to liking*. These effects apply to all perceived objects and companies are no exceptions.

When explaining the perception of companies, one of the most interesting phenomena is **anthropomorphization**, which is defined as 'attributing humanlike properties, characteristics, or mental states to real or imagined nonhuman agents and objects' (Epley *et al.* 2007, 865). It is a form of inductive inference used by people in order to understand stimuli through perception of a better-known similar stimulus so that an inanimate object gets human characteristics and becomes a subject. Mithen and Boyer (1996) explain anthropomorphism as a combination of perception errors that are natural and inevitable. Anthropomorphism is a tendency to personify objects and the inanimate world around us and is a universal human quality which helps individuals to reduce the complexity of the environment and experience, thus making their life easier. Stakeholders that have no problems attributing human characteristics to companies are likely to anthropomorphize because of the desire for expected interactions and apparent foreseeability that enhances the understanding of the object in the present and relations with it in the future (Epley *et al.* 2007).

9.3 Identity traits

Because companies communicate very specific messages, people tend to create similar networks of perceptions and associations about a company that they create about other people. In both cases, people use cognitive and emotional structures to create images. These are internal perceptions or schemes, usually of a collective nature, that have been constructed through social learning and conformity. According to the implicit theory, people use the same **set of constructs** to describe and evaluate other people that they use for themselves. Similarly, individuals have 'unique sets of abilities, inclinations, values and experiences that help to shape their individual impressions' (Bromley 2001, 320). Because of the influence of conformity and individuality on description or evaluation assignments (either of people or companies), the attributes are distributed in a typical J-curve. A high frequency of attributes points at shared experience and the conformity effect, while low frequencies and idiosyncratic attributes designate the influence of uniqueness (Bromley 1993, 2001). This means that cognitive maps of individuals are, when describing people or companies, composed of a small number of attributes that are shared by the majority of respondents and a large number of attributes that appear individually.

Beside the distribution of attributes in cognitive maps, what is also important is the content of attributes. Shared content is expressed through language designations that people use for description or evaluation of other people and companies. According to Spector (1961), there are two major categories of language designations, attributes or traits that can be used to describe people and companies.

- Language designations, used to describe **determinants of identity characteristics** or identity traits. This category includes the results of an individual's behaviour as well as any other thing that can be directly perceived with regard to the individual (Dijksterhuis and Bargh 2001). These attributes enable a person to implicitly infer the identity traits of an entity when he/she is in contact with it.
- A group of language designations describing perceived **identity characteristics** or the psychological traits of an entity. These traits are not perceived directly because the observer makes inferences about their existence from his/her perception of the entity's behaviour in a given time and space. This means that identity traits and their dimensions are cognitive constructions of the observers and not psychological characteristics of the observed. Inferring identity traits is a spontaneous, unconscious and constant process and an integral part of everyday social perceptions (Dijksterhuis and Bargh 2001).

By dividing attributes into two groups, namely identity characteristics and determinants of identity characteristics, we see that among unique attributes (both for individuals and for companies) attributes of the 'identity characteristics determinants' group prevail, while most of the shared attributes are from the 'identity characteristics' group (see Figure 9.1). However, the mentioned similarities in cognition

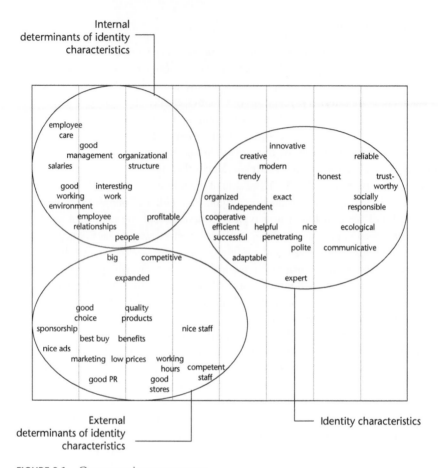

Internal
determinants of identity
characteristics

External
determinants of identity
characteristics

Identity characteristics

FIGURE 9.1   Corporate image structure

formation, structure and organization should not mislead us into mistaking them for semantic similarity. Several studies have shown that respondents only rarely share attributes when describing people or companies and that, in most cases, they use very different attributes. That is why special care is needed when transferring expressions and dimensions that designate perceived personal characteristics of people to the corporate level (Davies and Chun 2003).

It is interesting to see that the same traits are used to describe different entities. But perhaps in this context an even more important finding is that the more someone uses 'identity characteristics' attributes to describe people (and companies), the less they use attributes from the category 'determinants of identity characteristics'. Also, the more that someone uses identity characteristics to describe companies, the more often they will use them to describe people; the same is true for the determinants of identity characteristics. That means that on the macro level, there are two groups of people (Podnar 2002, 2004):

- The first group consists of respondents that tend to describe entities using identity characteristics.
- The second group tends to describe entities using determinants of identity characteristics.

When we are dealing with concrete perceptions of companies, especially if we want to measure the perceptions, we must keep in mind that formation of associations is not a one-dimensional process. A **one-dimensional process** would mean that we are only interested in what a person thinks about a perceived entity based on information directly transmitted by the entity, while completely ignoring what the person thinks that the entity thinks about him/her. This information can radically change an individual's perception and his/her evaluation of the perceived entity and that is why we must always keep in mind the **two-dimensional process** of forming associations. The formation of corporate associations is not an end in itself but is important because corporate associations strongly influence the decisions and behaviour of an individual, regardless of his/her stakeholder position. As research shows (Maathuis 1999), the single fact that a person has an opinion about the company and not only about its products or services can lead to the desired effect that the products and services of such companies are evaluated better than similar products or services of companies about which this person has no opinion. This effect can only take place if the company is congruent with its products and services (Madrigal 2000).

9.4 Corporate image

The influence of corporate associations on consumer decisions and behaviour in relationship to companies is the main reason why company (or corporate) image and its management is one of the most studied fields in marketing. However, one should deal with this multitude of research with a certain degree of caution because there are many different methods and approaches to the study of corporate image. Roughly, literature dealing with corporate image can be divided according to two criteria: firstly, according to the type of image (image of a company, subsidiary or branch, brand image, etc.) and secondly, according to the focus: whether the studies concentrate on the entity that transmits the image (in which case image is understood as something to be transmitted) or on the recipients of the image (in which case image is understood as a mental construct). Another approach is to study the interpretation of the images, or studying 'beliefs about beliefs'. Even though these approaches seem very heterogeneous, a chronological overview of different definitions of corporate image (Podnar 2002, 2004) reveals that all approaches have common elements.

In the literature, **image** is most often understood as a mental conception of the company made in the consumer's mind. Images are perceptions or sets of beliefs, attitudes and impressions of an individual about an object which are created in the consumer's mind when they think about a company or its products/services. Image is often defined as an immediate mental conception of an individual about an organization (Ind 1990; Balmer 1997). Image defined as an impression or a scheme made by an individual about the subject with which he/she interacts socially influences the behaviour of the individual in relation to others (Bromley 1993, 24–25). Image is expressed through a set of meanings that are typical of the object and that people often use to describe, memorize or relate to the object. It is a result of interactions among beliefs, ideas, emotions and impressions of an individual about the object which, according to time and circumstances, rapidly changes – that is why it is described as a dynamic concept. Images are not stable and change according to the reference framework of the observer. Image is a composition of objective and subjective, correct and false perceptions, attitudes and experiences about an object. Mental images are created through direct or indirect experience and can be rational or irrational, correct or false. What is also evident is that corporate image differs from one person to another and that different groups have different images about one company. As such, image has two major components: functional and emotional (Kennedy 1977). While the functional component relates to the tangible properties of the perceived entity, the emotional component relates to the ascribed psychological characteristics of the perceived entity that are manifested through emotions and relationships to the company (Nguyen and Leblanc 2001).

Studies of corporate image must take into consideration the hierarchical model of receiving and organizing information, meaning that researchers should pay attention to whether respondents know the company they are to evaluate or not. The knowledge of the company is, according to some authors (Bayton 1959; Carlson 1963), a precondition for the evaluation of corporate image. Knowledge is a necessary condition for an individual to create a corporate image; however knowledge alone is not enough. Hence, Macleod (1967) says that corporate image has three hierarchy levels that are interdependent; the first level is knowledge, the second positive attitude, while the third consists of special and specific attributes that are connected with the company and exist in people's minds.

A person that has never heard of a company has no notion of its image. Someone that has information about a company but the information is incomplete or insufficient is confused on hearing the company's name because this person is uncertain of how to evaluate and classify the company. Only after **recognition** of the company's name has been well established, can we go on to build corporate image. But even after this step has been made and individuals recognize the company unambiguously, its corporate image can still be unclear. When people recognize a company and are able to recall its characteristics, they become familiar with it. The better they know the company, the more detailed corporate image can they recall. Also, a person who knows a company well is more likely to have a positive attitude toward the company. The more positive image a person has of a company, the more positive their behaviour toward the company is. Positive attitude also significantly influences the 'perception and articulation of attributes, specific to the company in question' (Macleod 1967, 19). If a certain image seems stable and if reference groups around the individual support the image, the individual will resist internal and external factors that might contradict this image. This third level of corporate image is multidimensional and consists of product opinions, the company's market position, relationship to consumers and employees, the company's ethics, and other dimensions.

Corporate images are created on the basis of the collection of all experiences of the entity and of other factors that the entity is unable to control. The number of channels through which a person gets information about the company positively influences the stability and strength of the corporate image. Corporate image changes significantly according to the source of experience that people have with the company and according to the reference frame of the observer. For example, people who are personally acquainted with employees of a company have a more positive and detailed image of a company compared to people with no acquaintances in the company. Moreover, better informed respondents change their relationship with the company less often than respondents who have less information about the company.

Barich and Kotler (1991) write that a company has many images because construction of an image depends on many factors such as business success, the company's contribution to society, attitude toward employees, quality of products and services, the company's communications, sales team, distribution channels and services that support the company's relationship with the stakeholders. Garbett (1988) similarly writes that every company, regardless if it is aware of it or not, has an identity and therefore projects a certain image (Garbett 1988, 3). According to Garbett (1988), corporate image is influenced by six factors. The relationship between these factors, reality (R), newsworthiness (N), diversity (D), communication efforts (C), time (T) and memory decay (M), and their influence on the corporate image (I) is represented in the simple formula:

$$\frac{R+N}{D \times C \times T} \; M = I.$$

The following factors in the above formula influence corporate image (Garbett 1988).

- *Reality* of a company (R). This category includes company characteristics, such as size, structure, branch of industry, products and services, employees and their interactions with the environment.
- *Newsworthiness* of a company and its activities (N). A company can be newsworthy either in a positive or in a negative way. However, in most cases, the public is not interested in the company at all, so the organization must make an effort to achieve positive publicity and to attract positive attention through its operations.
- *Diversity* of a company (D). A diverse company communicates very diverse messages. Consequently it is harder to be cohesive and to create a consistent corporate image.

- *Communication effort* (C). There is a strong connection between efforts invested in communications and recognition and a positive corporate image.
- *Time* (T). Rome wasn't built in a day and nor is a positive corporate image. Communication efforts should be made over a longer period of time in order to create a strong corporate image.
- *Memory decay* (M). Garbett (1988, 4–5) says that memory decay of the public is a serious problem. A lot of communication effort is needed to keep the company in people's minds, let alone to improve its position.

By studying corporate image, the processes of its construction and the factors influencing it, companies have discovered that, in spite of the fact that the image is constructed by the individual, companies can manage image by controlling their public appearance and their manner of communication. Today, every programme designed to influence a company's public appearance must be based on a clearly defined corporate identity. It is impossible to create a suitable programme to communicate the desired corporate image if the management does not understand who the company is, what the vision is and what its future plans are.

At the same time, corporate image should be measured. We must analyse carefully and continuously what the current corporate image of the organization is in the eyes of different groups of stakeholders and target consumer groups. Bernstein (1984) writes that corporate image is important but not in that manner that it should be 'produced' but because we can use it to examine whether our messages are received according to expectations and to investigate if the image corresponds with the company's image in the eyes of management. A company needs to identify different images and reference points that exist in the minds of people of different groups and communities. A company's management must decide on which images to measure and who will do the measuring. In this phase, some questions are of special importance: 'Which factors will be measured?', 'Which offers will be measured?', 'Which publics will be included in the survey?', 'How many respondents, and which specific respondents from each of the stakeholder groups will be in the sample?', 'Who is the relevant competition?', 'How frequent should the measurement be repeated?', etc.

Only after these questions have been considered, can a survey be designed and carried out to gather desired information. Based on the analysis, appropriate steps can be taken in order to reach goals set by the organization and meet the expectations of stakeholders.

9.5 Measuring corporate image

Winick (1960) was one of the first scholars to offer an overview of possible methods of corporate **image measurement**. He suggested three approaches to empirical examination, namely projection techniques, open questions and structured questionnaires. The first two approaches were supposed to give the best and most realistic results, thanks to unstructured answers, but a quantitative analysis of such results can be a difficult and costly undertaking. The third approach is, according to the author, 'the most scientific one' and enables quantification of data. However, the third approach could be used only after one of the first two has been tested. Winick also suggests using linguistic-associative techniques like the semantic differential, Q-sort, adjective cards, visual techniques, thermometer techniques, etc.

Winick (1960) points out that every researcher faces the dilemma of whether to present the results individually for each of the measured image dimensions for similar companies or as a complete image construct for each of the companies in comparison. If a company wants to draw benefits from its corporate image studies, image measurements should use understandable characteristics that measure dimensions used by respondents when evaluating corporate image. Similarly, van Riel and colleagues (1998) establish that there is not one single and uniform way to measure corporate image, and that the selection of the best suited method can be a difficult task. That is why they make an overview and comparison of some of the most often used open and closed methods of corporate image measurement, including attitude measurement, Q-sort, photo sort, laddering, Kelly method and natural sort. The authors established that the decision for the open or closed method depends on the purpose of the corporate image study. Similarly to Winick's findings, open research methods were found suitable for discovering dimensions of image because they give rich and deep contextual data. Results obtained with open methods can be used to design closed research methods. The following **open techniques** can be very useful when measuring a company's image in the eyes of individuals.

1. *Association techniques*
   a. The first word that comes to mind on hearing the keyword.
   b. A series of words that come to mind on hearing the keyword (reaction time is measured, analysis shows whether there are negative associations, etc.).
2. *Completion techniques*
   a. Completion of a sentence (respondents are asked to complete an unfinished sentence about the company).
   b. Completion of a story (respondents are asked not only to complete a sentence but to continue a story about the company; it is up to the respondent's imagination how the story ends; analysis reveals which are the most common topics).
3. *Construction techniques*
   a. Comic (respondents write down what the people in the drawings say about a company).
   b. 'Third person' technique (respondents answer questions about what certain people, for example, a typical consumer, think about the company).

Closed methods of measuring corporate image are considered to be more suitable in instances when research goals are longitudinal measurement or comparison to competition. **Closed methods** also allow for measuring differences in stakeholders' perception of important image dimensions. The most important closed methods are well known in the attitude measuring methodology, namely the Likert scale, semantic differential and range scale.

The *Likert scale* is relatively easy to use (both for the data collector and for the respondent) and to interpret; this is why it is the most frequently used attitudinal scale. Respondents mark or write down a level to which they agree or disagree with each listed item that describes the object of interest. The scale consists of the same number of agreement/disagreement choices separated by a neutral choice. A range scale is used when respondents range individual items, in our case companies, according to different criteria such as general quality, price to value ratio, etc.

Range scale measures give important hints about which fields of a company's activity can be improved. *Semantic differential* is, similarly to the Likert scale, easy to design and use. The scale consists of bipolar adjectives (e.g. good–bad, hot–cold, expensive–cheap) placed on each side of the odd-numbered (usually 5- or 7-point) item. Respondents evaluate the object (product, company, etc.) by selecting a point in the continuum that best describes their feelings or beliefs. The 'original' semantic differential should measure three dimensions of the studied concept:

a.   evaluation, e.g. beautiful–ugly, good–bad;
b.   strength, e.g. big–small, strong–weak;
c.   activeness, e.g. fast–slow, loud–silent.

An important advantage of the semantic differential over other techniques is that it enables a graphic representation of the object of research. Semantic differentials can be used in many scenarios, for example, to compare consumers' perception of competitive companies or as an indicator of possible improvements inside the company (by comparing the perception of the 'actual' company to the perception of the 'ideal' company).

Since its development in the 1950s and 1960s (Osgood *et al.* 1957; Clevenger *et al.* 1965), the semantic differential has been the most popular method used in studying corporate image because it provides the researcher with many dimensions of the image, does not give stereotypical answers and prevents some problems that could arise in the open questions method, for example vagueness (Mindak 1961, 29). Mindak (1961) also suggests some adaptations of the original version of the semantic differential, for example using phrases and nouns and not only adjectives, using not only strictly bipolar adjectives but milder versions and using non-standard scales adapted to a concrete problem. Semantic differentials can be used to measure general characteristics of a company, its identity traits or company values as perceived by individuals. Results of such studies can give us a useful answer and can be used for a basis for future communication activities which can narrow the gap between desired and measured corporate image.

Today corporate image measurements combine qualitative and quantitative methods. A useful approach to measure corporate image is based on the method for *social network analysis* which analyses connections among attributes that appear in combination with a company or a group of companies. There are a number of software packages (e.g. Pajek, Dex, igraph, (Python) NetworkX, Ora) that give great results, offer a graphic presentation of key attributes and connections among them, thus enabling the identification of central attributes in the cognitive network.

9.6 Critiques of corporate image

Riley and Levy (1963, 185–186) identified four key approaches to corporate image construction, according to whether a company reacts to internal or external stimuli and how it responds to the expectations of stakeholders.

- *The eclectic approach* is characteristic of companies that offer consumer goods. Companies gather information about changes in relationships and in buying behaviour from different outside sources. Companies try to respond to changes immediately by using the whole spectrum of communication tools to project a general image designed in such a way that it would appeal to most of the people most of the time.
- *The inductive approach* is typical of diversified companies that deal with several publics. Companies are focused on the future that is studied and predicted. Based on the studies, a selection of the appropriate corporate image is made.
- *The deductive approach* is typical of companies producing consumer goods and service companies. Image(s) is (are) constructed in accordance with public expectations in the specific sector. The decision whether to project one or more image is tactical and is easily changed through time.
- *The evolution approach* is characteristic of companies with a long tradition and a defined company mission. Corporate image is based on the past and adapts only slowly to the challenges of the present.

Eclectic and evolution approaches to corporate image, according to the authors, create **'general image'** while the inductive and deductive approaches create **'specific images'** adapted to different publics. Construction of the corporate image is not an end in itself but should be one of the long-term goals of the company. Also, corporate image is limited by the existing images of the stakeholders and, because of the company's desire to please, the management could be tempted to present a better corporate image than it really is. Already in the 1960s, encouraged by frequent companies' practices to communicate false images of themselves, Boorstin (1961) developed his **image theory**. Boorstin's main contribution is his separation between the real and the perceived, between the reality 'out there' and what we think and believe that is real. He discusses the contrast between the world and pseudo-world that is best illustrated by the difference between events and pseudo-events. Corporate image is, according to Boorstin, a pseudo-event and is as such pseudo-real, meaning that it is an artificial product, false and unreal. By managing corporate image, we influence reality that is becoming more and more unreal, a constructed reality. Image – as a pseudo-ideal – is in his opinion intrinsically artificial, probable, passive, intensive, simplified and ambiguous (Boorstin 1961).

- *An image is synthetic.* This means that image 'is planned: created especially to serve a purpose, to make a certain kind of impression' (Boorstin 1961, 185). It is not only about the trademark, design, slogan or memorable visual identity, but is about the carefully constructed personal profile of a person, institution, company, product or service constructed and established with the latest techniques of the graphic revolution. Such definition of image allows for differentiation between what is seen and what is really there (Boorstin 1961, 186). The author suggests the difference between the visible 'public personality' and the invisible 'private character'. According to Boorstin (1961), such an image can always be – more or less successfully – made, controlled, repaired, renovated and improved, which, however, cannot be done with the 'original' that this image represents.

- *An image is believable.* This means that 'it serves no purpose if people do not believe it. In their own head they must make it stand for the person or institution imagined' (Boorstin 1961, 188). According to Boorstin (1961), the most successful images are those that are constructed in a very believable manner. The best technique in constructing such images is to moderately reflect reality.

- *An image is passive.* Because image should be congruent with reality, the one who makes the image is expected to adjust to the existing image rather than fight it. The same is true for the receiver or the 'image user'. Once a probable, convincing and popular image has been constructed, people suppose that it originates from real life. 'In the beginning the image is a likeness of the corporation; finally the corporation becomes a likeness of the image. The image (unlike actual conduct) can be perfect. It can be a precise pattern which will satisfy everybody' (Boorstin 1961, 189). In his book, Boorstin also warns that companies that renovate their corporate image do not decide on a 'change of heart' but more on a 'change of face'. Because image is passive it does not have much to do with the activities of the real company. Due to its passivity, image leads to conformity.

- *An image is vivid and concrete.* This means that image serves its purpose best if it addresses our senses. It has to be precise. 'It is not enough if the product, the man, or the institution has many good qualities appropriate to it. One or a few must be selected for vivid portrayal' (Boorstin 1961, 193).

- *An image is simplified.* This means that an image has to be simpler than the object that is represented in order to separate desired aspects of the image from undesired ones. 'The most effective image is one simple and distinctive enough to be remembered, yet not so handy as to seem the natural symbol for the whole class of objects it describes' (Boorstin 1961, 193).

- *An image is ambiguous.* This means that image 'floats somewhere between the imagination and the senses, between expectation and reality' (Boorstin 1961,

193). It needs to correspond with unexpected future goals and unexpected changes of taste. At the same time it needs to suit the present and future desires of different groups of people (Boorstin 1961, 193–194).

Under the influence of Boorstin's theory, Bernays (1977) went so far as to write an article titled 'Down With Image, Up With Reality' in which he claims that the use of the term *image* should be prohibited in public relations because the term suggests that PR deals with illusions. Grunig (1993) later jumps on the bandwagon by differentiating between symbolic (communication) and behavioural relationships between an organization and its stakeholders and argues against the use of the word 'image' in those two contexts. One of his arguments against the word is its pejorative meaning. Image was supposed to have a negative connotation, denoting the opposite of reality, an imitation of something, an illusion that has nothing to do with the real behaviour of an organization because it is artificial, constructed and projected without any substance. Grunig (1993) also believed that image was one of the reasons why the public relations sector had a bad reputation at that time. Grunig differentiated between symbolic (image) and behavioural (substance) relationships but believed that both are complementary concepts and should not be separated one from the other. If we concentrate only on symbolic relationships (communication) and neglect much more important behavioural relationships, PR becomes an image builder.

> Public relations practitioners ... offer little of value to the organizations they advise because they suggest the problems in relationships with publics can be solved by using the proper message – disseminated through publicity or media relations – to change an image of an organization.
>
> *(Grunig 1993, 136)*

9.7 Achieving desired corporate image

Keeping that in mind, it is now more than ever advisable that the projected image of a company should be based on characteristics and identities that are real.

> If an image fails to be individual and distinctive, it will have no relation to reality i.e., the actual corporate personality. It will be only a fabrication. As such, it negates one major premise of its existence – that an offered image can make up for the public's lack of direct contact and represents an attempt to make people think what the corporation wants to think, rather than to give them a grasp of what the corporation is really like.
>
> *(Finn 1961, 136)*

Theories dealing with the persuasive power of messages suggest that messages that are perceived as honest tend to be received faster and have a greater influence on the receivers. In the organizational context, *honesty* means that a company shares with the public all information that relates to real attributes of the company. A company must also be capable of giving an exact and *unbiased image* of itself.

The third condition that needs to be met in order to create a desired image in the eyes of stakeholders is *consistency*. The more consistently that identity characteristics are expressed through time, the more stakeholders can create a stable image of the company (van Halderen and van Riel 2006, 6–12). Van Halderen and van Riel (2006) in their corporate expressiveness model suggest indicators that influence honest, transparent and consistent expression.

In order to be perceived as honest, companies tend to express their identity by revealing organizational values to confirm the norms, expectations and values of stakeholders. Consequently, companies that defend socially acceptable values but do not support their disposition with actions tend to be perceived as dishonest. Companies must also make sure that their identity is *authentic* and that it has been a part of the company for a certain period of time. One of the tools that can convince people of the company's authenticity is referring to the company's history. But in doing so, companies must employ a certain degree of self-criticism and, in case of mistakes or dishonesty, must assume responsibility for their actions. Companies must evaluate their identity and behaviour self-critically and must be ready for constant improvements.

Companies should also work toward *transparency* and be able to reveal all general information about them. Companies should provide their stakeholders with all necessary information needed to evaluate the company in order to satisfy their need for information. Necessary pieces of information are:

- strategic and social goals;
- current business in relation to those goals;
- future goals and activities, undertaken by a company to achieve desired results.

Companies must vouch for the *reliability and relevance* of information. Regardless of the quantity of information sent to the public, stakeholders doubt its reliability and relevance. To reduce scepticism, companies could present to the public the manner in which the information is prepared and shared. Reliability of information could be enhanced if information is additionally presented by an independent source. It is also necessary that a company, besides leading a continuous dialogue with its stakeholders, creates a proactive communications strategy, meaning that openness for dialogue is included in all corporate communications and that stakeholders' feedback on the company's activities is publicly revealed.

In order to achieve the desired image, companies must be *consistent* in creating their corporate messages. Although different corporate messages may be addressed to different publics, they should, on the whole, have a common identity. Because the company's identity is usually expressed through the company vision, mission, values and slogan, a consistent image is created by repeatedly relating to the so-called identity elements.

But consistency when expressing corporate identity in corporate messages is not enough to create a desired image in the stakeholders' eyes. Companies must also express consistency through time. Stakeholders will doubt the sincerity of the identity if it changes very often. Research has shown that there is a strong correlation between the actual nature of the company and the image that a company wants to project. Corporate image is a part of reality and not its substitute. If a company is faced with problems regarding corporate associations and image, its main concern should be the congruity between its real identity and the things that the company says about itself. Corporate image, even though exclusively a product of individual perception, must be a part of the objective reality and not its substitute. Only after an individual has no more problems recognizing the company, has a clear idea of its characteristics, knows what the company is and what it stands for, and — most importantly — likes this image, only then can corporate associations become a good basis for the formation of corporate reputation and all the other benefits that come with a good name.

CASE: SI.MOBIL

The mobile operator Si.mobil was founded in 1997 by four Slovenian companies. It presented its services to users in March 1999 by offering a prepaid service, Halo. The company had just over 130 employees and was the sole competitor to the only other mobile operator in Slovenia, which had been on the market since 1991. The Si.mobil brand expressed modernity, youth, future but also quality and affordable prices. The service was launched accompanied with a well-received marketing campaign featuring the then Miss Slovenia. But in the first year only 17,000 users began to use its services, most of them because they were not happy with the market's leading operator. Perception studies have shown that Si.mobil's main weaknesses, compared to the leading operator, were poor access and image.

In 2001, when a third company entered Slovenia's mobile market, mobilkom austria became a part owner of Si.mobil. Si.mobil's management redefined its strategic guidelines and renovated the company's visual identity. A new slogan was coined 'Always for me' (sl. Vedno zame). The company's vision was formulated, stating that Si.mobil wanted to become the most popular Slovenian mobile operator which would, with responsibility and excellence, meet every need of its users. In its marketing communications the company stressed its individuality, determination and simple but useful products at affordable prices. In 2002 Si.mobil launched a new service ORTO aimed at the price-sensitive youth segment. After three years of intensive presence on the market, Si.mobil gained over 300,000 users and a market share of 22 per cent. Respondents saw Si.mobil as a mobile operator which is still behind the leading company but offers good service, is price efficient, young and fresh.

Because of the Austrian majority owner, in 2003 Si.mobil became a partner to the biggest mobile operator in Europe – Vodafone. All marketing activities were now under a common brand Si.mobil – Vodafone and with a new slogan 'Catch the world' (sl. Ujemi svet). Corporate messages emphasized the benefits of this strategic connection for the consumer, quality services and favourable price. The company wanted to become the most attractive mobile operator in Slovenia and started to introduce its first socially responsible campaigns. In 2004 Si.mobil reached green figures for the first time in its history. Users described Si.mobil as a company that 'offers best suited services', 'meets expectations', 'has attractive offers', 'is nice', 'communicates well with its users', 'makes nice advertisements' and, most of all, has 'favourable call charges', 'good connections to foreign operators' and 'speaks to young people'.

In 2006, mobilkom austria became the sole owner of the company, which in the same year acquired the UMTS frequency, was named the Slovenian advertiser of the year and gained over 400,000 users.

In the following year the company appointed a new Chairman of the Management Board who continued the strategy of quality services for optimum prices. Si.mobil started to exhaustively stress its commitment to operating in a socially responsible way. It received the 'Reputable Employer' award and the 'Family-friendly company' certificate. Si.mobil launched in-company activities implementing small but important ideas about everyday decisions, actions and attitudes trying to persuade individuals into following a responsible way of life. The project was named Re.think (sl. Re.misli) and became one of Si.mobil's brands. The company modernized the corporate brand visually and substantially and again started to appear on the market individually with its slogan 'Say something beautiful'. The company renovated its brand architecture and its service packages. The number of users reached 500,000 and income increased from €122 million to over €180 million. Although in 2007 Si.mobil's image was still slightly behind its only competitor, the following characteristics were highlighted: Si.mobil was an operator with favourable call charges where users get the most for their money, has attractive services and mobile phones and is dynamic and modern.

The company continued to consistently stress its social responsibility and supported it by opening the first environmentally friendly store, environmental certificate ISO 14001 and founding an independent non-profit organization Si.voda whose aim is to support the efforts in keeping water in Slovenia clean and healthy. Si.mobil users could donate €1 with an SMS or could join the Re.think project and donate €1 every month. The year 2009 was full of awards not only for the company (Golden Thread Award for best employers, advertiser of the year, Excel Merit Award, Gold Quill Award, Business Issue Award, most innovative staff practice, etc.) but also for the Chairman of the Management Board, Dejan Turk, who was selected as Best Director 2009 by business journalists.

Si.mobil currently employs over 350 people, has over 600,000 users and creates an income of over €200 million annually. It is the leading mobile operator in some segments (young people). For the first time in the company's history, Si.mobil is rated better in almost all features according to Si.mobil users, in comparison to its main competitor. Also it has caught up with its main competitor in the field of perceived social responsibility which was until recently the domain of the leading mobile operator. The general public perceives Si.mobil in some categories as better than the leading operator. The company's image includes the following attributes: 'favourable call and service charges', 'passionate and daring', 'offers much for the price that users pay', 'rewards loyalty', 'trendy', 'offers quality phones at favourable prices', 'dynamic', 'offers calls from abroad at favourable prices', 'is a member of a global group', 'holds its promises' and is 'honest'. Some independent studies have shown that it is one of the most reputable and most socially responsible companies in Slovenia.

Key terms

Corporate associations. This term denotes all information that an individual has about a company. Corporate associations comprise the general perception of a company and its identity traits, as well as its image, reputation and trust.

Perception. A sensory comprehension of the material world or in other words a selection, organization and interpretation of sensory impulses by an individual in order to make sense of his/her environment. It is a process of combining, integrating and interpreting information about the other in order to be able to understand it.

Cognitive schemes and scripts. Schemes are abstract knowledge structures saved in memory, or neural networks in the brain that enable organization and interpretation of information about a perceived entity. A scheme is an organized set of information about an object, phenomenon or event. A script is the organization of information about an action. Schemes and scripts are results of past experience and knowledge from various sources.

Anthropomorphization. A process of attributing human-like properties, characteristics or mental states to real or imagined non-human agents and objects. It is a form of inductive inference used by people in order to understand stimuli through perception of a better-known similar stimulus so that an inanimate object gets human characteristics and becomes a subject.

Identity traits. Enduring patterns of perceiving, relating to and thinking about the particular entity. According to the implicit theory, people use the same set of constructs to describe and evaluate other people that they use for themselves. Similar traits are used to describe different entities.

Corporate image. A personal impression or mental picture about a perceived entity. It is a mental conception of the organization made in the consumer's mind. Images are perceptions or sets of beliefs, attitudes and impressions of an individual about an object which are created in the individual's mind when they think about a company or its products/services. Image is a composition of objective and subjective, correct and false perceptions, attitudes and experiences about an object. Mental images are created through direct or indirect experience and can be rational or irrational, correct or false.

REVIEW QUESTIONS

- What is corporate association and why it is important?
- What are the key determinants of company perceptions? What is athropomorphization? What are the similarities and differences between perceptions of humans and companies?
- Define corporate image, make a critical reflection of the concept and, with the help of Garbett's formula, explain its key determinants.
- How can corporate image be measured and 'managed'?

Discuss how Si.mobil has changed its corporate image. Is it possible to change corporate image without changing corporate identity? How can corporate communication respond to critics that corporate image is a pseudo-event, which has nothing to do with reality?

References

Balmer, John M. T. 1997. Corporate identity: what is it? What of it? And what is next? *Corporate Reputation Review* 1 (2): 183–188.

Barich, Howard and Philip Kotler. 1991. A framework for marketing image management. *Sloan Management Review* 32 (2): 94–104.

Bayton, James. 1959. Researching the corporate image. *Public Relations Journal* 4 (10): 3–8.

Berens, Guido A. J. M. 2004. *Corporate Branding: The Development of Corporate Associations and their Influence on Stakeholder Reactions*. Rotterdam: Erasmus Research Institute of Management, Erasmus University Rotterdam.

Bernays, Edward L. 1977. Down with image, up with reality. *Public Relations Quarterly* 22 (1): 12–14.

Bernstein, David. 1984. *Company Image and Reality: A Critique of Corporate Communications*. Eastbourne: Holt, Rinehart and Winston Ltd.

Boorstin, Daniel J. 1961. *The Image: A Guide to Pseudo-events in America*. New York: Random House.

Bromley, Dennis Basil. 1993. *Reputation, Image and Impression Management.* Chichester: John Wiley.

———2001. Relationships between personal and corporate reputation. *European Journal of Marketing* 35 (3/4): 316–334.

Brown, Tom J. and Edwin Cox. 1997. Corporate associations in marketing and consumer research: a review. *Corporate Reputation Review* 1 (1/2): 34–38.

Brown, Tom J. in Peter A. Dacin. 1997. The company and the product: corporate associations and consumer product responses. *Journal of Marketing* 61 (1): 68–84.

Carlson, Robert O. 1963. The nature of corporate images. In *The Corporation and its Publics: Essays on the Corporate Image,* eds. John W. Riley, Jr. and Marguerite F. Levy. New York: John Wiley and Sons, 24–47.

Clevenger, Theodore, Gilbert A. Lazier and Margaret Leitner Clark. 1965. Measurement of corporate images by the semantic differential. *Journal of Marketing Research* 2 (1): 80–82.

Davies, Gary and Rosa Chun. 2003. The use of metaphor in the exploration of the brand concept. *Journal of Marketing Management* 19 (1/2): 45–72.

Dijksterhuis, Ap and John A. Bargh. 2001. The perception-behavior expressway: automatic effects of social perception on social behavior. *Advances in Experimental Social Psychology* 33: 1–40.

Epley, Nicholas, Adam Waytz and John T. Cacioppo. 2007. On seeing human: a three-factor theory of anthropomorphism. *Psychological Review* 114 (4): 864–886.

Finn, Alan. 1961. The price of corporate vanity. *Harvard Business Review* 39 (4): 135–143.

Garbett, Thomas F. 1988. *How to Build a Corporation's Identity and Project its Image.* Lexington, MA: Lexington Books.

Grunig, James E. 1993. Image and substance: from symbolic to behavioral relationships. *Public Relations Review* 19 (2): 121–139.

Ind, Nicholas. 1990. *The Corporate Image: Strategies for Effective Identity Programmes.* London: Kogan Page.

Kennedy, Sherril H. 1977. Nurturing corporate images. *European Journal of Marketing* 11 (3): 120–164.

Maathuis, Onno Johannes Maria. 1999. *Corporate branding: the value of the corporate brand to customers and managers.* Unpublished PhD thesis. Rotterdam: Erasmus University.

Macleod, Jennifer. 1967. The emphasis is on corporate reputation. *Public Relations Journal* 18 (8): 18–20.

Madrigal, Robert. 2000. The role of corporate associations in new product evaluation. *Advances in Consumer Research* 27 (1): 80–86.

Mindak, William A. 1961. Fitting the semantic differential to the marketing problem. *Journal of Marketing* 25: 28–33.

Mithen, Stephen and Pascal Boyer. 1996. Anthropomorphism and the evolution of cognition. *The Journal of the Royal Anthropological Institute* 2 (4): 717–721.

Nguyen, Nha and Gaston Leblanc. 2001. Corporate image and corporate reputation in customers' retention decisions in services. *Journal of Retailing and Consumer Services* 8 (4): 227–236.

Osgood, Charles E., George J. Suci and Percy H. Tannenbaum. 1957. *The Measurement of Meaning.* Urbana: University of Illinois Press.

Podnar, Klement. 2002. *Resničnost in neresničnost identitete podjetja: analiza teoretskega okvira upravljanja korporativne identitete. Magistrsko delo.* Ljubljana: Fakulteta za družbene vede.

———2004. *Ugled, organizacijska identifikacija in zavezanost zaposlenih.* Doktorska disertacija. Ljubljana: Fakulteta za družbene vede.

Riley, John W. and Margaret F. Levy. 1963. The image in perspective. In *The Corporation and its Publics,* ed. John W. Riley. New York: John Wiley and Sons, 176–189.

Spector, Aaron J. 1961. Basic dimensions of the corporate image. *Journal of Marketing* 25 (6): 47–51.

van Halderen, Mignon D. and Cees B. M. van Riel. 2006. *Developing a corporate expressiveness model for managing favorable impressions among stakeholders.* Available at: http://www.reputationinstitute.com/members/nyc06/Riel_Halderen_2006.pdf (21 October 2010).

van Riel, Cees B. M., Natasha Stroeker and Onno Maathus. 1998. Measuring corporate images. *Corporate Reputation Review* 1 (4): 313–326.

Winick, Charles. 1960. How to find out what kind of image you have. In *Developing the Corporate Image*, ed. Lee Hastings Bristol. New York: Charles Scribner's Sons, 23–40.

10

CORPORATE ASSOCIATIONS

Reputation and trust

CONTENTS

Chapter 10 continues with a discussion on special forms of corporate associations, namely reputation and trust. It defines corporate reputation and presents its dimensions and key management issues. We emphasize the role of perceived external prestige of the company and discuss the consequences of reputation to illustrate why reputation is the most valuable intangible asset of the company. In the final part of the chapter, we stress the importance of stakeholders' trust in the company. We operationalize the concept using reliability, honesty and benevolence, and present actions that can lead to mistrust, scepticism or cynicism of stakeholders.

10.1 Corporate reputation

Although the literature long held corporate image and reputation as synonyms, today they are treated as two closely related but different types of corporate associations. Both concepts are dynamic in nature but a relevant difference between the two concepts is that corporate image relates to an individual's momentary perception of a company, while corporate reputation is formed over time and is based on what the organization has done and how it has behaved (Balmer 2003, 177). Both concepts are interconnected; on the one hand, reputation in the public to a large extent depends on day-to-day images that individuals make about a company, while on the other the existing reputation (or absence of it), along with other factors, influences day-to-day corporate image creation. The relationship between image and reputation is parallel to the relationship between an individual and a social group that the individual belongs to. When individuals construct an image of a company based on information they get from the company, they supplement their knowledge with information from other sources, while they check the correctness, congruity and cohesion of their construction within the social group or public of which they are a member. The process, in which individuals check whether their constructions match with those of their social group, is called the accreditation process. During this process, an individual makes the group accept part of the attributes of his/her construction. An individual first constructs an image of an organization, which through time by selection of image elements (through the filter of social norms) reflects in a general evaluation residing as a social entity in the public. This means that reputation is wholly a social category, an active abstract, that exists independently as long as a group of people have it in common (Podnar 2000).

Reputation or public image (Bromley 1993) is understood as an overall evaluation and, to a certain degree, a simplified estimation of a company by its stakeholders (Fombrun 1996). Reputation relates to the question of how specific publics evaluate the company in terms of social standards, beliefs and values (Podnar 2000). Reputation is about categorizing companies according to certain criteria, which as a whole (which is more than a sum of its parts) create a relative position of an organization in the eyes of its stakeholders (Shenkar and Yuchtman-Yaar 1997, 1362). Dowling (2001, 19) relates to the corporate reputation attributed values (such as authenticity, honesty, responsibility and integrity) evoked from the person's corporate image. Reputation *per se* includes judgements, with which the company evaluates itself, and judgement of attributes that a certain public associates with the company. Reputation is a complete and evaluated impression of an organization that reflects perceptions of individual stakeholder groups (Fombrun and Shanley 1990). According to Herbig and Milewicz (1993), a company's reputation is formed in a process of accumulation of opinions and estimations of multiple groups that interact with the company through time. Fombrun's (1996) definition is similar, defining reputation as a perception of past actions and future expectations of a company that describe the overall attractiveness of a company in comparison to the competition in the eyes of its key stakeholders. The reputation that constituents ascribe to a company is the aggregate of many personal judgements about the company's credibility, reliability, responsibility and trustworthiness (Fombrun 1996, 72). Fombrun describes reputation as a net of perceptions of a firm's capabilities to meet the expectations of all its stakeholders (Fombrun *et al.* 2000, 13). Corporate reputation thus by definition relates to the estimation of *capabilities, activities and achievements* of a company or perception and beliefs about the company. Necessary conditions for reputation are, beside the company's activeness, the perception of the company by stakeholder groups, their direct or indirect experience, and a context of values in which the company is evaluated. It is interesting that reputation has an exclusively positive connotation and can be in this sense distinguished from fame. Companies and other entities can be famous because of recognizable positive or negative characteristics, which are not necessarily true, while reputation can only be gained with socially acceptable behaviour.

10.2 Dimensions of corporate reputation

When trying to understand, measure and manage corporate reputation, it is important to note that different publics and stakeholders establish different reputations of the company, and that they evaluate the company according to specific criteria that they see as relevant (Fombrun 1996). This means that different publics and stakeholders perceive a different reputation of the same company, which is based on their economic, social or personal background (Gotsi and Wilson 2001). Another view that is in line with those mentioned above is Caruana's (1997; Caruana and Chircop 2000) who says that reputation consists of general evaluations of the public and specific evaluations that pertain to a specific object of evaluation and differ one from another according to the stakeholder group. As was established very early on by Martineau (1958), differences among various groups occur because of differences in their perceptions, expectations and desires that individuals have with respect to the company. In his overview of different approaches to 'reputation scales' (cf. Sobol *et al.* 1992) that are executed and published by business media, supervision organs or trade associations, Fombrun established that most of them operate with non-systematic criteria, usually covering narrow views, specific only for some stakeholder groups. That is why findings of such research are difficult to generalize since different methods produce different results. Attention to criteria that would best explain the reputation construct is therefore much needed. Identification of such criteria enables the development of a methodological tool that would enable and facilitate the comparison of results. That is why Bromley (1993) speaks of 'the general factor (or set of factors) common to most or all the attributes of reputation [that] provides a valuable, quantitative, operational definition of reputation for making comparisons between entities' (Bromley 1993, 183). A true **reputation index** should include a representative sample of various stakeholders and their criteria. It should be based on an assumption that companies can be positively ranked by consumers, investors, general public and employees, and on a standardized set of attributes (see Figure 10.1) that include the social, emotional, financial and organizational traits of a company. A foundation on which this could be constructed is Fombrun's establishment of a relatively limited set of criteria used for the evaluation of company reputation, that is, an aggregate of stakeholder interests (Fombrun 1998, 338).

There are many examples of overall reputation measurement of companies (for an overview see Cravens *et al.* 2003). One of the more interesting examples is the ORC model that identifies six elements of reputation (Greyser 1999, 179):

- *competitive effectiveness* (such as quality management, R&D investments, financial strength);
- *market leadership* (such as market position within industry, differentiated products, connections to the market);
- *consumer focus* (such as high quality for a good price, commitment to consumers);

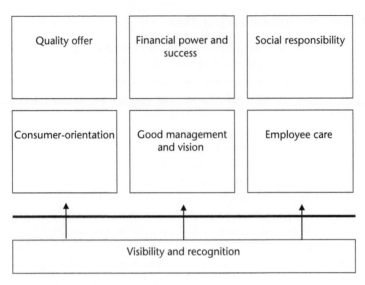

FIGURE 10.1 Reputation dimensions

- *familiarity* or *favourability*;
- *corporate culture* (such as high ethical standards, visible social responsibility, skilled employees);
- *communications* (such as advertising, sponsorships, event management).

The Harris/Fombrun Corporate Reputation Quotient (RQ), one of the best known models tested in almost all Western countries, is a six-dimensional measuring instrument (Fombrun *et al.* 2000, 253; Fombrun and van Riel 2004):

- *emotional appeal* (trust, respect, admiration, feeling good about the company);
- *products and services* (high quality, innovativeness, value for the money, guarantee);
- *financial performance* (profitability, low degree of investment risk, growth, edge over competition);
- *vision and leadership* (market opportunities, excellent leadership, clear vision for the future);
- *workplace environment* (good management, work environment and employees);
- *social responsibility* (support of good causes, responsibility toward environment and community).

Measurements have shown that the factor with the most influence on reputation is emotional appeal, which is, in particular for the general public, the main 'driver' of reputation. The Reputation Institute further developed RQ with the Reptrak model, which is a standardized model of measuring reputation applied in many countries and among multiple stakeholders, and surmounts several measuring difficulties typical of RQ, such as validity and reliability of the model. The model retained six dimensions that are related to the company: acting as a good citizen, the company's management, successfulness, products and services, innovativeness and business environment (van Riel and Fombrun 2007).

The latest research (Walsh *et al.* 2009) in measuring reputation in the eyes of consumers (as one of the most important stakeholder groups for every company) discovered that dimensions of reputation include indicators that measure a company's attitude toward consumers, its relationship with employees, perceptions of the company's reliability and financial stability, perceived quality of products and services, and the company's social and environmental responsibility.

As we can see, different scales reflect findings of empirical studies where reputation is a result of consumer perceptions, which are influenced by a number of factors, such as profitability, intensity of communication, company size, accounting risk, amount of dividends, market success, ownership structure, media appearance, social responsibility and the company's attitude toward society (Fombrun and Shanley 1990). We should add also a positive relationship between a company's media appearance and reputation, mutual influence between the reputation of the management and reputation of the company, and the influence of branch reputation on the company reputation, which further supports the claim of what a highly complex task reputation management is.

10.3 Corporate reputation management

A successful approach to **reputation management** always starts with knowing the expectations of stakeholders well and their perceptions of the company. At its core, especially in terms of its management, reputation must always be *based on corporate identity* and on the capability of managers to convince stakeholders of the excellence and unique capacities of the company. Also, it needs to be clearly defined how to act in relationships with each individual *stakeholder*. Fombrun's (1996) research defined the main identity traits on which to build reputation in the eyes of key stakeholders. For a company to be reputable in the eyes of its employees, it should develop trust, give authority and arouse pride. Such traits enable development of a belief that the company is a trustworthy partner. With respect to investors, the key identity traits are profitability, maintenance of stability and potential for growth, which make the company credible. To be seen as reliable with respect to consumers, two key factors are excellence and quality of products and services, and good relationships with consumers. In terms of relationships with society, it is important to be socially responsible, to serve the community and to care for the environment, which makes the company's overall actions responsible (Fombrun 1996). Companies must also pay attention to the *relationship between positive and negative aspects of reality and perceptions*, and any deviations harming positive reality must be remedied immediately. When a company's actions are better than perceived and estimated actions, it should communicate intensively, and when its perceived actions are better than actual ones, the company should do anything it can to deserve such a positive evaluation.

Reputation is gained and built through consistent activities and although the building up of reputation is a long and continuous process, it can quickly be destroyed. Because reputation is a result of the previous actions of a company and of stakeholders' expectations based on those actions, the company is always scrutinized whether it holds its promises and commitments or not. In all cases, reputation is a result of hard work and many efforts, and a company has to earn it. Besides, the company has no direct control over reputation because it is attributed by specific audiences, or not.

10.4 Perceived external prestige of a company

The important influence of the overall reputation and its management on different stakeholders and their perceptions and responses is reflected in the concept of **perceived external prestige**. The concept was defined by Dutton and Dukerich (1991) as a way in which the organization members think that others (non-members, external audiences) see the organization, what they think about it and how they evaluate it. Or, as has been formulated by Dutton et al. (1994), perceived external prestige relates to 'a member's beliefs about the outsiders' perceptions of the organization' (Dutton et al. 1994, 248). Prestige is seen as an (external) reputation as evaluated by the organization's internal members. It can be a consequence of information from different sources, for example, reference group opinions, publicity, controlled external communications, and even the company's internal communication about how it is perceived by external audiences. Most often, perceived external prestige is treated as a variable on the level of an individual that signifies their interpretation and estimation of a company's reputation based on their own exposure to information about the organization. That is why different members can have varying perceptions of external prestige or reputation (Smidts et al. 2001, 1052). But perceived external prestige is more than just information about the possible social evaluation of the company. It provides an answer to members' questions such as 'How do outsiders think of me because of my association with this organization?' (Dutton et al. 1994, 248–249). Perceived external prestige functions as a powerful mirror that gives members of an organization an image of how the organization and behaviour of its members are seen by external audiences. Elsbach and Kramer (1996) undertook research that included members of 20 of the most prestigious business schools and established that individuals change and adjust their own perceptions of organizational identity based on available information about how others see the organization. In the study, respondents could change and correct their opinions according to the discrepancy between their original evaluations and information they received about how others see the organization.

The importance of perceived external prestige lies in the fact that Brennan drew attention to decades ago: it is the human nature of employees that they want to be proud of the company they work for and of the products and services they produce (Brennan 1960, 42). Creation of images and pride of employees is not only influenced by their direct experience and perception of corporate and organizational identity, as established by Bergami and Bagozzi (2000), but also by how the employees see that others perceive their company. Reputation does not only differentiate one company from others and facilitate needs of individuals to categorize themselves and others, it also influences, through perceived external prestige, the second important need within the **social identity approach**, that is the improvement of self-image (Bergami and Bagozzi 2000).

Dutton *et al.* (1994, 251) use findings of the social identity approach to relate external reputation with:

- *self-continuity of the individual*: if members believe outsiders view the organizational reputation in terms that are close to how they see themselves, then membership provides an opportunity to maintain a coherent and consistent sense of self;
- *self-distinctiveness of the individual*: perceived external prestige that enhances a member's distinctiveness in interpersonal contexts is seen as more attractive, because its fulfils the member's need to be different to the others (outsiders);
- *self-enhancement of the individual*: a member bases their positive self-concept on appraisals of the company by external publics.

Dutton *et al.* (1994) point out that perceived external prestige of a company is in a close relationship with the social identity of an individual.

> When members construe the external image as attractive – meaning that they believe this image has elements that others are likely to value – then organizational affiliation creates a positive social identity that increases the level of overlap between how a member defines him- or herself and the organization.
>
> *(Dutton et al. 1994, 250)*

This means that perceived external prestige increases the identification of employees with the organization, because individuals inherently like to see themselves in a positive way since positive self-image increases self-respect (Bhattacharya and Sen 2003). Similarly, several other theories, such as social interactionism, media studies and the marketing approach, also discuss the influence of others and their opinions on the identification of individuals.

10.5 Consequences of corporate reputation

Reputation is treated by marketing literature as the basis of social stratification and as a result of objective and subjective social reality, saying that there is a relevant heterogeneity of subjective perceptions of reputation by social actors (Czellar 2002). In terms of a company, this means that reputation differentiates one company from others and brings competitive advantages. Reputation secures to a company its perceived position or ranking in relation to the competition. As formulated by van Riel (1997), reputation is not an isolated goal for a company. 'Reputation is a vital condition for, and means of, creating a sound commercial basis from which the success of the company eventually stems' (van Riel 1997, 297–298). In order to acquire this commercial basis, the company has to win positive attitudes and the cooperation of multiple stakeholders; reputation can provide significant help in this process. That is why reputation is seen as a **competitive advantage** and an intangible asset for the company. There is consensus among authors, supported by research, that reputation brings advantages and benefits in a company's relationship with different stakeholders. Yoon *et al.* (1993) took an overview of empirical research studying the influence of reputation on consumers, and established that reputation influences the expectations about the quality of the offer, reduces purchase risks, sustains loyalty, supports market share, acts as an entry barrier for new actors in the market, raises effectiveness of communications, while also supporting the positive relationship between reputation and purchase intention.

Shenkar and Yuchtman-Yaar (1997) established a connection between reputation and the higher price of products. Reputation is also a helpful tool when launching a new product on the market (Garud and Lampel 1997). Furthermore, reputation influences acceptance of advertising messages and trust in such messages (Goldberg and Hatwick 1990), raises credibility of a provider and loyalty to a retailer (Ganesan 1994), raises credibility of a company (Goldsmith *et al.* 2000) and influences profitability and the gaining of market advantage (Fombrun and Shanley 1990; Roberts and Dowling 1997). Reputation also influences investors' perceptions and evaluations of a company (Srivastava *et al.* 1997; Brown 1998), attracts better employees (Sobol *et al.* 1992), motivates employees and increases their identification and loyalty (Bhattacharya *et al.* 1995; Podnar 2004).

Fombrun and Shanley (1990) list further research in support of the thesis that reputation facilitates access to capital markets, attracts investors and reduces the cost of capital. Reputation helps companies in times of crisis (Jones *et al.* 2000). Fombrun and van Riel (2004, 5) describe reputation as a magnet that attracts different constituents of a company, for example, employees (reputation makes jobs more attractive, motivates hard work, customers (encourages repeat purchases, builds market share), investors (lowers capital costs, attracts new investments), media journalists (generates more favourable media coverage) or financial analysts (affects content of coverage and recommendations).

The multiple influences of reputation are consolidated by Greyser (1999, 178) into three main strategic advantages for a company:

- stakeholders' preference in doing business with a company;
- support for a company in times of crisis;
- a company's value in the financial marketplace.

Several authors (Sobol *et al.* 1992; Dukerich and Carter 2000) consider the concern for reputation management as a way of enlightened egoism because, as we have illustrated, good reputation (see also Shenkar and Yuchtman-Yaar 1997) brings a number of benefits and positive influences to the company. These benefits are the reason why the company should try to earn a good reputation, even though the 'price to pay' is a true concern for company identity, transparency and honesty, ethical attitude toward stakeholders, investment in natural and social environment, and being a good and responsible citizen. Most of all, it is important to consistently realize communicated topics in everyday actions, together with involvement of stakeholders in organizational processes and decision making. By doing that, companies must give up potential myopic profitability and other unethical decisions that are often present in competitive battles and the drive for success. In this way, corporate reputation arouses, builds and affirms the trust of key stakeholders in the company.

10.6 Forms and roles of trust

In the last three decades, trust – a feeling that you can rely on somebody in some ways – became an important research concept in social sciences. Reasons for that can be found, according to Viklund (2003), in the works of Luhmann (1979) and Giddens (1990), who claim that trust significantly reduces complexity and instability in modern society, in which technical and abstract systems are not completely comprehended even by experts. Authors believe that it is trust among social actors that is the main factor for effectiveness, adaptability and even survival in our complex modern society (Rotter 1967). As such, trust is a key element in stable relationships in society, because (mis)trust is an important factor in interpersonal and group behaviours and in relationships among institutions.

Kenning (2008) writes that business literature treats trust from four different points of view. The first view is interpersonal trust dealing with trust among human beings. The second area covers trust among institutions, while the third deals with trust within organizations. The fourth area covers trust with respect to technologies. In our book, we will deal with trust of individuals with respect to companies, which is an important form of corporate association.

Although there are different aspects of trust to consider, one aspect is extremely important for our discussion on a broader approach to corporate associations; we are talking about 'specific trust', which relates to an individual situation and specific entity (Kennedy *et al.* 2001, 74). This is a concrete relation between a company and its stakeholders that can be influenced by marketing and communication activities. **Specific trust** is a category that is different from general or **initial trust** (which is also called moral trust), which is a principled orientation toward building trust in someone or something, which happens at an early stage in childhood and is from then on an important part of a personality (Morrow *et al.* 2004). It is a fact that an individual can trust a company due to the person's general trustfulness, but this is not the same phenomenon as when the trust of an individual is influenced by a company's actions. A logical question here is why individuals enter into such relationships. For example, Ring (1996) distinguishes between rational and emotional trust. While **emotional trust** is based on personal experience, emotional involvement, and information from within the relationship, rational or **calculative trust** is based on rational estimation of risks, rewards, controls, and information gained outside the relationship, and it assumes an estimation of one side that selfish behaviour from the other side (that is, the company) would be disadvantageous (Ring 1996). This means that trust can originate from an individual's social ties or from their self-interest (Saparito *et al.* 2004). However, some authors reject this calculative component of trust, because this would contradict the specific and intimate nature of the relationship that is based on trust (Williamson 1993).

Similarly we can distinguish between trust based on personal characteristics, institutional trust, and trust based on processes (Zucker 1986), which puts forward that stakeholder trust can originate from different sources. According to Johnson and Grayson (2000), trust can be based on **'generalized trust'** that is typical for certain environments and prevailing expectations of general moral principles, specific behaviour norms, and responsibilities in this environment. We can also talk about **'systemic trust'** that relates to the rule of law and describes the trust of individuals in regulative and legislative authorities who believe in legislative provisions and their implementation and believe that breaking the law will be sanctioned. The trust of individuals can be a result of a 'process' or individual expectations and their outcomes, as they happen among actors in transactions and situations. Trust can also be 'personal' if an individual is trustful, which is a personality characteristic resulting from their socialization.

In relationships among social actors, trust increases security, reduces disturbances and defensive behaviour, and creates an atmosphere in which people can share their feelings and desires (Stinnett and Walters 1977). Trust also reduces transaction costs in relationships and exchanges among social actors, and is effective in reducing insecurity of stakeholders. Trust helps to build up commitment, improves communication and enables better cooperation, mutual adjustments and satisfaction with interactions (Tyler and Stanley 2007, 335). Especially in the service economy, companies could not do business without users' trust in services and their providers. Trust between a customer and a company is obligatory, because a customer buys a product or a service before experiencing it (Berry and Parasuraman 1991, 144).

10.7 Definition of trust

For the purpose of this book, **trust** is defined as a reliance of a person, group or organization on a voluntarily accepted duty of another person, group or organization to recognize and protect the rights of everybody involved in mutual efforts or economic exchange (Hosmer 1995). In this sense, trust is the amount of confidence that individuals have in institutions, either when getting real information about risks or when directly or indirectly managing risk (Cha 2000). Trust is an optimistic expectation of an outcome of an event or of an entity's behaviour, or a belief from one side that the other will behave or respond in a way that is expected and acceptable for both sides (Sako 1992, 37). Trust is accompanied by the assumption of accepted duty that the rights and interests of the other should be protected. This happens when the actor involved has confidence in their partner's reliability and honesty (Morgan and Hunt 1994, 23). Trust is a result of true, just and honest behaviour that recognizes and protects the rights and interests of others in society (Hosmer 1995). Trust depends on the level to which an individual believes other individuals to be well-meaning and honest (Larzelere and Huston 1980, 596). Although trust develops through progressive familiarization and better understanding of the other and especially through immediate experience (Dwyer *et al.* 1987), Thorelli (1986) points out that trust, even though a consequence of previous interaction among companies, is a future-oriented concept. Tyler and Stanley (2007, 335) summarize the key components of multiple definitions of trust that are important in terms of corporate marketing and communication.

- As a cognitive or affective belief held by one party that its partner will not exploit their vulnerability.
- As a behaviour or behavioural intention of a party to act in a way that inclines it toward risk, uncertainty or increases its vulnerability to another.
- As a willingness to rely on a partner in whom one has confidence.
- As a recognition of importance and interconnection of the belief component and behavioural component, but maintaining that these are distinct phenomena.
- As a broad, socially defined phenomenon relating to the management and atmosphere of effective interaction as a whole (sociological perspective approach).

We have shown that trust arises when interests of individuals are vulnerable and dependent on other people's behaviour, and that trust is related to voluntary, unforced cooperation and benefits arising from cooperation. This means that trust is a quality that cannot be acquired by force.

10.8 Dimensions of trust

The literature has defined several different dimensions of trust. Writers use a number of similar concepts and qualities that help them to describe the concept of trust. Some of the most frequently mentioned dimensions of trust are competence, reliability, honesty and benevolence.

- **Reliability** is the perceived ability to keep an implicit or explicit promise (Selnes and Gønhaug 2000, 259) or act competently. Competence is based on the belief of one partner about the other partner's knowledge and skills in a specific field of activities, and on the belief that the other partner will execute a specific activity in accordance with expectations (Cook and Wall 1980). Reliability is therefore a perceived capacity of an entity to keep its promises.

- **Honesty** is an evaluation of a person about the extent to which they can believe their partner about their future intentions (Larzelere and Huston 1980, 596). Honesty relates to characteristics that convince somebody that he/she can rely on another person and includes traits such as reliability, keeping their word and keeping promises (Kumar *et al.* 1995), fulfilling duties, and sincerity (Linksold 1978). Benbasat and Wang (2005) define honesty as a belief in an individual's conviction that the other person in the exchange will stick firmly to their principles, which they accepted in accordance with its possibility, and will stick to in any case. Honesty is not so much a question of an entity's capability of keeping its promises, but its honest intention to keep them (Berens 2004). This relates not to the ability of an actor to fulfil its promises but to its intentions to fulfil promises.

- **Benevolence** denotes an expectation that the activities of the trusted party will operate to the benefit and in accordance with the interests of the trusting party (Kumar *et al.* 1995). It is founded on the qualities, intentions and characteristics of the trusted entity, and not on the entity's specific behaviour (Rempel *et al.* 1985). It relates to the interests of the exchange partners and on their genuine orientation toward the well-being of the other, not only toward satisfying their own interests. In the case of companies, this means an orientation toward reciprocal exchange and not only following their own partial interests (Mayer *et al.* 1995). The key factor is the willingness to act to the benefit of all sides involved (Doney and Cannon 1997).

While reliability and benevolence deal with the likelihood that a company will fulfil the explicit promises that it makes, honesty deals with the likelihood that a company will behave in a cooperative manner, independent of promises (Berens 2004, 36).

10.9 Consequences of bad reputation and mistrust

Trust is the 'foundation stone of a strategic partnership' (Spekman 1988, 79) and as such, extremely important for exchange and relationships. Greenberg *et al.* (2007) list a number of studies showing that people do not trust institutions if they are not competent, do not share their values or do not operate honestly. The reasons for not trusting institutions or companies are many. For example, management has little respect for other sides that are involved in the exchange with the company but have less power; or, institutional leaders cannot or will not keep their promises to work on a desired level. Also, companies are not trusted when they create such circumstances that lead to inequality among exchange partners and to unjust distribution of benefits and costs, and when risks connected with the exchange are very high and consequences of exchange durable. Further reasons for mistrust are attempts by institutions to cover up information about their problems and failures, or the lack of competence in employees who cannot keep up with the complexity of processes and procedures.

For a company, a lack of reputation does not only make the company less trusted, but it also strengthens the scepticism of stakeholders. Scepticism in this context means a negative attitude toward the motives, claims and activities of companies. It is a cognitive response of an individual to doubt the credibility of different forms of marketing communication (Obermiller and Spangenberg 1998). An individual always asks questions, regardless of what a company does, about the honesty and sincerity of a company's actions. Scepticism leads the way to cynicism, which is a stable personality trait that occurs when people see that other people, but also companies, act solely based on selfish motives (Mohr *et al.* 1998, 33). Transactions with such stakeholders only rarely grow into an exchange that is based on a mutual and reciprocal relationship, because communications become ineffective, and the operation extremely difficult.

We are faced today with diminishing trust in institutions, companies and complete industries, and at the same time with rising scepticism of stakeholders. Despite the enormous importance of trust in our society for the activities of companies, research show that the trust of multiple stakeholders and citizen groups in companies has never been lower, a phenomenon which is present across the world, above all in developed countries. This important signal predicts a deep management crisis but at the same time warns managers and owners that they must show more responsibility in their business operations. But it seems that companies are not very aware of how extremely unstable trust is, and that once betrayed, it is hard to build up again. Only exceptionally and in special circumstances do people trust again or reinstate their trust. In terms of corporate and other brands, each individual trust and opinion is valuable, since trust is formed not only from our own experience but also from recommendations of others. If a person trusts someone, then he/she can transfer his or her trust to a brand that is recommended by them. Managers should be more mindful of this fact in order to avoid mistrust, scepticism and cynicism in stakeholders, and to create positive corporate associations that help to build up the company's most valuable intangible asset of all, that is, its reputation.

CASE: BP

The story of BP, one of the largest oil companies in the world, starts in 1908 when a British adventurer, William D'Arcy, found oil in the Persian Gulf. The following year, D'Arcy and the Burmah Oil society founded Anglo-Persian Oil, and in 1914 the British government took over 51 per cent of its share. In 1954, the company was renamed British Petroleum. In 1998, British Petroleum merged with an oil company Amoco and was again renamed, this time as BP Amoco. Around the year 2000, the company took over several other companies, including ARCO and Castrol and shortened the name of the corporation to BP. In a press release, the corporation promoted the new name with an argument that BP is a well-known name that is reflected through the new company's mission: 'Better People, Better Products, Big Picture, Beyond Petroleum'.

In the 1990s, BP was involved in a number of environmental scandals. One such story was that BP played an active role in efforts to convince the US government to allow drilling in Alaska, in the area of the Arctic National Wildlife Reserve. The non-governmental organization Corporate Watch said in 1999 that BP's emissions of air pollutants are larger than those of Canada or Great Britain. After the company had taken over several other oil companies, it was reportedly responsible for emissions of 3 per cent of all greenhouse gases in the world.

Despite the fact that the company, throughout its history, had a reputation for consequently causing deterioration of the natural environment in which it was active and trampling down human rights in developing countries, BP maintained its reputation of being an environmentally progressive company. One of the moves that were important for the preservation of such reputation was the decision of the company's President Lord John Browne to withdraw from the 'Global Climate Coalition', which was formed by oil giants that denied global warning. After BP had left the coalition, it said publicly that global warming is indeed a big global problem. John Sawhill, one of the leading managers of the American BP, said that President Browne saw here an opportunity to distinct BP from other companies in the industry. The decision to leave the coalition was made precisely at the moment when the company was criticized heavily for its business in Colombia.

Simultaneously with the change of name to BP, the corporate brand was also repositioned. Advertising agency Ogilvy Worldwide revitalized the logo and equipped it with the tagline 'Beyond Petroleum'. The agency claimed that the change of name repositioned the company into a global energy company of a new era that is ready to face challenges such as the conflict between environmental and energy needs and that carries out activities that are much more positive (those that one would expect from an oil company). In cooperation with the agency, BP launched a global communication campaign worth over US$600 million and presented itself as a new, environmentally aware energy company. In 2001, the campaign received many awards for being one of the best PR campaigns.

Even more was done for BP's reputation in the USA, where the company wanted to profile itself among competitors. An extensive reputation-building programme was created on which a special team of people was working. Goals were to raise reputation, to increase the value of shares, to raise sales and to get new investors. The goal was also to convince employees to identify with the 'new' company, and not with company history. Outside commentators reported that the programme was very similar to a political campaign.

Some very explicit goals were to increase reputation with opinion leaders, raise recognition rate from 70 per cent to 90 per cent and to be among the top 5 companies listed in the Fortune 500 list, before Shell and Exxon Mobil. A number of studies were carried out among various stakeholder groups to define key messages that were to be communicated through a variety of communication tools. As a result, a 200-page reputation management manual was published with instructions for managers who could use the manual as a sort of 'cookbook'.

Activities brought great results; spontaneous brand recall increased to 49 per cent in the general public; the company was rated high among investors and opinion leaders. There were a great deal more opinion leaders that believed that BP produced clearer energy, that BP is a leading environmentalist in the industry, that BP redefines energy business and that BP is a company attractive to investments. But the best result was the position on the Fortune list, which campaign managers believed to be the best indicator of company reputation – in 2001, BP reached fourth place in its industry, while in 2003 it reached first place in its industry. Despite its success in the industry, BP did not reach the top 25 in the overall category.

Although PR experts repeatedly claim that the campaign was well planned, there were numerous warnings from the media and NGOs that BP was not doing things in the way it had said it would. The most-heard criticism was that it neglected security of oil drilling operations. Robert Eccles, an expert on crisis communications, wrote for *Harvard Business Review* that 'when the reputation of a company is more positive than its underlying reality, this gap poses a substantial risk ... BP appears to be learning this the hard way'. In 2005 and 2006 the company faced two major accidents in Texas and in Alaska, followed by a much larger accident in the Gulf of Mexico. BP's reputation plummeted drastically. Furthermore, reports show that only 2 per cent of BP's revenue came from alternative energy sources, despite the main message upon which the corporate reputation has been built, being 'Beyond Petroleum'.

Key terms

Corporate reputation or public image. An overall evaluation and, to a certain degree, a simplified estimation of a company by its stakeholders. Reputation relates to the question of how specific publics evaluate the company in terms of social standards, beliefs and values. It refers to the categorization of companies according to certain criteria, which as a whole (which is more than a sum of its parts) create a relative position of an organization in the eyes of its stakeholders.

Perceived external prestige. A way in which the organization members think that others (non-members, external audiences) see the organization, what they think about it and how they evaluate it. As such it relates to a member's beliefs about the outsiders' perceptions of the organization.

Trust. Optimistic feeling of someone, that he or she can rely on somebody in some ways. It is a reliance of a person, group or organization on a voluntarily accepted duty of another person, group or organization to recognize and protect the rights of everybody involved in mutual efforts or economic exchange. In this sense, trust is the amount of confidence that individuals have in institutions, either when getting real information about risks or when directly or indirectly managing risk.

Reliability. The perceived ability or capacity of an identity to keep an implicit or explicit promise (or act competently).

Honesty. Refers to an evaluation of a person about the extent to which they can believe their partner about their future intentions. It is not so much a question of an entity's capability of keeping its promises, but its honest intention to keep them. This relates not to the ability of an actor to fulfil its promises but to its intentions to fulfil promises.

Benevolence. Denotes an expectation that the activities of the trusted party will operate to the benefit and in accordance with the interests of the trusting party. It relates to the interests of the exchange partners and on their genuine orientation toward the well-being of the other, not only toward satisfying their own interests.

REVIEW QUESTIONS

- Define corporate reputation, its dimensions and its consequences.
- What is perceived external prestige and why it is important?
- What is corporate trust, its dimensions and how can they be managed?
- What are the possible consequences of corporate scepticism and cynicism?

Visit BP's global website and review how it addresses its environmental impact. Do you think that companies in particular industries with a negative image, such as the oil industry, tobacco, chemistry, etc. can gain public trust regarding their sustainability? Think about industries and companies which have problems with their reputations. What strategies can they use to gain the trust of the public?

References

Balmer, John M. T. 2003. *Revealing the Corporation.* London; New York: Routledge.

Benbasat, Izak and Weiquan Wang. 2005. Trust in and adoption of online recommendation agents. *Journal of the Association for Information Systems* 6 (3): 72–101.

Berens, Guido A. J. M. 2004. *Corporate Branding: The Development of Corporate Associations and their Influence on Stakeholder Reactions.* Rotterdam: Erasmus Research Institute of Management, Erasmus University Rotterdam.

Bergami, Massimo and Richard P. Bagozzi. 2000. Self-categorization, affective commitment, and group self-esteem as distinct aspects of social identity in the organization. *British Journal of Social Psychology* 39 (7): 555–577.

Berry, Leonard L. and A. Parasuraman. 1991. *Marketing Services: Competing Through Quality*. New York: Free Press.

Bhattacharya, C. B. and Sankar Sen. 2003. Consumer–company identification: a framework for understanding consumers' relationships with brands. *Journal of Marketing* 67 (2): 76–88.

Bhattacharya, C. B., Hayagreeva Rao and Mary Ann Glynn. 1995. Understanding the bond of identification: an investigation of its correlates among art museum members. *The Journal of Marketing* 59 (4): 46–57.

Brennan, William. 1960. The image among your employees. In *Developing the Corporate Image*, ed. Lee Hastings Bristol. New York: Charles Scribner's Sons, 41–48.

Bromley, Dennis Basil. 1993. *Reputation, Image and Impression Management*. Chichester: John Wiley and Sons.

Brown, Tom J. 1998. Corporate associations in marketing: antecedents and consequences. *Corporate Reputation Review* 1 (3): 215–233.

Caruana, Albert. 1997. Corporate reputation: concept and measurement. *Journal of Product and Brand Management* 6 (2): 109–118.

Caruana, Albert and Saviour Chircop. 2000. Measuring corporate reputation: a case example. *Corporate Reputation Review* 3 (1): 43–57.

Cha, Yong-Jin. 2000. Risk perception in Korea: a comparison with Japan and the United States. *Journal of Risk Research* 3 (4): 321–332.

Cook, John and Toby Wall. 1980. New work attitude measures of trust, organizational commitment and personal need non-fulfillment. *Journal of Occupational Psychology* 53 (1): 39–52.

Cravens, Karen, Elizabeth Goad Oliver and Sridhar Ramamoorti. 2003. The reputation index: measuring and managing corporate reputation. *European Management Journal* 21 (2): 201–212.

Czellar, Sandor. 2002. *An Exploratory Inquiry on the Antecedents of Prestige Judgments. Conference Proceedings*. Austin, TX: Society for Consumer Psychology.

Doney, Patricia M. and Joseph P. Cannon. 1997. An examination of the nature of trust in buyer–seller relationships. *Journal of Marketing* 61 (2): 35–51.

Dowling, Grahame. 2001. *Creating Corporate Reputations: Identity, Image and Performance*. Oxford: Oxford University Press.

Dukerich, Janet M. and Suzanne M. Carter. 2000. Distorted images and reputation repair. In *The Expressive Organization: Linking Identity, Reputation and the Corporate Brand*, eds. Maijken Schulz, Mary Jane Hatch and Mogens Holten Larsen. Oxford: Oxford University Press, 97–112.

Dutton, Jane E. and Janet M. Dukerich. 1991. Keeping an eye on the mirror: image and identity in organizational adaption. *Academy of Management Journal* 34 (1): 517–554.

Dutton, Jane E., Janet M. Dukerich and Celia V. Harquail. 1994. Organizational images and member identification. *Administrative Science Quarterly* 39 (2): 239–263.

Dwyer, Robert F., Paul H. Schurr and Sejo Oh. 1987. Developing buyer-seller relationships. *Journal of Marketing* 51 (2): 11–27.

Elsbach, Kimberly D. and Roderick M. Kramer. 1996. Members' responses to organizational identity threats: encountering and countering the business week rankings. *Administrative Science Quarterly* 41 (3): 442–476.

Fombrun, Charles J. 1996. *Reputation: Realizing Value from the Corporate Image*. Boston, MA: Harvard Business School Press.

——1998. Indices of corporate reputation: an analysis of media rankings and social monitors' ratings. *Corporate Reputation Review* 1 (4): 327–340.

Fombrun, Charles J. and Mark Shanley. 1990. What's in a name: reputation building and corporate strategy. *Academy of Management Journal* 33 (2): 233–258.

Fombrun, Charles J. and Cees B. M. van Riel. 2004. *Fame and Fortune: How Successful Companies Build Winning Reputations*. London: Pearson Financial Times.

Fombrun, Charles J., Naomi A. Gardberg and Joy M. Sever. 2000. The reputation quotient: a multi-stakeholder measure of corporate reputation. *The Journal of Brand Management* 7 (4): 241–255.

Ganesan, Shankar. 1994. Determinants of long-term orientation in buyer-seller relationship. *Journal of Marketing* 58 (2): 1–19.

Garud, Raghu and Joseph Lampel. 1997. Product announcements and corporate reputations. *Corporate Reputation Review* 1 (1/2): 114–118.

Giddens, Anthony. 1990. *The Consequences of Modernity*. Stanford, CT: Stanford University Press.

Goldberg, Marvin E. and Jon Hartwick. 1990. The effects of advertiser reputation and extremity of advertising claim on advertising effectiveness. *Journal of Consumer Research* 17 (2): 172–179.

Goldsmith, Ronald, Barbara Lafferty and Stephen Newell. 2000. The influence of corporate credibility on consumer attitudes and purchase intent. *Corporate Reputation Review* 3 (4): 304–319.

Gotsi, Manto and Alan Wilson. 2001. Corporate reputation management: living the brand. *Management Decision* 39 (2): 99–104.

Greenberg, Penelope Sue, Ralph H. Greenberg and Yvonne Lederer Antonucci. 2007. Creating and sustaining trust in virtual teams. *Business Horizons* 50 (4): 325–333.

Greyser, Stephen A. 1999. Advancing and enhancing corporate reputation. *Corporate Communications* 4 (4): 177–181.

Herbig, Paul and John Milewicz. 1993. The relationship of reputation and credibility to brand success. *Journal of Consumer Marketing* 10 (3): 18–24.

Hosmer, Larue Tone. 1995. Trust: the connecting link between organizational theory and philosophical ethics. *Academy of Management Review* 20 (2): 379–403.

Johnson, Devon and Kent Grayson. 2000. Sources and dimensions of trust in service relationships. In *Handbook of Services Marketing*, eds. Dawn Iacobucci and Teresa Swartz. Thousand Oaks, CA: Sage, 357–370.

Jones, Gary H., Beth H. Jones and Philip Little. 2000. Reputation as reservoir: buffering against loss in times of economic crisis. *Corporate Reputation Review* 3 (1): 21–29.

Kennedy, Mary S., Linda K. Ferrel and Debbie T. LeClair. 2001. Consumers' trust of salesperson and manufacturer: an empirical study. *Journal of Business Research* 51 (1): 73–86.

Kenning, Peter. 2008. The influence of general trust and specific trust on buying behaviour. *International Journal of Retail & Distribution Management* 36 (6): 461–476.

Kumar, Nirmalya, Lisa K. Scheer and Jan-Benedict E. M. Steenkamp. 1995. The effects of supplier fairness on vulnerable resellers. *Journal of Marketing Research* 32 (1): 54–65.

Larzelere, Robert E. and Ted L. Huston. 1980. The dyadic trust scale: toward understanding interpersonal trust in close relationships. *Journal of Marriage and the Family* 42 (3): 595–604.

Linksold, Svenn. 1978. Trust development, the GRIT proposal and the effects of conciliatory acts on conflict and cooperation. *Psychological Bulletin* 85 (4): 772–793.

Luhmann, Niklas. 1979. *Trust and Power*. Chichester: John Wiley.

Martineau, Pierre. 1958. Sharper focus for the corporate image. *Harvard Business Review* 36 (6): 49–58.

Mayer, Roger C., James H. Davis and David F. Schoorman. 1995. An integrative model of organizational trust. *Academy of Management Review* 20 (3): 709–734.

Mohr, Lois A., Dogan Eroglu and Pam Scholder Ellen. 1998. The development and testing of a measure of skepticism toward environmental claims in marketers' communications. *Journal of Consumer Affairs* 32 (1): 30–55.

Morgan, Robert M. and Shelby D. Hunt. 1994. The commitment-trust theory of relationship marketing. *Journal of Marketing* 58 (3): 20–38.

Morrow, J. L., Jr., Mark H. Hansen and Allison W. Pearson. 2004. The cognitive and affective antecedents of general trust within cooperative organizations. *Journal of Managerial Issues* 16 (1): 48–64.

Obermiller, Carl and Spangenberg, E. R. 1998. Development of a scale to measure consumer skepticism toward advertising. *Journal of Consumer Psychology* 7 (2): 159–186.

Podnar, Klement. 2000. Korporativna identiteta, imidž in ugled. In *Vregov zbornik*, ed. Slavko Splichal. Ljubljana: Evropski inštitut za komuniciranje in kulturo: Fakulteta za družbene vede, 173–181.

——2004. *Ugled, organizacijska identifikacija in zavezanost zaposlenih*. Doktorska disertacija. Ljubljana: Fakulteta za družbene vede.

Rempel, John K., John G. Holmes and Mark P. Zanna. 1985. Trust in close relationships. *Journal of Personality and Social Psychology* 49 (1): 95–112.

Ring, Peter Smith. 1996. Fragile and resilient trust and their roles in economic exchange business society. *Business Society June* 35 (2): 148–175.

Roberts, Peter W. and Grahame R. Dowling. 1997. The value of a firm's corporate reputation. *Corporate Reputation Review* 1 (1): 72–76.

Rotter, Julian B. 1967. A new scale for measurement of interpersonal trust. *Journal of Personality* 35 (4): 651–665.

Sako, Mari. 1992. *Prices, Quality, and Trust: Inter-firm Relations in Britain and Japan*. Cambridge: Cambridge University Press.

Saparito, Patrick A., Chao C. Chen and Harry J. Sapienza. 2004. The role of relational trust in bank–small firm relationships. *Academy of Management Journal* 47 (3): 400–410.

Selnes, Fred and Kjell Gønhaug. 2000. Effects of supplier reliability and benevolence in business marketing. *Journal of Business Research* 49 (3): 259–271.

Shenkar, Oded and Ephrainm Yuchtman-Yaar. 1997. Reputation, image, prestige and goodwill: an interdisciplinary approach to organizational standing. *Human Relations* 50 (11): 1361–1381.

Smidts, Ale, Ad Th. H. Pruyn and Cees B. M. van Riel. 2001. The impact of employee communication and perceived external prestige on organizational identification. *Academy of Management Journal* 44 (5): 1051–1062.

Sobol, Marion, Gail Farrelly and Jessica Taper. 1992. *Shaping the Corporate Image*. New York: Quorum Books.

Spekman, Robert E. 1988. Strategic supplier selection: understanding long-term buyer relationships. *Business Horizons* 31 (4): 75–81.

Srivastava, Rajendra K., Thomas H. McInish, Robert A. Wood and Anthony J. Capraro. 1997. The value of corporate reputation: evidence from the equity markets. *Corporate Reputation Review* 1 (1): 62–68.

Stinnett, Nick and James Walters. 1977. *Relationships in Marriage and Family*. New York: Macmillan.

Thorelli, Hans B. 1986. Networks: between markets and hierarchies. *Strategic Management Journal* 7 (1): 37–51.

Tyler, Katherine and Edmund Stanley. 2007. The role of trust in financial services business relationships. *Journal of Services Marketing* 21 (5): 334–344.

van Riel, Cees B. M. 1997. Research in corporate communication: an overview of an emerging field. *Management Communication Quarterly* 11 (2): 288–309.

van Riel, Cees B. M. and Charles J. Fombrun. 2007. *Essentials of Corporate Communication: Implementing Practices for Effective Reputation Management.* London; New York: Routledge.

Viklund, Mattias J. 2003. Trust and risk perception in Western Europe: a cross-national study. *Risk Analysis* 23 (4): 727–738.

Walsh, Gianfranco, Sharon E. Beatty and Edward M. K. Shiu. 2009. The customer-based corporate reputation scale: replication and short form. *Journal of Business Research* 62 (10): 924–930.

Williamson, Oliver E. 1993. Calculativeness, trust and economic organisation. *Journal of Law and Economics* 36 (1): 453–486.

Yoon, Eunsang, Hugh J. Guffey and Valerie Kijewski. 1993. The effects of information and company reputation on intentions to buy a business service. *Journal of Business Research* 27 (3): 215–228.

Zucker, Lynne Goodman. 1986. Production of trust: institutional sources of economic structure. *Research in Organizational Behaviour* 8 (1): 53–111.

11

ORGANIZATIONAL IDENTIFICATION

CONTENTS

In this chapter, we present identification as one of the key consequences of corporate communication with important effects on stakeholders and the organization. First, we present the main characteristics of identification, then specifically the identification of organizational members with the organization. Further, we discuss issues in connection with the identification of external stakeholders, such as consumers. The chapter concludes with an overview of the main consequences of organizational identification.

11.1 Identification: main characteristics

Organizational identification is a social and psychological bond that associates stakeholders with an organization. In this process, personal goals become more integrated and congruent with the goals of an organization. From the management's point of view, this is the process of internal and external persuasion and exertion of influence which make the interests of an individual congruent with the interests of the organization.

Identification is seen as a critical communication process that not only affects the stakeholder's perception of an organization but also influences the organization's decisions. In the process, individuals perceive characteristics that they share with other organization members and with the company, which results in supporting behaviour and solidarity with the organization.

Because this is a basic psycho-social human process that has a major impact on the commitment and loyalty of stakeholders with the company and that influences stakeholder behaviour, organizational identification should be one of the most important tasks of companies and managers. The process of identification can occur spontaneously, of course, but this process can also be accompanied by a negative identification (dis-identification), which can have destructive effects on the relationship between two social entities. Hence, organizational identification should not be left completely to chance, even though there cannot be complete control over the phenomenon.

Identification of an individual is an elementary human mechanism that is closely related to the psychic and social development of an individual. It is seen as an individual's sense of oneness with an entity with which he/she is in a relationship. It accompanies a person, in different forms and circumstances, throughout the entire life during which he/she identifies with different individuals, groups, and other entities and categories. Identification is seen as a process through which the society enters into a person, thus making him/her a social and symbolic being, not only a biological one. Psychology defines identification as a natural psychological process of social learning of adaptation, development and defence, and sees it as an individual's emotional attachment to person(s) where the individual assumes and adopts characteristics of the other and changes completely or partly, according to the model and object of identification. Although psychology treats identification primarily in the context of interpersonal human relationships, it also posits that individuals deal with different types of identification. In those cases we are faced with an application of primary identification patterns that are inherent to humans and closely related to their instincts which develop at the earliest stage of human life. As such, identification has important effects on the thinking and behaviour of individuals, both in relation to themselves and to the entity with which they identify.

Identification is seen as a means for construction and manipulation of an individual's own identity. An individual draws his/her own (social) identity from social identifications with different categories that are most often entirely concrete, but can also be very abstract groups of people. Physical presence in the group is established as a factor that strengthens social identification, but is not a necessary condition for identification. The feeling of a person that he/she is a member of a category (or a desire to become a member) is enough for the process of identification. In combination with **social categorization**, which is a process of arranging and ranking the social environment, social identification is a continuous and spontaneous process. There can be as many social identifications as there are categories, among which an individual can choose and feel one with. Identifications are contextual, non-fixed, related hierarchically with one another, not necessarily synchronous, and distinguished according to the strength and symbolic meaning they have for an individual and his/her identity. Identifications are in a close relationship with human self-image and self-respect.

Besides being a mechanism for the construction of identity, identification is also one of the important processes of social influence. By getting people to identify with our entity, we influence more easily the change of opinions, beliefs and behaviours, because the more a person identifies with somebody or something, the more susceptible they are to their suggestions. The process of identification is based on the likeness perceived by an individual between him/herself and an object. The greater the perceived similarity, the easier the process of identification and consequently the influence is stronger. Thus, identification influences behavioural dispositions and the behaviour of individuals, especially in the sense of their positive responses and reactions to entities with which they identify. An entity with which a person identifies becomes a part of this person, who favours that entity in their thoughts and in behaviour. Such a person responds to events that happened to someone else as if they happened to him/her (Kagan 1958, 298).

11.2 Identifications in the work environment

A discussion on identification of individuals in relation to their work environment and the company with which they are in an employment relationship must take into consideration the many different objects of identification and therefore diversified identifications of an individual. 'In theory, the process of identification begins simply with knowing that one is a member of an organization' (Bartel and Dutton 2001, 115). However, contemporary views emphasize that organizational membership is less a question of being in or out of an organization than knowing when and to what degree one is a member (Bartel and Dutton 2001, 116) and to what extent and on what basis they identify with a specific entity or category. Possible objects or levels of identification within the work environment are profession, union, co-workers, work place, work groups, reference groups, subgroups, tasks, work department, hierarchical level, friendly groups, demographic groups, management, consumers, owners and other shareholders, and even the strategies, goals and geographic units of the organization (Reichers 1985; Scott 1997; Russo 1998; Bhattacharya and Sen 2003; Connaughton and Daly 2004). In order to successfully understand and manage identification, it is not so important to know all the categories and objects of identification, but to understand their simultaneousness, consistency, compatibility or competitiveness. Morrow (1982) and Russo (1998), and Reichers (1985) before that, posit that identification is not an all-or-nothing phenomenon, although it is possible that one form of identification could be in conflict with another, for example, organizational identification could interfere with the professional one.

That is why a distinction must be made between **situated identification** and **deep structure identification** (Russo 1998). Mael and Ashforth (2001) suggest that we can distinguish between the two according to the criteria of permanence and stability. Situational identification is a result of individuals' perception of mutual benefits or a need for joint actions in order to achieve a specific, mutually desired effect, and is time-specific. Structural identifications are permanent and accompany relationships through time and in changing circumstances.

Ashforth and Johnson (2001) explain the relationship among different aspects of identification by introducing the criterion of importance that defines hierarchy in relationships among identification. The importance of a specific identification is defined by the subjective meaning and situational relevance (Ashforth 2001).

> A subjectively important identity is one that is highly central to an individual's global or core sense of self or is otherwise highly relevant to his or her goals, values, or other key attributes. A situationally relevant identity is one that is socially appropriate to a given context. Whereas subjective importance is defined by internal preferences, situational relevance is defined by external norms.
>
> *(Ashforth and Johnson 2001, 32)*

According to importance, Ashforth and Johnson (2001) classify organization-related identifications into two major groups called nested and cross-cutting identifications. In the given organizational context, individuals select among them and position themselves and others into them. Although Ashforth and Johnson primarily concentrate on organizational identifications, they suggest that we can also treat in a similar way identifications that are beyond the narrow organizational framework.

Ashforth and Johnson (2001, 31–41) classified nested identifications from high-order to low-order identifications. Examples of **high-order identifications** are identification with the whole organization and a division within an organization, whereas **low-order identifications** are related to work and work groups. Inside an organization, nested identifications are connected to formal social categories institutionalized in the organizational context (e.g. individual elements of the organization's formal structure can be independent objects of identification). It is characteristic of nested identifications that they 'form a means-end chain in that a given identity is both the means to a higher order identity and the end of a lower order identity' (Ashforth and Johnson 2001, 32). In this sense, identifications are nested one in another.

Low-order identifications do not contain high-order identifications. Identification relates to whether an individual meets a very concrete condition. For this reason, low-order identifications are explicitly exclusive in comparison to high-order identifications that are, by definition, inclusive because they include all low-order identifications. This postulates that an individual can identify with an organization regardless of his/her position, work or work group. However, an individual can hardly identify with work that he/she did not, does not and will not do. Low-order identifications are more concrete than high-order identifications, which are abstract because they include diversified types of low-order identifications. Organizational identities are therefore defined more or less universally and are mostly related to the basic values and mission of an organization. It has been established that the larger and more diversified an organization is, the more abstract are its identity and related identifications. Owing to their abstract nature, the influence of higher order identifications is more indirect and long term in comparison to the effects of low-order identifications that function directly with short-term effects, and are therefore proximal. While high-order identifications represent a basic psychological framework defined by some key guidelines that direct the functioning of an individual, low-order identifications represent an operationalization and concrete instructions of the same psychological framework. Low-order identifications are more subjectively important and situationally relevant for an individual than high-order identifications. However, organizations have tools to make high-order identifications equally or even more important than low-order identifications (Albert and Whetten 1985).

Cross-cutting identifications include categories that are either formal or informal.

> Formal cross-cutting social categories may include committees, task forces, local unions, and so on, whereas informal categories may include friendship cliques, common interest social groups, demographic clusters, and so on. They may be external to the organization and overlap only partially with membership in the organization itself. Cross-cutting identities are analogous to lower order identities in that they tend to be relatively exclusive, concrete and proximal.
>
> *(Ashforth and Johnson 2001, 41)*

How important identifications are for an individual varies according to their current subjective meaning and situational relevance. Identifications reach beyond formal categories and between various levels of identification.

Ashforth and Johnson (2001) claim that it is desirable that there be as few contradictions as possible among different forms of identifications. The more that cross-cutting identities are linked to formal identifications, the greater the congruity among them, and the harder it is to separate them. This phenomenon is called the generalization of the identification, and reduces the differences between formal and informal parts. Ashforth and Johnson's model (2001) conveys an important message that different identifications can overlap and exist simultaneously in one person, regardless of whether they are low- or high-order identifications.

Dukerich *et al.* (1998) suggest discussing the organizational identification through the use of orthogonal dimension, firmly putting complete identification on one side of the equation, and its counterpart, dis-identification, on the opposite side. Elsbach and Bhattacharya (2001; see also Bhattacharya and Elsbach 2002) have accordingly noted that in the same way that individuals can define their self-image through the sense of oneness with an organization, they can also create it by distinguishing and differentiating themselves from the organization. In the words of Elsbach and Bhattacharya: 'individuals sometimes find it easier to define themselves through the social groups they do *not* belong to than those to which they do belong' (Elsbach and Bhattacharya 2001, 394). Based on case study analyses, Elsbach and Bhattacharya (2001, 397) define **organizational dis-identification** as a self-perception that is based on:

- a cognitive separation between one's identity and one's perception of the identity of an organization; and
- a negative relational categorization of oneself and the organization.

Such a definition implies that organizational dis-identification is indicated by the level to which an individual defines his/herself as someone that does not share the same or similar attributes that are typical of an organization. Such definition also implies a relationship or a relational categorization between an individual and an organization that has a negative form (in the sense of competition, adversary, etc.). Further, it distinguishes dis-identification from cognitive apathy, which is also a stance that an individual can have toward an organization, and occurs if an individual does not make connections or distinctions between his/her own identity and an organization. Elsbach and Bhattacharya (2001) call this phenomenon not-identification.

Dis-identification is also different from **de-identification** that is defined by Ashforth as 'selectively denying or forgetting those aspects of a previously valued identity that impede mobilization toward a new identity' (Ashforth 1998, 218), and is important especially when (re)constructing a (new) identification (Chreim 2001). As pointed out by Pratt (2001), dis-identification is not the breaking of an identification, but rather 'identification with a set of values and beliefs that are antithetical to those of a group' (Pratt 2001, 20; see also Chreim 2001), or in other words, contrary to those of the organization.

Dis-identification is different from identification in the sense that it is focused on differences between an individual and an organization, rather than on similarities. Pratt (2001) notes that, beside dis-identifications, there are also conflicting or contradictory identifications (Elsbach 1999). These occur when individuals are 'both attracted to and repulsed by their organization' (Pratt 2001, 20).

11.3 Corporate and group identification of employees

Employee–organization identification is arguably one of the most important forms of identifications in the work environment. It is defined as an individual's perception of oneness with the organization and the experience of the organization's success and failures as one's own (Mael and Ashforth 1992). **Organizational identification** is a cognitive connection between an individual and an organization in which an individual sees him- or herself in close psychological connection to the organization's fate (Wan-Huggins *et al.* 1998). Identification is therefore seen as a 'communicative process through which individuals either align themselves with or distance themselves from one or both of the targets/sources of identity' (Larson and Pepper 2003), which are, in this context, interwoven realities of the company, such as a group of co-workers and/or companies as social or working entities. The central issue of the employee–organization identification is the extent to which an individual defines him- or herself through an organization, either as a part of a group of co-workers, as a part of the social entity, or as a part of both. In other words, the extent to which an individual understands, feels and describes an organization (as an entity and/or a community of people) as a part of him- or herself (Dutton *et al.* 1994).

This means that in terms of companies or other formal organizations, a distinction must be made between group and corporate identification. **Group identification** is identification of an individual with co-workers and the company's employees, and is defined as the individual's perception of shared attributes with the group of people, which the individual believes or wants to be a member of, or as the individual's perception of oneness with an organization as a group of people (Mael and Tetrick 1992). People identify with co-workers or other individuals who function as a group within the organization or in connection with it. **Corporate identification** is defined in a similar way as the individual's perception of shared attributes with the company or company's identity, or as the individual's perception of oneness with a company as a social entity (Dutton *et al.* 1994). In this case, we talk about identification with a company, which operates in relation to an individual as a functioning unit; a sort of a pseudo-person with whom an employee is in a mutually dependent relationship.

In the above paragraph, we introduced two different approaches to organizational identification that, according to Alvesson (2000), are based on two different premises; the aspect of identification based on the institution, and the community or the aspect of identification based on the community (Brewer and Gardner 1996; Kaptein and Wempe 2002). In the first case, the primary object of employee identification is the corporate identity, while in the latter it is the group identity. In the latter case, identification takes place through personal interactions among members of a group (low-order identification) and is very concrete. In the first case, identification can occur independently from personal interaction and from cohesion among the organization's members and is much more abstract (Ashforth and Mael 1989; Alvesson 2000). It is therefore high-order identification in the terminology of Ashforth and Johnson (2001).

When trying to provide a definition of organizational identification, we must consider both facts – and make a distinction between them – because they both exert an influence on an employee or organization's member in the form of two interconnected realities. Both realities of the company – the company as a community of people and the company as a social entity – are perceived simultaneously by an individual. In everyday activities, the organization as a group of people (co-workers) is in primary focus. However, when managing personal matters connected to the relationship with the company and its representation in the public, the corporate identification gains the upper hand.

It is important to distinguish between the two categories of organizational identification because each has its own effects on the reality of an organization (see Figure 11.1). Measuring the two categories of identification separately can help us segment employees, which is very useful information for human resource management. From the managerial point of view, it is important to consider which of the two forms of identification should be emphasized and expressed more clearly in our own organization. We believe that organizations without any group and/or corporate identification cannot exist for long in such a form. A company's management must question its human resources policies and begin to employ such workers who will be able to identify with the company and/or completely change the company's

	Group identification	
	HIGH	LOW
HIGH Corporate identification	Company builds success on the corporate community	Company builds success on the corporate community
LOW	Low employee productivity	Problems, company's breakdown

FIGURE 11.1   Forms of organizational identification and their consequences for the company

identity. Encouraging only group identification in small and middle enterprises is not recommended because it can have negative effects on the organization. In such instances, a group is very cohesive, and employees consequently pursue the goals of their group and not those of the organization. Emphasized group identification is also not desirable in times of active downsizing because it can lead to a collective response and revolt of all members of the organization. On the other hand, the sole emphasis on corporate identification can also have some negative effects, such as individualism and exaggerated competiveness among employees, which weakens teamwork and reduces creativity that is a consequence of group dynamics. Furthermore, employees who identify exclusively with the corporate element can have a negative effect on interpersonal relations in an organization. But despite some negative effects of emphasized corporate identification, our research (Podnar 2004) has shown that corporate identification has a substantial influence on soliciting responses from individuals that are beneficial for an organization and its goals. In normal conditions, both dimensions of organizational identification are in harmony, so that a company has an organizational community that is based on the corporate brand, in which case one identification type supports another. The company's management must accordingly devote its attention to both forms of organizational identification.

11.4 Consumer identification

For an organization, it is important that not only its formal members, such as employees, but also external stakeholders identify with the organization. Consumers are the most prominent example, although they are not an organization's formal members. Consumers can use identification with a corporate brand and its semantics to define their self-image and communicate it to others. Marketing literature identifies four sources on which a personal relationship between a company and a consumer can occur and form a basis for consumer identification:

- basic values
- shared identity traits
- common goals
- satisfaction of consumer needs by the company.

A corporate brand and other companies' brands can play an important role in satisfying the needs of individuals for a sense of a stable self-image, distinction from others, likeability and belonging. An individual can achieve a stable, lasting and consistent self-image by means of identification with such a brand that is perceived as having identity traits that are congruent with his/her personal attributes. Often, the uniqueness of an individual is constructed on these perceived similarities, because brands can help satisfy human needs for differentiation through their use of original personal stories. The more an individual recognizes the originality of a brand, the easier can he/she identify with it and use the brand for emphasizing his/her own individuality in relation to other people and brands. The brand which a person identifies with becomes a means of attracting admiration and recognition from others. Because individuals feel a need to have a positive self-image, they connect themselves with such brands, persons and groups that have a positive public image. Members of such groups often have in common the use of a certain brand. Identification with a brand enables individuals to become part of a group, or it gives them a sense of belonging to a certain group, which they communicate outwards through the brand that unites the group. At the same time, the membership in such a group enables differentiation in relation to other individuals that are not members of the group. This makes the circle of the individual's construction of identity through its personal and social dimensions complete.

Corporate brands have, similar to service and product brands, two important functions: being an object of personal identification through a relationship between an individual and a brand aimed at shaping an individual's uniqueness and particularity; and being an object of social identification, which is based on the need of an individual to belong and identify with a community around the brand. While the first case emphasizes individuality, it is in the latter case, similarity with others, that is in the foreground. Here, we must consider the psychological law of similarity positing that the closer the perceived similarity and connection between a company and an individual, the more attractive will an individual find the company, and the easier it will be for him/her to identify with the company.

Fournier (1998) studied in what way a corporate brand can be legitimized as a partner in interaction with an individual and established that first we need to discover how brands are animated, humanized and personalized. As it has been pointed out before in this book, research shows that individuals have no problems with ascribing human attributes to brands, regardless of whether they are product brands (Levy 1959; Plummer 1985; Aaker 1997) or companies (Davis *et al.* 2002; Podnar 2004). Personification of inanimate objects is, particularly, a basic process that enables identification of an individual with an inanimate object, such as a brand. Fournier (1998, 345) discusses three basic processes or ways in which inanimate objects get personified and identified with.

- The first way is to fill the entity with the spirit of the past or with the presence of another person, by means of a celebrity endorsement. Such people act and speak in the name of the entity to the entity's benefit.
- The second way is more intimate, because it involves a transfer of personal characteristics of people close to the consumer (family, friends) to the entity itself. Examples include building relationships with brands that were used by our parents, grandparents, brands that we used in the early childhood, and brands that we received as a gift.
- The third way is that of a total anthropomorphization of an entity as such, which is most often stimulated by marketing communications and by the intrinsic human inclination to personify the inanimate world.

In order to get people to anthropomorphize brands, and to achieve their identification through anthropomorphization, many marketing tools have been developed, for example, strategic tools, such as positioning (Bhat and Reddy 2001), to more specific techniques of transferring meanings and constructing association networks within marketing communications. The emphasis is on the construction of the differentiated contents of the brand, which happens in the following ways.

- We can emphasize the nostalgic value of the brand by stressing the past connection between a consumer and an entity. We try to arouse pleasant memories and past feelings in connection with the entity.
- We can connect a brand with other brands, people, places, organizations, activities, events or issues by means of communication and visibility. In this way, we influence the image of a brand in the mind of a consumer. However, the sensory appeal relating to the visual attractiveness and other qualities of a brand, such as the touch, taste, scent and sound of products, must be under the complete control of a company. From a strategic point of view, it is very important that a company relevantly estimates how stakeholders feel about it and want to feel about it.
- We can emphasize the symbolic value of brands that possess a social and status appeal and can help a consumer to construct his/her own identity. Such examples include adding human attributes to entities, either in a physical form (drawing eyes on cars), by giving names to things, or by ascribing brands with human attributes.

- An important technique is interactivity, meaning that an individual gains participation through the use of a certain brand by investing psychological, emotional and physical energy. Interactivity is achieved by strengthening an individual's sense of control and choice. It is important that an individual attains a feeling that the brand will help them to reach certain goals, realize their dreams, or help them in any other way to fulfil any tasks or missions they might have. At the same time, we create circumstances that support the need or necessity to have a relationship with a company. More precisely, we emphasize that an individual really could not manage without a certain product (e.g. glasses, because they can't see without them) or think they couldn't manage without them (because eye-glasses of a brand XY match their image).

11.5 Brand communities

Beside personal identification with a company, we must also consider social identifications from an individual. There are four basic approaches used by companies to strengthen the social identification of consumers (Underwood *et al.* 2001):

- Organization and management of common experiences in relation to the company or its brands.
- Emphasizing common history and experience that individuals have with a company and its brands.
- The use of physical evidence in connection with the company and its services.
- Rituals in connection with the purchase and use of the company's products.

These factors strengthen the social identification of individuals, which leads to a directed community created around a certain symbol and its users. A **brand community** is defined as a 'specialized, non-geographically bound community, based on a structured set of social relations among admirers of a brand' (Muniz and O'Guinn 2001, 412). At the centre of the community is a company, its offer or the company's brands.

Muniz and O'Guinn (2001) identified three key characteristics of brand communities:

- belonging to a group that is tied together by a brand;
- provability of rituals and traditions surrounding a brand;
- 'feeling of obligation' toward the group and its members typical of the group members.

For the creation and functioning of brand communities, neither physical contacts nor formal membership of an organization are necessary. Besides groups based on physical membership and interactions between members, there are also brand communities that are imaginary (Muniz and O'Guinn 2001). To be a group member, an individual must only feel that he/she is a member, that is why such groups can exist when there are absolutely no social contacts. Carlson *et al.* (2008) speak not only of social but also of psychological brand communities. For such communities to form, it is enough that an individual knows of other brand-admirers and that he/she identifies with them, but does not necessarily have physical or personal contact with them (Anderson 1983). We are talking about a community that exists in the minds of consumers, but for them it is as real as a physical community.

Brand communities that exist both in physical as well as in virtual and psychological environments are defined by a common attribute, namely that such communities can only arise around a single entity and must not be confused with homogenous segments of lifestyles or with groups of consumers with similar or identical purchase habits, and are not to be confused with reference groups either. In brand communities, the only link between members is a company or a brand. What is also important is that within brand communities, it is not only personal identification with a company or its brands but also group identification among community members, which makes the brand community a foundation for an individual's social identifications. Although community members are most commonly 'active loyals' (Gruen and Ferguson 1994) and 'hyper-loyals' (McAlexander and Schouten 1998), the benefits of those communities are not only for companies but for members as well. Communities can act as a representation of consumers, which can, in such a constellation, have a stronger position in relationship with the brand's owners than they would have individually. For individuals, brand communities represent an important source of information, they support the construction of their own identity and social distinction, represent an important source of social interaction, fortify such interaction, and offer a place for social withdrawal. Muniz and O'Guinn (2001) claims that the relationship between a brand community and a brand is and must be two-dimensional and reciprocal, because in the same way that a brand influences its consumers and their social identification, consumers also influence the brand and its identity.

11.6 Effects of organizational identification

As Barker (1998) puts it, a company has no reason to worry about the extent to which its employees and other stakeholders identify with it. The concern of the company is to what extent identification with a company manifests in employees' actions that influence the company. Based on this, a company rewards or punishes the employee (Barker 1998, 260). This notion may also be one of the reasons why so many theoretical considerations and empirical studies have been made to investigate the effects of organizational identification on actions of employees and other stakeholders.

Mael and Ashforth (2001) write that identification can have a positive influence on an individual's improvement of self-image, the transcendence of their self-concept, the meaning of their life, meeting the needs of belonging, and raising their aspirations and goals. According to Glynn, 'organizational identification is functional, helping individuals to make sense of their organizational environment and to maintain positive social identities' (Glynn 1998, 241). Based on the social identity theory, Ashforth and Mael (1989, 25–26) suggest four **main consequences of organizational identification** for the employees.

- Individuals tend to choose activities congruent with salient aspects of their identities, and they support the institutions embodying those identities. Thus, it is likely that identification with an organization enhances support for and commitment to it.
- A second and related consequence is that social identification affects the outcomes conventionally associated with group formation, including intragroup cohesion, cooperation and altruism, and positive evaluations of the group. This means that one may like other group members, despite their negative personal attributes, simply by virtue of the common membership.
- Identification also may engender internalization of, and adherence to, group values and norms and homogeneity in attitudes and behaviour.
- It is likely that social identification will reinforce the very antecedents of identification, including the distinctiveness of the group, group prestige, competition with other groups, etc.

The above general effects of identification manifest in some very specific consequences, namely in the motivation of employees, work satisfaction, effectiveness, organization-beneficial decisions, fulfilling tasks, reducing the number of conflicts, intensifying interactions between employees, better provision of services and accepting roles within an organization (Cheney 1983; Dutton *et al.* 1994). Peteraf and Shanley (1997) postulated that organizational identification positively influences capacity for teamwork, fosters exchange of information and strengthens the reputation of group members.

Furthermore, organizational identification influences the decisions of individuals and their making sense of an organization in such a manner that their way of thinking becomes congruent with the values and goals of a company (Pratt 2001) and is closely connected with the individual's intention of staying a member of the organization. The basic goal to be achieved through organizational identification is a long-term commitment to a company, in the widest meaning of the term commitment, thus achieving positive consequences for the company. Commitment can reflect in being loyal to a company or its products, defending the company, rejecting negative information about the company, having a feeling of owning a company, or in many other ways. Organizational identification helps organizations keep control over their members and to keep them motivated. However, control and motivation come from employees themselves, because they are satisfied with their work and are committed because of their identification with the company.

Similar effects of identification can also be observed in consumers and their relationship with a company and its brands. Several studies discovered that identification directly influences consumers' brand preference (Tildesley and Coote 2009), purchase decisions (Ahearne *et al.* 2005), willingness to pay a premium price (del Rio *et al.* 2001), satisfaction (Kuenzel and Halliday 2008), willingness to make repeated purchases (Kuenzel and Halliday 2008), loyalty (Kim *et al.* 2001), sharing recommendations and positive word of mouth (del Rio *et al.* 2001) and resistance to negative information. However, the last effect must be handled with caution; when negative information and actions cross a certain level, then not even identification can prevent negative reactions from consumers. The main goal of getting consumers (as well as employees and other stakeholders) to identify with a company is to get affective commitment and related positive effects, which we can only achieve with appropriate management.

CASE: HARLEY-DAVIDSON

When William S. Harley, his brother Walter and Arthur Davidson made their first motorcycle in 1903 in Milwaukee, they probably did not believe that Harley-Davidson, the company they'd just founded, would become a legendary brand and almost a synonym for freedom. But the first years were modest; the company sold barely 3,000 motorcycles until 1910. The first major growth came during WWI when the company manufactured more than 20,000 motorcycles for the military. The company was one of the few that survived the Great Depression of the 1930s. During WWII it had already produced 90,000 motorcycles for the US military.

In 1953 Harley-Davidson was the only American motorcycle manufacturer on the global market. Owing to the film *The Wild One* starring Marlon Brando, the motorcycle brand acquired the image of an uncompromising rebel, a perfect image of 1950s USA. By the end of the 1960s Harley-Davidson climbed to 80 per cent market share in the USA. However, less than a decade later, the introduction of Japanese competitors to the American market (Honda, Yamaha, Kawasaki) caused intensive price competition. Harley-Davidson reduced costs of production by lowering the quality of motorcycles, which quickly reflected in the falling market share, first to 20 per cent and later to only 3 per cent. The company was almost bankrupt.

The company responded to domination of foreign competition in the American market by filing an appeal to the US International Trade Commission in the 1980s. Subsequently, the Reagan administration raised tariffs on imported motorcycles with over 700 cc engine capacity from 4 per cent to 40 per cent. Company management together with Arthur Davidson's grandson bought the company and introduced the Japanese model of managing, including complete quality control. They also involved employees and stakeholders in the efforts to save the company. This was a basis upon which the brand was repositioned and intensive marketing activities were launched. The company's research had shown that three out of four people that bought a Harley-Davidson would eventually repeat the purchase. The company's logo was also one of the most popular tattoo motifs.

Management finally realized that there were organic communities of users who shared the joy at riding and the shared values that they ascribed to the brand. At the same time, the brand became a synonym for Hell's Angels, which was not a desirable profile. To gain control over the use of the logo and turn the high commitment to the company's advantage, they made a then unique step by organizing and sponsoring the 'Harley Owners Group' (HOG). The main purpose of this motorcycle club was to connect employees, distributers and consumers and allow them to exchange experiences of driving a Harley-Davidson bike. The company launched a campaign, 'Super Ride', in which they authorized over 600 dealers who could invite people for a test ride and an experience with a Harley-Davidson. Members of HOG received a one-year free membership, while the company organized mass meetings of members and group rides, sent free motorcycling magazines, organized receptions in Daytona, offered favourable conditions for insurances, road assistance and other services. The company started to sell other products related to motorcycles from apparel to motorcycle equipment, souvenirs and even a Harley-Davidson Visa card. These products were very popular and helped grow membership in HOG. Harley-Davidson bikes and equipment found buyers among doctors, lawyers, bankers and managers, collectively called rich urban bikers or rubies, who were not discouraged by high prices. This group of consumers was responsible for the fact that in the 1990s the company again became the market leader in the segment of heavy motorcycles. From 1989 to 1995, Harley-Davidson reached cult status and doubled its sales. By the end of the 1990s, buyers had to wait up to two years for the fulfilment of their orders.

In 1987, HOG had 73,000 registered members, in 2000 there were over 500,000, while today it has over a million members and 1,458 sections worldwide. To promote membership in the club, Harley-Davidson emphasizes feelings of joy at riding, fun and belonging to a large family. Company communications stress the experience and not the product and talk about the brand as a way of life by suggesting freedom, diversity and individuality as the key values. When the company celebrated its 100th anniversary, the central event in Milwaukee attracted almost one million visitors committed to the brand and in love with the experience offered by Harley-Davidson, including the sound of motors, apparel and iconography. The company runs the Harley-Davidson museum where fans learn about company history, visit the restaurant, organize private events and receive the whole brand experience. The company organizes factory visits, motorcycle meets and other events. It has over 100 licence agreements for the use of logo with companies producing toys, pet

products, bicycles, shoes, knives, lighters, clothes, etc. The company emphasizes its social responsibility, supports the Muscular Dystrophy Association and
runs a foundation that invests in various local communities. The company also
runs special programmes for distributors, most loyal users, veterans riding
Harley-Davidson bikes, and it also devotes special attention to women, youth
and students.

Because almost 90 per cent of Harley-Davidson customers are men just
under 50, the company now increasingly uses social media to reach a younger
population. Distributers carry out mobile campaigns to attract and retain
customers. The company uses its website to encourage visitors to share their
experiences through MySpace, Twitter or Facebook, where Harley-Davidson
has almost 4 million fans. The company that has almost $5 billion annual
revenue still understands the family of Harley-Davidson riders and their commitment to the brand as the company's most valuable asset and potential,
while the company's greatest challenge and responsibility for the future are
attracting and maintaining new and younger consumers and their commitment. Management says that their strategy is multigenerational and multi-
cultural. Beside developing and fortifying existing networks and partnerships,
classical values have to be respected and fulfilled as well. This means, of course,
freedom and individuality but also the following: telling the truth, keeping
their promises, respecting the individual, encouraging intellectual curiosity
and fairness.

Key terms

Organizational identification. This is a social and psychological bond that associates
stakeholders with an organization. It is an elementary human mechanism that is
closely related to the psychic and social development of an individual. It is seen
as an individual's sense of oneness with an entity with which he/she is in a relationship. Identification is seen as a means for construction and manipulation of an
individual's own identity.

Organizational dis-identification. This is indicated by the level to which an individual
defines his/herself as someone that does not share the same or similar attributes that
are typical of an organization. Dis-identification is not the breaking of an identification, but rather identification with a set of values contrary to those of the organization or a group within the organization.

Group identification. Identification of an individual with co-workers and the company's employees, and is defined as the individual's perception of shared attributes
with the group of people, which the individual believes or wants to be a member
of, or as the individual's perception of oneness with an organization as a group of

people. People identify with co-workers or other individuals who function as a group within the organization or in connection with it.

Corporate identification. This is the individual's perception of shared attributes with the company or company's identity, or as the individual's perception of oneness with a company as a social entity. Identification with a company, which operates in relation to an individual as a functioning unit, a sort of a pseudo-person with whom an employee is in a mutually dependent relationship.

Anthropomorphism or personification. The attribution of human characteristics to anything other than a human being. Individuals have no problems with ascribing human attributes to brands, regardless of whether they are product brands or companies. Personification of inanimate objects is, particularly, a basic process that enables identification of an individual with an inanimate object, such as a brand.

A brand community. A specialized, non-geographically bound community, based on a structured set of social relations among admirers of a brand. At the centre of the community is a company, its offer or the company's brands. For the creation and functioning of brand communities, neither physical contacts nor formal membership of an organization are necessary. Brand communities that exist both in physical as well as in virtual and psychological environments are defined by a common attribute, namely that such communities can only arise around a single entity and must not be confused with homogenous segments of lifestyles or with groups of consumers with similar or identical purchase habits, and are not to be confused with reference groups either. In brand communities, the only link between members is a company or a brand.

REVIEW QUESTIONS

- What is identification and why it is important for companies? Define dis-identification.
- What is the distinction between corporate and group identification and which one is more important for corporations?
- What methods can be used to strengthen consumers' identification with the company?
- What are characteristics of brand communities?

Browse the web and discover how Harley-Davidson builds its brand community. Consider the strengths and weaknesses of Harley-Davidson brand management. What communication tools do they use? Visit the local Harley-Davidson club and discover how its members express their identification with the brand. Discuss whether it is possible to fully control the brand community.

References

Aaker, Jennifer L. 1997. Building dimensions of brand personality. *Journal of Marketing Research* 23 (11): 347–356.

Ahearne, Michael, C. B. Bhattacharya and Thomas Gruen. 2005. Antecedents and consequences of customer–company identification: expanding the role of relationship marketing. *Journal of Applied Psychology* 90 (3): 574–585.

Albert, Stuart and David A. Whetten. 1985. Organizational identity. *Research in Organizational Behavior* 7: 263–295.

Alvesson, Mats. 2000. Social identity and the problem of loyalty in knowledge-intensive companies. *Journal of Management Studies* 37 (6): 1101–1123.

Anderson, Benedict. 1983. *Imagined Community*. London: Verso.

Ashforth, Blake E. 1998. Becoming: how does the process of identification unfold? In *Identity in Organizations: Building Theory Through Conversations*, eds. David A. Whetten and Paul C. Godfrey. Thousand Oaks, CA: Sage, 213–222.

——2001. *Role Transitions in Organizational Life: An Identity-based Perspective*. Mahwah, NJ: Erlbaum.

Ashforth, Blake E. and Scott A. Johnson. 2001. Which hat to wear? The relative salience of multiple identities in organizational contexts. In *Social Identity Processes in Organizational Contexts*, eds. Michael A. Hogg and Deborah J. Terry. Philadelphia: Psychology Press, 31–48.

Ashforth, Blake E. and Fred Mael. 1989. Social identity theory and the organization. *The Academy of Management Review* 14 (1): 20–39.

Barker, James R. 1998. Managing identification. In *Identity in Organizations: Building Theory Through Conversations*, eds. David Allred Whetten and Paul C. Godfrey. Thousand Oaks, CA: Sage Publications, 257–267.

Bartel, Caroline and Jane Dutton. 2001. Ambiguous organizational memberships: constructing organizational identities in interactions with others. In *Social Identity Processes in Organizational Contexts*, eds. Michael A. Hogg and Deborah J. Terry. Philadelphia: Psychology Press, 115–130.

Bhat, Sobodh and Srinivas K. Reddy. 2001. The impact of parental brand attribute associations and affect on brand extension evaluation. *Journal of Business Research* 53 (3): 111–122.

Bhattacharya, C. B. and Kimberly D. Elsbach. 2002. Us versus them: the roles of organizational identification and disidentification in social marketing initiatives. *Journal of Public Policy & Marketing* 21 (1): 26–36.

Bhattacharya, C. B. and Sankar Sen. 2003. Consumer–company identification: a framework for understanding consumers' relationships with brands. *Journal of Marketing* 67 (2): 76–88.

Brewer, Marilynn B. and Wendi Gardner. 1996. Who is this 'we'? Levels of collective identity and self representations. *Journal of Personality and Social Psychology* 71 (1): 83–93.

Carlson, Brad Dean, Tracy A. Suter and Tom J. Brown. 2008. Social versus psychological brand community: the role of psychological sense of brand community. *Journal of Business Research* 61 (49): 284–291.

Cheney, George. 1983. On the various and changing meanings of organizational membership: a field study of organizational identification. *Communication Monographs* 50: 342–362.

Chreim, Samia. 2001. *Organizational de-identification during major change: the dynamics of dissociation and re-association*. Working paper ODC B1. Briarcliff Manor, NY: Academy of Management.

Connaughton, Stacey L. and John A. Daly. 2004. Identification with leader: a comparison of perceptions of identification among geographically dispersed and co-located teams. *Corporate Communications: An International Journal* 9 (2): 89–103.

Davis, Gary, Rosa Chun, Rui Vinhas Da Silva and Stuart Roper. 2002. *Corporate Reputation and Competitiveness*. London; New York: Routledge.

del Rio, A. Belen, Rodolfo Vazquez and Victor Iglesias. 2001. The effects of brand associations on consumer response. *Marketing Science* 25 (6): 740–759.

Dukerich, Janet M., Roderick Kramer and Judi McLean Parks. 1998. The dark side of organizational identification. In *Identity in Organizations: Building Theory Through Conversations*, eds. David A. Whetten and Paul C. Godfrey. Thousand Oaks, CA: Sage, 245–256.

Dutton, Jane E., Janet M. Dukerich and Celia V. Harquail. 1994. Organizational images and member identification. *Administrative Science Quarterly* 39 (2): 239–263.

Elsbach, Kimberly D. 1999. An expanded model of organizational identification. *Research in Organizational Behavior* 21: 163–200.

Elsbach, Kimberly D. and C. B. Bhattacharya. 2001. Defining who you are by what you're not: organizational disidentification and the National Rifle Association. *Organization Science* 12 (4): 393–413.

Fournier, Susan. 1998. Consumers and their brands: developing relationship theory in consumer research. *Journal of Consumer Research* 24 (4): 343–373.

Glynn, Mary Ann. 1998. Individuals' need for organizational identification (nOID): speculations on individual differences in the propensity to identify. In *Identity in Organizations: Building Theory Through Conversations*, eds. David A. Whetten and Paul C. Godfrey. Thousand Oaks, CA: Sage, 238–244.

Gruen, Thomas and Jeffery Ferguson. 1994. Using membership as a marketing tool: issues and applications. In *Relationship Marketing: Theory, Methods and Applications*, eds. Jagdish N. Sheth and Atul Parvatiyar. Atlanta: Emory Center for Relationship Marketing, 60–64.

Kagan, Jerom. 1958. The concept of identification. *Psychological Review* 65 (5): 296–305.

Kaptein, Muel and Johan Wempe. 2002. *The Balanced Company: A Theory of Corporate Integrity*. Oxford: Oxford University Press.

Kim, A. Chung, Han Dongchul and Park Aeung-Bae. 2001. The effect of brand personality and brand identification on brand loyalty: applying the theory of social identification. *Japanese Psychological Research* 43 (4): 195–206.

Kuenzel, Sven and Sue Vaux Halliday. 2008. Investigating antecendents and consequences of brand identification. *Journal of Product & Brand Management* 17 (5): 293–304.

Larson, Gregory S. and Gerald L. Pepper. 2003. Strategies for managing multiple organizational identifications: a case of competing identities. *Management Communication Quarterly* 16 (4): 528–557.

Levy, Sidney J. 1959. Symbols for sale. *Harvard Business Review* 37 (4): 117–124.

Mael, Fred A. and Blake E. Ashforth. 1992. Alumni and their alma mater: a partial test of the reformulated model of organizational identification. *Journal of Organizational Behavior* 13 (2): 103–123.

——2001. Identification in work, war, sports, and religion: contrasting the benefits and risks. *Journal for the Theory of Social Behaviour* 31 (2): 197–222.

Mael, Fred A. and Lois E. Tetrick. 1992. Identifying organizational identification. *Educational and Psychological Measurement* 52 (4): 813–824.

McAlexander, James H. and John W. Schouten. 1998. Brandfests: servicescapes for the cultivation of brand equity. In *Servicescapes: The Concept of Place in Contemporary Markets*, ed. John F. Sherry Jr. Chicago: American Marketing Association, 377–402.

Morrow, Paula C. 1982. Concept redundancy and organizational research: the case of work commitment. *Academy of Management Review* 8 (4): 486–500.

Muniz, Albert M., Jr. and Thomas C. O'Guinn. 2001. Brand community. *Journal of Consumer Research* 27 (4): 412–432.

Peteraf, Margaret and Mark Shanley. 1997. Getting to know you: a theory of strategic group identity. *Strategic Management Journal* 18: 165–186.

Plummer, Joseph T. 1985. *Brand personality: A strategic concept for multinational advertising.* Paper presented to the AMA Winter Marketing Educators' Conference. New York: Young and Rubican.

Podnar, Klement. 2004. *Ugled, organizacijska identifikacija in zavezanost zaposlenih.* Doktorska disertacija. Ljubljana: Fakulteta za družbene vede.

Pratt, Michael G. 2001. Social identity dynamics in modern organizations: an organizational psychology/organizational behavior perspective. In *Social Identity Processes in Organizational Contexts*, eds. Michael A. Hogg and Deborah J. Terry. Philadelphia: Psychology Press, 13–30.

Reichers, Arnon E. 1985. A review and reconceptualization of organizational commitment. *Academy of Management Review* 10 (3): 465–476.

Russo, Tracy Callaway. 1998. Organizational and professional identification: a case of newspaper journalists. *Management Communication Quarterly* 12 (1): 72–111.

Scott, Craig R. 1997. Identification with multiple targets in a geographically dispersed organization. *Management Communication Quarterly* 10 (4): 491–522.

Tildesley, Amy E. and Leonard V. Coote. 2009. This brand is me: a social identity based measure of brand identification. *Advances in Consumer Research* 36: 627–628.

Underwood, Robert, Edward Bond and Robert Baer. 2001. Building service brands via social identity: lessons from the sports marketplace. *Journal of Marketing Theory and Practice* 9 (1): 1–12.

Wan-Huggins, Veronica N., Christine M. Riordan and Rodger W. Griffeth. 1998. The development and longitudinal test of a model of organizational identification. *Journal of Applied Social Psychology* 28 (8): 724–749.

12

ORGANIZATIONAL COMMITMENT AND SOCIAL ACCEPTABILITY

CONTENTS

The first part of the chapter deals with commitment to a company. We discuss several approaches to studying commitment and present how the phenomenon is understood in the contemporary literature. We describe the main differences between affective, continuance and normative commitment, and explain the most important consequences of commitment. In the second part, we deal with the concept of social acceptance, which companies have to take into consideration when planning their activities.

12.1 Influence of organizational identification on commitment

Marketing literature has long treated identification as a part of commitment or commitment as a part of identification (Podnar 2004), but the latest studies show that these are two closely related but different concepts. Pratt (1998) writes that the most obvious difference between organizational identification and organizational commitment lies in the fact that identification explains the relationship between an individual and an organization in terms of an individual's self-concept, while this is not applicable to organizational commitment (Pratt 1998, 178). **Organizational commitment** relates to the question of happiness and satisfaction in a relationship with a company, and whether a continuation of a relationship is desirable, whereas organizational identification deals with how individuals perceive themselves in a relationship with a company (Pratt 1998). Similarly, Ashforth (1998) writes that both commitment and identification describe a relationship between an individual and the environment, but commitment, however, does not answer the question of how an individual (at least partly) defines his- or herself through an organization.

Russo (1998) suggests that organizational commitment is a manifestation of organizational identification. 'Identification is considered the substance of the relationship; commitment is the form' (Russo 1998, 77). Such understanding shifts the focus away from differences between the two concepts to the cause and effect relationship. Siegel and Sisaye's (1997, 150) definition of differences and relationships between the concepts is similar; commitment is a behavioural type of construct and is a function of the organizational identification, which is a cognitive-affective construct. Research undertaken by Siegel and Sisaye (1997) suggest that there is a strong positive influence of organizational identification on commitment. Ellemers *et al.* (1997) also provided empirical evidence for the notion that individuals who identify more intensively with a company in terms of their behaviour and responses show greater commitment to the company than people who identify less intensively. Even decades before them, Scholl established that 'if we stick to the concept of commitment as a force leading to consistency of action, it seems reasonable to view identification as a process that increases commitment' (Scholl 1981, 595).

12.2 Understanding organizational commitment

One of the most important consequences of personal and social identifications of an individual with a company is organizational commitment, which is one of the central relation variables that define the relationship between a company and its stakeholders (Gundlach *et al.* 1995). The terms commitment, belonging and devotion denote a form of psychological connection, or a relationship between an individual and a company, and express a form of an individual's involvement with or affiliation to a company.

In their literature review, Yoon *et al.* (1994) point out that inside the theoretical discussion of the terms commitment and belonging there are two distinct lines of research (see also Meyer and Allen 1997, 8). The first line focuses on objects to which an individual develops a feeling of belonging and/or acts in such a way, meaning that an individual is committed to the object. Individuals can develop a feeling of belonging to an organization, in which case we talk about organizational commitment, which is the commitment of employees to an organization in the role of the employer (Sano 1999), but also the commitment of consumers to a company in the role of a product and service provider (Bansal *et al.* 2004). The second line of literature refers to the nature and the orientation of commitment (Yoon *et al.* 1994, 332). This branch has two subgroups that signify two main approaches to studying commitment (Morris and Sherman 1981) and are called psychological and exchange approaches (Stevens *et al.* 1978).

The **psychological approach** is generally very close to the concept of identification and explains commitment as an active and positive affection of an individual toward an organization. One example of such an explanation is a definition suggested by Porter *et al.* (1974) that commitment can be defined 'in terms of the strength of an individual's identification with and involvement in a particular organization' (Porter *et al.* 1974, 604). Three factors of commitment are proposed (Porter *et al.* 1974, 604):

* a strong belief in and acceptance of the organization's goals and values;
* a willingness to exert considerable effort on behalf of the organization;
* a definite desire to maintain organizational membership.

This approach emphasizes the psychological connection that an individual feels in the relationship with an organization.

The **exchange approach**, on the other hand, sees commitment as the result of transactions of inducements or contributions between an individual and an organization, 'with an explicit emphasis on the instrumentalities of membership as the primary determinant of the member's accrual of advantage or disadvantage in the ongoing process of exchange' (Morris and Sherman 1981, 513). This approach emphasizes investments in the exchange as factors defining the nature of the relationship between the two exchange partners. One notable example is Becker's definition postulating that commitment is a tendency to preserve a consistent existing course of activities because the perceived costs of doing that in any other way are higher (Meyer *et al.* 1989, 152). According to Beck, the more that individuals invest in an organization, or the more they can lose by leaving an organization, the greater their commitment to the organization. Commitment thus refers to a string of reciprocal obligation between a company and an individual (Marsh and Mannari 1977).

The psychological approach, according to Blau and Boal (1987), defines commitment as an attitude, while the exchange approach defines commitment as behaviour (see also Mowday *et al.* 1982). Both approaches try to describe the nature of the relationship between an individual and a company. If commitment is viewed as a type of behaviour, then

> the individual is viewed as committed to an organization if he/she is bound by past actions of sunk costs. Thus, an individual becomes committed to an organization because it has become too costly for him/her to leave … In contrast, in the attitudinal approach, organizational commitment is viewed as a more positive individual orientation toward the organization.
>
> *(Blau and Boal 1987, 290)*

Vardi *et al.* (1989) also use two approaches to studying commitment, namely an **instrumental-calculative approach** and a **normative approach**. The first approach explains commitment as an individual's intent to stay in a relationship with an organization, the main factor for such a decision being their own interests. Own interests in this context are understood as a cost–benefit ratio if the relationship with an organization is preserved, and a cost–benefit ratio if this relationship is terminated. The normative approach defines commitment as a sum of internalized normative pressures on the individual to operate in a manner that is in concordance with the interests of an organization. This approach relates commitment to terms such as pride, moral obligations, duty, sacrifice, etc. (Vardi *et al.* 1989, 27; see also Gaertner and Nollen 1989; Bielby 1992).

Marketing science brings an interesting point of view to the understanding of commitment and its development. It sees commitment as a continuum, where there is transaction commitment at one end and relational commitment at the other (Iniesta and Sanchez 2003, 206). **Transaction commitment** is stimulated by the communication and promotion activities of a company and is related solely to the implementation of the transaction, in the process of which an individual does not think about repeating transactions or entering into a relationship with a company. Transaction commitment can – but not necessarily – develop into **relational commitment**, which does include transactions, but shifts the focus to interactions and to creating and keeping a long-term relationship. A relationship implies an exclusive cooperation between the two exchange partners because ties between partners are so strong that they demand cooperation in all potential exchange processes.

12.3 Dimensions of commitment

One good attempt at integrating psychological and exchange approaches to commitment is the work of Natalie Allen and John Meyer (1990), and of Meyer *et al.* (1984, 1989, 1990). Allen and Meyer (1990) define commitment in the context of a relationship between a company and its employees as a psychological state, and the concrete activities of individuals that expresses their attitude toward the organization; the consequence of commitment is the decision whether an individual would stay a member of an organization or not. Many studies confirmed that 'employees who are strongly committed are those who are least likely to leave the organization' (Allen and Meyer 1990, 1), or would not be willing to terminate their employment. This is in concordance with the notion that commitment is the determination of an individual to continue with a certain activity and is, as such, explicitly related to an individual's behaviour at a specific time (Bielby 1992). Upon this shared attribute, the authors formulated three types of commitment, namely affective, continuance or calculative, and normative commitment. 'Affective, continuance and normative commitment are psychological states that characterize the person's relationship with the entity in question and have implications for the decisions to remain involved with it' (Meyer and Allen 1997, 93). Emphasized is the individual's wish to stay a member of an organization and to continue the relationship (see Figure 12.1).

- **Affective commitment** was explained on the basis on the psychological definition of the need to belong. It is defined by the fact that affectively committed employees stay in an organization because they 'want' to. Individuals' commitment is thus based on their wish.
- **Continuance or calculative commitment** is based on the exchange approach. Employees, for whom continuance commitment is typical, stay in an

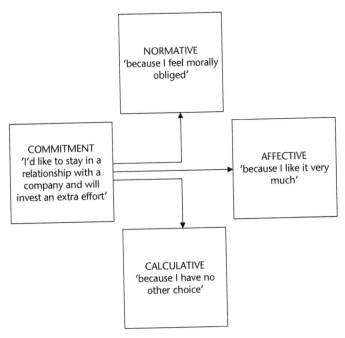

FIGURE 12.1   Types of commitment to a company
Adapted from Meyer and Allen (1997)

organization because they 'have no better choice' (Meyer and Allen 1984; Meyer *et al.* 1989, 1990). Such commitment is based on the feeling of necessity.

- Beside the two views, Wiener (1982) suggests the third, the **normative approach to commitment**, which involves not only identification, costs and benefits, but also ethical norms and moral standards. Those function as the third factor that influences an individual's commitment to a company for which they work. This approach includes concepts such as moral obligation, sense of duty and responsibility, which were subsequently studied by Meyer and Allen (1997; Meyer *et al.* 1990) and recognized as a third dimension of organizational commitment. The normatively committed employees remain members of an organization because they 'have to' or feel morally obliged to stay. Normative commitment develops in the process of socialization when individuals internalize the set of norms of 'suitable' behaviour (Meyer and Allen 1997).

The above model presenting three dimensions of commitment was not only tested on a relationship between a company and its employees (Podnar 2004) but also on a relationship between a company and its external stakeholders, such as consumers. A study by Gruen *et al.* (2000) supported the validity and reliability of the proposed model in the field of classical marketing. Bansal *et al.* (2004) came to a similar conclusion when applying the model to study the relationship between consumers' commitment and a change of service provider and established that to understand customer retention, we need to consider all three types of commitment (see also Meyer and Herscovitch 2001).

- *Emotional or affective commitment* of a consumer to a company is based on the desire to be connected or to have an emotional connection to the company (Gruen *et al.* 2000, 37).
- We speak of *normative commitment* when customers stay with a company that offers them products or services, because they feel they 'should stay' and have an inclination toward loyalty originating in their ethical codex. Because loyalty is an important value for them, such consumers remain committed to the company (Bansal *et al.* 2004).
- *Continuance commitment* can be seen as a 'forced' relationship because consumers remain in a relationship with a company because they feel they must and are in a sense locked up in the relationship (Meyer and Herscovitch 2001). Consumers believe that the relationship cannot be terminated due to economic, social or psychological costs (Bendapudi and Berry 1997). A relationship can also be preserved due to a rational estimation of economic costs incurred by the termination of the relationship or change of a provider (Gilliland and Bello 2002). Consumers can also stay in a relationship when they do not see a better choice (Bendapudi and Berry 1997).

To sum up the basic characteristics, we can say that affectively committed individuals wish to keep a relationship with a company because they identify with it or have positive feelings about it. Individuals with continuance commitment maintain relationships because they have no better alternative. The defining characteristic of the third type, the normative commitment, is that relationships are preserved because individuals were taught that this was right and believe that it should stay so. However, they would be to a same degree committed to any other company if they were in a relationship with it.

The above forms or dimensions of commitment interweave in an individual, and some aspects are dominant, others less apparent. Empirical studies have demonstrated that there is even mutual influence among different dimensions. For example, affective commitment can influence the creation of normative commitment, because a consumer with emotional ties to a company can begin to feel an obligation to maintain this relationship (Bansal *et al.* 2004, 239); and a reverse process is also possible. It has also been established that continuance commitment reduces the influence of emotional commitment on the behaviour of individuals (Meyer and Herscovitch 2001). Regardless of its type, however, commitment only occurs when a relationship is considered important, and when partners are willing to make an effort to keep the relationship running (Morgan and Hunt 1994, 22–23).

12.4 Effects of commitment

It is commitment that makes people cooperate with their exchange partners and invest in the maintenance of a relationship. Commitment improves resistance to attractive short-term alternatives by offering long-term benefits if the present relationship is preserved, and it also reduces risks by guaranteeing that the exchange partner would not behave opportunistically. In a relationship based on trust and commitment, which are the basic conditions for a stable relationship, other benefits appear, namely effectiveness, productivity and successfulness (Morgan and Hunt 1994, 22–23). As the most important ingredient of a relationship, commitment directly influences consumers' behaviour toward a company, and their decisions with regard to preserving or terminating a relationship (Bansal *et al.* 2004, 245). As it has been put forward by Buchanan (1974), commitment in the literature means a willingness to devote effort in a relationship with an organization, a strong desire to stay in a relationship, a high level of loyalty, acceptance of organizational goals and values, and a positive estimation of an organization together with a reciprocal set of obligations between a company and an individual (Marsh and Mannari 1977, 57–58).

Clearly, three different types of commitment have different **effects and consequences** (Cohen and Kirchmeyer 1995; Meyer and Allen 1997). The most common and most studied positive effects for employees are lower absence from work, higher productivity, not terminating employment, responsible acting, extra effort and satisfaction with work. The greatest positive influence on the above consequences comes from the affective commitment.

Research by Bansal *et al.* (2004) also confirmed that commitment plays an important role in shaping the behaviour of individuals. Their research measuring influences of different dimensions of commitment on consumers established that all three dimensions have negative correlation with intent to change a provider of services. Further, the research reveals that the influence of emotional commitment to the intent to change a provider is indirect because it is mediated by normative commitment (Bansal *et al.* 2004, 244–245). Further studies established that there is a direct and positive influence of commitment on the retention of customers (Morgan and Hunt 1994), and on the loyalty of stakeholders (Iniesta and Sanchez 2003). Loyalty is understood as a deeply rooted preference and a stable obligation to purchase a certain product or service in the future, regardless of the situational influences and market pressures to change consumer behaviour (Oliver 1997, 392).

Research results show that commitment is in correlation with a higher level of employee retention, but also with keeping existing customers and their loyalty, and is therefore a factor that influences the intentions of consumers to preserve the existing relationship (Bansal *et al.* 2004, 234). As mentioned, the correlation between commitment and intent to terminate a relationship is explicitly negative (Mathieu and Zajac 1990). An overview of the above research reveals that from a company's point of view, the most desirable is affective, and partly also normative commitment, but not continuance commitment (Meyer *et al.* 1989; McFarlane Shore and Wayne 1993). Even though all three have a positive influence on a willingness to remain in a relationship with a company, it is even more important to get a desirable response from an individual in exchange situations with a company.

12.5 Social acceptability

It would not be realistic to expect that companies would have a great number of stakeholders who would be committed and loyal to a company and its activities. Because stakeholders have various interests, and because companies are variegated and complex entities that can act in a way that is unpopular with certain audiences, complete commitment and loyalty is impossible. That is why companies must ensure their overall operation and concrete actions are socially accepted. In social sciences, the term **social acceptance** has no clear definition (Brunsson and Sahlin-Andersson 2000), and is most commonly used in situations where there is no consensus on what is right and what is wrong, or even where there are conflicting opinions. In the context of social acceptance, the term *social* refers to a network of interpersonal relationships, or to a community that, due to its attitude toward certain issues, is activated and thus becomes a public and thereby an important factor in planning and placing various activities in the local environment. The term *public* denotes a group of people who are involved in the issue, recognize the problem, are faced with no obstructions in the problem solving, and whose main concern is the mutuality among the interest groups within the public itself. *Acceptance* means a minimal degree of content with or suitability of the largest level of change that could be accepted or approved.

From a company's point of view, this means that decisions about every action, for which conflicting opinions of the public are expected, must be made by taking into consideration what the consequences of the support or opposition of the public would be.

Social acceptance is a result of judgement through which individuals, in the words of Brunsson and Sahlin-Andersson (2000):

1.   compare perceived reality with any alternatives they know;
2.   make a decision on whether the existing condition is better than, or at least satisfactory likeness to, the best alternative conditions.

It is important not to substitute acceptance with affection, enthusiasm for a certain issue or even with a desire to please everyone with everything. What makes acceptance different from these concepts is the fact that acceptance includes a behavioural component that reflects the attitudes of an individual (Brunsson and Sahlin-Andersson 2000). Social acceptance is an opinional process that involves a comparison of known alternatives and (not) acting on their basis. It is seen as a readiness to consider certain issues in question as possible alternatives. Clausen and Schroeder (2004) add a behavioural component to the concept, by saying that social acceptance manifests in behaviour; a socially accepted policy or a concrete measure means that such policies or measures are explicitly and implicitly supported by the majority of the public, to which this measure or policy is a concern, and is reflected in a behavioural intent.

After an individual has accepted an evaluation, they decide what to do in response. It is very probable that if a state or activity is estimated as positive or neutral, they would not do anything. In case the estimation is negative, they must decide whether the condition is so unacceptable that an action must be taken. If people see an existing condition as unsatisfactory, they will commit to such activities that are believed to change conditions toward a more acceptable alternative (Brunsson and Sahlin-Andersson 2000). In the context of companies, this is manifested through different forms of passive and active activism, citizen and consumer initiatives, petitions, referendums, exerting influence through other institutions and stakeholders, boycotts and consumer terrorism.

Brunsson and Sahlin-Andersson (2000) believe that a condition is only unchangeable when an individual decides that it has to respond to it with their own action. This means that changeability is not necessarily related only to enthusiastic approval, but it represents conditions that an individual can still tolerate. That is why it is so important that social acceptance is understood as a behavioural intent. Although it is difficult to study social acceptance as such, we can make accurate assumptions about it by measuring the presence or absence of events that point at whether something is socially accepted or not.

The above reasoning points at a conclusion that social acceptance should never be seen as a dichotomous or exclusive category (in the sense, there is or there is no social acceptance), but should be considered as a continuum, because the level of acceptance changes through time. That is why some of the examples of measuring social acceptance use as a measure willingness to negotiate, which is seen as evidence of social acceptance (Wolfe *et al.* 2002). Negotiations about a certain issue can deal with the issue itself or with a number of related topics, such as the level of involvement in the decision-making processes, questions of compensation and other topics related to the issue (Wolfe *et al.* 2002). The continuum thus stretches from total acceptance on one side to complete blockade or non-acceptance on the other, and not only includes problematic topics and actions, but also processes related to them. Companies should therefore, besides being attractive and fulfilling the needs and desires of consumers, always make sure that their business processes are legitimate because of the stakeholders' belief that the decision-making process should be open and honest (Moore 1995), and that companies decide about their actions in accordance with ethical standards (Easterling 1992). The legitimacy of a process is defined as congruence between the results of actions by decision-makers and the value patterns of the relevant system or the people who are influenced by the results. Here, psychological traits are ascribed to a person, institution or a social procedure, which leads concerned people to the belief that this person, institution or social procedure is suitable, ideal and honest (Tyler and de Cremer 2005). Only in such a way can companies get a licence to operate, which enables them not only to do business successfully, but to do business at all.

CASE: COCA-COLA

The history of the Coca-Cola Company starts in 1886, when John Pemberton, a pharmacist from Atlanta, first mixed a caramel drink, took it to Jacob's Pharmacy where soda was added, and the drink was then offered to customers to taste. Everybody agreed that the drink was something special. It was sold for five cents a glass. Frank Robinson, Pemberton's bookkeeper, named the drink Coca-Cola and wrote the name down in his typical handwriting. This typeface has remained a distinctive trade mark up to this day. Pemberton died two years later and did not live to see the success of his drink. Between 1888 and 1891, an Atlanta businessman, Griggs Candler, managed to secure rights of production and sale of Coca-Cola with an investment of $2,300. He became the first president of the company and was the first to develop a long-term vision for the development of the Coca-Cola brand. Coca-Cola has developed from a drink that sold nine glasses per day, to one of the best-known world brands, with 1.4 billion bottles sold every day. It is available in 200 countries. Its philosophy is the focus on local markets, with special attention being paid to the specialties of each local market. Coca-Cola cooperates with local partners that fill the bottles and sell it in their own markets.

In the 1980s, when Coca-Cola was on the brink of its 100th birthday, it was a large and successful international company. Its most important milestones of that era were the acquisition of Columbia Pictures (1982) and the launch of Diet Coke (1982). But nonetheless, troubles were ahead: Coca-Cola started to lose market share to its main competitor, Pepsi. In 1984, it only had a 4.9 per cent market share advantage over Pepsi and it seemed that Coca-Cola would become only the second most popular drink. Coca-Cola spent more money on advertising than Pepsi, but it seemed that the latter was more efficient. Furthermore, blind tests showed that consumers preferred the taste of Pepsi to that of Coca-Cola. The only advantage that Coca-Cola had was its presence on the market – due to the long years of intense distribution, Coca-Cola was everywhere. Even people who wanted Pepsi could mostly buy only Coca-Cola. It was also served in the McDonald's chain.

In autumn of 1983, Coca-Cola started to think about introducing a new formula and changing the taste. Consumer focus groups were against such an idea. But when analysing results of focus group studies, another problem was identified. Coca-Cola was officially the favourite drink, but people actually drank sometimes Pepsi, sometimes Coca-Cola, and at other times, a different generic drink. In September 1984, Coca-Cola finally thought it had a solution. Production technicians developed a taste that beat Pepsi in blind tests. In April 1985, the 'New Coke' was pompously introduced to the American market but consumers did not like it. Their reaction was quick and humiliating: Coca-Cola was compared to furniture polisher, or even to a two-day old Pepsi. Customers started to stockpile the old Coca-Cola. The price for a bottle of an old Coca-Cola skyrocketed on the black market and reached prices of up to $30. There were even ideas to import Coca-Cola from other countries. There were boycotts, civil initiatives and protests. The notion of changing Coca-Cola wounded the American pride; loyal customers were shocked and personally offended. Most journalists of almost all major media reacted similarly and showed contempt for the decision and the actions of the company's management. Despite the fact that the company continued to lose popularity and that the market rejected the new taste, the management insisted for some time that it had really invented a great new formula. The taste of Coca-Cola did change over the years (for example, caffeine and sugar content), but this was never presented as a repositioning of the brand. The management finally admitted that repositioning of the most popular and most successful brand in American history was a mistake. The company apologized to consumers and removed the new product from stores. The ensuing campaign 'The real thing' strengthened its leading position on the market.

In 2004, there was another unpleasant reaction to Coca-Cola's activities. In that year, Coca-Cola introduced a bottled spring water, Dasani, to the British market and spent £7 million on a communications campaign with the slogan 'As pure as water can get'. However, customers found out that the bottles contained normal tap water from London suburbs and almost all mainstream media picked up the story. Some customers even called Health Inspection to test the water. Coca-Cola responded with a statement that Dasani was indeed tap water and that it was never claimed that it was being sourced from a spring. They marketed it as extremely pure because Dasani used a special purification procedure developed by NASA. However, again, the media reported that a very simple procedure of reverse osmosis was used. The same month, there was another blow to Dasani: a two times higher than allowed concentration of bromate, a cancerous chemical, was found in the product. Coca-Cola immediately recalled all bottles from the market in order to prevent harm to consumers.

Key terms

Organizational commitment. Belonging and devotion denote a form of psychological connection, or a relationship between an individual and a company, and express a form of an individual's involvement with or affiliation to a company. It is willingness to devote effort in a relationship with an organization and a strong desire to stay in a relationship with it. It is a psychological state and the concrete activities of individuals that expresses their attitude toward the organization; the consequence of commitment is the decision whether an individual would stay a member of an organization or not.

Affective commitment. Affectively committed employees stay in an organization because they 'want' to. Individuals' commitment is thus based on their wish.

Continuance or calculative commitment. Continuance committed employees stay in an organization because they have no better choice. Individuals' commitment is thus based on their feeling of necessity.

Normative commitment. Normative committed employees stay in an organization because they 'have to' or feel morally obliged to stay. Individuals' commitment is thus based and develops on their moral obligation.

Social acceptance. An opinional process that involves a comparison of known alternatives and (not) acting on their basis. It is seen as a readiness to consider certain issues in question as possible alternatives. It is a result of judgement through which individuals compare perceived reality with any alternatives they know; make a decision on whether the existing condition is better than, or at least of satisfactory likeness to, the best alternative conditions. Because stakeholders have various interests, and because companies are variegated and complex entities that can act in a way that is unpopular with certain audiences, they must ensure their overall operation and concrete actions are socially accepted.

REVIEW QUESTIONS

- What is organizational commitment?
- What are affective, normative and continuance commitment and why is the distinction between different types of commitment important for organizations?
- What are the most important consequences of organizational commitment?
- Explain the meaning and importance of corporate social acceptability.

Visit the Coca-Cola company website. Discover the ways how this company builds its employee commitment. How is this done in the company that you work for? Throughout its history Coca-Cola confronted several crises related to the social acceptability of its products. Try to identify some of them. What danger, if any, may Coca-Cola witness in relation to the social acceptability of its products that contain high levels of sugar?

References

Allen, Natalie J. and John P. Meyer. 1990. The measurement and antecedents of affective, continuance and normative commitment to the organization. *Journal of Occupational Psychology* 63 (1): 1–18.

Ashforth, Blake E. 1998. Becoming: how does the process of identification unfold? *Identity in Organizations: Building Theory Through Conversations*, eds. David A. Whetten and Paul C. Godfrey. Thousand Oaks, CA: Sage, 213–222.

Bansal, Harvir S., Gregory P. Irving and Shirley F. Taylor. 2004. A three-component model of customer commitment to service providers. *Journal of the Academy of Marketing Science* 32 (3): 234–250.

Bendapudi, Neeli and Leonard L. Berry. 1997. Customers' motivations for maintaining relationships with service providers. *Journal of Retailing* 73 (1): 15–37.

Bielby, Denise D. 1992. Commitment to work and family. *Annual Review of Sociology* 18: 281–302.

Blau, Gary J. and Kimberly B. Boal. 1987. Conceptualizing how job involvement and organizational commitment affect turnover and absenteeism. *Academy of Management Review* 12 (2): 288–300.

Brunsson, Nils and Kerstin Sahlin-Andersson. 2000. Constructing organizations: the example of public sector reform. *Organization Studies* 21 (4): 721–746.

Buchanan, Bruce. 1974. Building organizational commitment: the socialization of managers in work organizations. *Administrative Science Quarterly* 19 (4): 533–546.

Clausen, Debra L. and Robert F. Schroeder. 2004. *Social Acceptability of Alternatives to Clearcutting: Discussion and Literature Review with Emphasis on Southeast Alaska*. Portland, OR: US Department of Agriculture, Forest Service, Pacific Northwest Research Station. Available at: http://www.fs.fed.us/pnw/pubs/pnw_gtr594.pdf (14 October 2010).

Cohen, Aaron and Catherine Kirchmeyer. 1995. A multidimensional approach to the relation between organizational commitment and non-work participation. *Journal of Vocational Behavior* 46 (2): 189–202.

Easterling, Douglas. 1992. Fair rules for siting a high-level nuclear waste repository. *Journal of Policy Analysis and Management* 11 (3): 442–475.

Ellemers, Naomi, Wendy van Rijswijk, Marlene Roefs and Catrien Simons. 1997. Bias in intergroup perceptions: balancing group identity with social reality. *Personality and Social Psychology Bulletin* 23 (2): 186–198.

Gaertner, Karen N. and Stanley D. Nollen. 1989. Career experiences, perceptions of employment practices, and psychological commitment to the organization. *Human Relations* 42 (11): 975–991.

Gilliland, David I. and Daniel C. Bello. 2002. Two sides to attitudinal commitment: the effect of calculative and loyalty commitment on enforcement mechanisms in distribution channels. *Journal of the Academy of Marketing Science* 30 (1): 24–43.

Gruen, Thomas W., John O. Summers and Frank Acito. 2000. Relationship marketing activities, commitment, and membership behaviors in professional associations. *Journal of Marketing* 64 (3): 34–49.

Gundlach, Gregory T., Ravi S. Achrol and John T. Mentzer. 1995. The structure of commitment in exchange. *Journal of Marketing* 59 (1): 72–92.

Iniesta M. Angeles and Manuel Sanchez. 2003. Client commitment relations towards financial entities. *International Journal of Retail & Distribution Management* 31 (4): 203–213

Marsh, Robert M. and Hiroshi Mannari. 1977. Organizational commitment and turnover: a prediction study. *Administrative Science Quarterly* 22 (1): 57–75.

Mathieu, John E. and Dennis M. Zajac. 1990. A review and metaanalysis of the antecedents, correlates, and consequences of organizational commitment. *Psychological Bulletin* 108 (2): 171–194.

McFarlane Shore, Lynn and Sandy J. Wayne. 1993. Commitment and employee behavior: comparison of affective commitment and continuance commitment with perceived organizational support. *Journal of Applied Psychology* 78 (5): 774–780.

Meyer, John P. and Natalie J. Allen. 1984. Testing the 'side-bet theory' of organizational commitment: some methodological considerations. *Journal of Applied Psychology* 69 (3): 372–378.

——1997. *Commitment in the Workplace: Theory, Research, and Application*. Thousand Oaks, CA: Sage.

Meyer, John P. and Lynne Herscovitch. 2001. Commitment in the workplace: toward a general model. *Human Resource Management Review* 11 (3): 299–326.

Meyer, John P., Sampo V. Paunonen, Ian R. Gellatly, Richard D. Goffin and Douglas N. Jackson. 1989. Organizational commitment and job performance: it's the nature of commitment that counts. *Journal of Applied Psychology* 74 (1): 152–156.

Meyer, John P., Natalie J. Allen and Ian R. Gellatly. 1990. Affective and continuance commitment to the organization: evaluation of measures and analysis of concurrent and time-lagged relations. *Journal of Applied Psychology* 75 (6): 710–720.

Moore, Susan A. 1995. The role of trust in social networks: formation, function, and fragility. In *Nature Conversation 4: The Role of Networks*, eds. Denis A. Saunders, John L. Craig and Elizabeth M. Mattiske. New South Wales: Surrey Beatty and Sons, Chipping Norton, 148–154.

Morgan, Robert M. and Shelby D. Hunt. 1994. The commitment-trust theory relationship marketing. *Journal of Marketing* 58 (3): 20–38.

Morris, H. James and Daniel J. Sherman. 1981. Generalizability of an organizational commitment model. *Academy of Management Journal* 24 (3): 512–526.

Mowday, Richard. T., Lyman M. Porter and Richard M. Steers. 1982. *Employee Organization Linkages: The Psychology of Commitment, Absenteeism and Turnover*. New York: Academic Press.

Oliver, Richard L. 1997. *Satisfaction: A Behavioral Perspective on the Consumer*. New York; London: McGraw Hill.

Podnar, Klement. 2004. *Ugled, organizacijska identifikacija in zavezanost zaposlenih*. Doktorska disertacija. Ljubljana: Fakulteta za družbene vede.

Porter, Lyman W., Richard M. Steers and Richard T. Mowday. 1974. Organizational commitment, job satisfaction, and turnover among psychiatric technicians. *Journal of Applied Psychology* 59 (5): 603–609.

Pratt, Michael G. 1998. To be or not to be: central questions in organizational identification. In *Identity in Organizations: Building Theory Through Conversations*, eds. David A. Whetten and Paul C. Godfrey. Thousand Oaks, CA: Sage, 171–207.

Russo, Tracy Callaway. 1998. Organizational and professional identification: a case of newspaper journalists. *Management Communication Quarterly* 12 (1): 72–111.

Sano, Yoko. 1999. Commitment. In *The IEBM Handbook of Human Resource Management*, eds. Michael Poole and Malcom Warner. London: International Thomson Business Press, 481–487.

Scholl, Richard W. 1981. Differentiating organizational commitment from expectancy as a motivating force. *Academy of Management Review* 6 (4): 589–599.

Siegel, Philip H. and Seleshi Sisaye. 1997. An analysis of the difference between organization identification and professional commitment: a study of certified public accountants. *Leadership and Organization Development Journal* 18 (3): 149–165.

Stevens, John M., Janice M. Beyer and Harrison M. Trice. 1978. Assessing personnel, role, and organizational predictors of managerial commitment. *The Academy of Management Journal* 21 (3): 380–396.

Tyler, Tom R. and David de Cremer. 2005. Process based leadership: fair procedures and reactions to organizational change. *The Leadership Quarterly* 16 (4): 529–545.

Vardi, Yoav, Yoash Wiener and Micha Popper. 1989. The value content of organizational mission as a factor in the commitment of members. *Psychological Reports* 65 (1): 27–34.

Wiener, Yoash. 1982. Commitment in organizations: a normative view. *Academy of Management Review* 7 (3): 418–428.

Wolfe, Amy K., David J. Bjornstad, Milton Russell and Nichole D. Kerchner. 2002. A framework for analyzing dialogues over the acceptability of controversial technologies. *Science Technology & Human Values* 27 (1): 134–159.

Yoon, Jeongkoo, Mouraine R. Baker and Jong-Wook Ko. 1994. Interpersonal attachment and organizational commitment: subgroup hypothesis revisited. *Human Relations* 47 (3): 329–351.

CONCLUSION

If there is one word that best sums up the contents of this book, than this word is 'credibility'. This book is about **corporate credibility**, which is a relation between what a company says it is (or will be) doing, and what its behaviour actually is. Thus, this is also a relationship between an expected and perceived congruity between a company's communications and a company's actions. The concept of credibility has two components: on one hand there is the feeling of the individual – that they have received what they have been promised; on the other, there are actual experiences, impressions, feelings and judgements in relation to the company. The credibility is thus based on integrity or honesty, and on the company's competencies. As studies in the field of spokespersons and market communications have shown, credibility of the source, to the largest extent, influences the reception of information and the receiver's attitude toward what is offered and transferred by the sender. Corporation credibility defines the attitude of the stakeholders toward a company's messages, products and services, and its responses to the needs and demands of the environment. This attitude is expressed as the level to which a company's stakeholders feel that the company has the knowledge and capacity to fulfil its promises and whether or not the company is communicating the truth. Without the necessary credibility, all resources invested in communications are lies and propaganda more than anything else, which never bring desired effects in the long term.

That is why successful corporate communication always has to start with the identity of the communication sender. We have to know, understand and, if necessary, change the nature of the social subject. Although this can be explained quite well with the metaphor of peeling an onion (which is getting smaller and smaller with removal of every layer) identity is nonetheless such a complex and unique composition that the studying of its components and structure gives fairly clear answers to questions of the substance of a company's promises and communications. Corporate identity is a matter from which we knead promises and commitments of

the company, which are then articulated through the process of internal and external branding and through conscious decisions that that company's actions will be
based on legal and social norms and moral commitments, regardless of the role that
the company is playing (either an employer, provider of products and services, tax
payer, investor or investment opportunity). Because in this phase we create contents
and directly influence the method of a company's management and its actions,
many authors reasonably claim that identity management is a key aspect of the
entire management and that instead of corporate communication we should speak
of corporate marketing.

The idea of corporate communication, and corporate marketing even more
so, diverts attention away from the consumers and products and services made
for them to a broader mix of stakeholders and various exchange processes that
an organization, as a complete and socially active unit, is involved in within its
many environments. The stakeholder theory has thus become the key postulation
in modern management, while relationship and communication with stakeholders
have become the key communication issue of the communication department in
the companies. Companies and other organizations are only pseudo-persons and
are as such constructed only through narration and people's interaction with such
entities. Internal and external stories where companies (or persons handling in
their name) perform as main actors in various plots with very real consequences
for involved individuals, are an important mechanism for construction of reality.
The understanding of a story's morphology not only helps us to create efficient
and convincing stories, but also helps us to analyse relationships among individual
actors performing in the story. Strategic stories are an efficient tool when it comes
to introduction of changes in an organization, and in times when a company has to
prevent or respond to a crisis. Approaches that companies use when communicating their stories are numerous. Although it is very difficult to achieve an absolute
consistency of content and a perfect harmony of communication, the integrated
approach is nonetheless becoming a real theoretical dogma. Not only must a company have complete control over what it says and how it talks about itself, it also has
to be mindful of what others say about it. Only in this way can a company expect
to have a desired public image and have a maximum influence on the associations
about the company in the minds of people. Good corporate image of a company
in the eyes of individuals is a key to good public reputation, which is one of the
most important intangible treasures of people and organizations and brings, among
other benefits, a resource that is more and more rare today – trust. Reputable and
trustworthy companies can expect that their stakeholders will identify with the
companies and be emotionally, morally and otherwise committed. Society, in which
companies, individuals and groups of individuals function, gives companies the
licence to operate. If a company wants to obtain, preserve and upgrade this licence
to operate, then corporate communication can substantially help lower opportunity costs for the organization and create competitive edge and partial monopolies,
which are the benefits of strong brands.

As has been put forward in the Introduction, this book follows Lasswell's model of communication that identifies the sender, the message, and communication codes, media and channels, receivers, and also the intention and consequences of the communication. The model is actually a return loop between the sender and the receiver. It shows a concluded circle, but actually this is a never-finished process of interactions among various exchange partners. Such a structure to the book enabled us to use elements of the communication model and express through them antecedents and consequences of individual concepts (that the book described) as well as steps of their strategic and tactical management. Further, with this structure we tried not only to illustrate the need for dialogue and strategic approach to management, and the need to understand numerous antecedents and consequences, but also to show that a unit as a whole has a greater impact than all its constituent parts individually and that it creates a special added value, just like strategically managed corporate communication and corporate marketing do. But, the latter concept is already a topic for the next book, or maybe for the extended version that you, dear reader, have just read.

AUTHOR INDEX

Page numbers in *italics* indicate a figure

Aaker, David A. 37, 38, 39
Aaker, Jennifer L. 186
Aaker *et al* 33
Aarts, M. N. C. 90
Aberg, Leif Eric Gustav 4
Ackerman, Laurence D. 22, 23
Adams, Carol 74, 75
Aguilera *et al* 68
Ahearne, Michael 190
Albert, Stuart 56, 181
Allen, Natalie J. 198, 200–201, 203
Allport, Gordon Willard 127
Alvesson, Mats 183
Ambler, Tim 50
Anderson, Benedict 188
Andrijanič, Boris 75
Ansoff, Igor H. 108
Aperia, Tomy 37
Argenti, Paul A. 5, 6–7, 9
Armenakis, Achilles A. 102
Ashforth, Blake E. 179–180, 181, 182, 183, 188–189, 197
Atkin, Charles 118
Aupperle *et al* 68

Back, Rolf 37
Backhaus, Kristin 51
Bagozzi, Richard P. 163
Baker, Michael J. 120
Balmer, John M. T. 5, 22–23, 24, 25, 32–33, 34, 120, 142, 157
Bansal *et al* 198, 202, 203

Bargh. John A. 139
Barich, Howard 143
Barker, James R. 188
Barrow, Simon 50
Bartel, Caroline 179
Basil, Michael D. 118
Basu, Kunal 63
Bayton, James 142
Beardwell *et al* 50
Belasen, Alan T. 108
Belk, Russell W. 118, 119
Bello, Daniel C. 202
Benbasat, Izak 168
Bendapudi, Neeli 202
Benoit, William I. 106–107
Berens, Guido A. J. M. 137, 168
Bergami, Massimo 163
Bergstrom *et al* 50, 53–54
Bernays, Edward L. 149
Bernstein, David 4, 144
Berry, Gregory R. 97
Berry, Leonard L. 166, 202
Berthon *et al* 54–55
Bhat, Sobodh 186
Bhattacharya, C. B. 70, 163, 164, 179, 181–182
Bickerton, David 33, 36, 37
Biehal, Gabriel J. 123
Bielby, Denise 200
Birkigt, Klaus 9, 10
Blau, Gary J. 199
Blauw, Ed 4–5

Block, Martin 118
Boal, Kimberly B. 199
Boin, Arjen 104
Boorstin, Daniel J. 116, 147–149
Bordia, Prashant 125, 127, 128
Bordia *et al* 103–104
Bourne, Lynda 85
Bowie, Norman E. 82
Boyer, Pascal 138
Brennan, William 162–163
Brewer, Marilynn B. 183
Bromley, Dennis Basil 139, 142, 158, 159
Brown, Andrew D. 103
Brown, Tom J. 137, 164
Brown, William J. 118
Brunsson, Nils 204, 205
Buchanan, Bruce 203
Buchanan, David 101
Buckner, Taylor H. 127–128
Burnett, John 7, 104, 105
Butlle, Francis A. 126
Byrne *et al* 118, 119

Cannon, Joseph P. 168
Carlson, Robert O. 142
Carroll, Archie B. 65, 67
Carter, Suzanne M. 165
Cartwright, Lisa 120
Caruana, Albert 159
Cha, Yong-Jin 167
Chase, Howard W. 108
Cheney, George 10, 189
Cheney *et al* 101
Chicop, Saviour 159
Choudhury, Pravat K. 65
Chreim, Samia 182
Christensen, Lars Thøger 10
Chun, Rosa 140
Clarkson, Max B. E. 83, 89
Clausen, Debra L. 204–205
Clevenger *et al* 146
Cohen, Aaron 203
Collins, Christopher J. 123
Collins, James, Charles 53
Connaughton, Stacey L. 179
Cook, John 168
Coombs, Timothy W. 106, 107
Cooper, Stuart Martin 81, 83
Coote, Leonard V. 190
CorpWatch 64
Cox, Edwin 137
Cravens *et al* 159
Currie, Graeme 103

Cutlip *et al* 7, 105
Czellar, Sandor 164

Dacin, Peter A. 137
Daly, Aidan 43
Daly, John A. 179
Daneshvary, Rennae 118
Davies, Gary 140
Davis *et al* 186
Dawson, Patrick 101
de Chernatony, Leslie 32, 39, 52, 55, 57
de Cremer, David 205
del Rio *et al* 190
Dennehy, Robert F. 98, 101
Dichter, Ernest 127
DiFonzo, Nicholas 125, 127, 128
Dijksterhuis, Ap 139
Dolphin, Richard 5
Donaldson, Thomas 82
Doney, Patricia M. 168
Dowling, Grahame 107–108, 158, 164
Downey, Stephen M. 18, 20–21
Dukerich, Janet M. 162, 165
Dukerich *et al* 181
Dutton, Jane E. 108, 162, 179
Dutton *et al* 162, 163, 182, 183, 189
Dwyer *et al* 167
Dyhr, Villy 68

Easterling, Douglas 205
Edwards, Lee 117
Einwiller, Sabine 34
Elfers, Joost 85
Ellemers *et al* 198
Elsbach, Kimberly D. 162, 181–182
Elving, Wim J. L. 102, 103
Epley *et al* 138

Fan, Ying 63
Farell *et al* 118
Farkas, Ferenc 52
Fearn-Banks, Kathleen 104
Ferguson, Jeffery 188
Ferris *et al* 116
Fill, Chris 87
Finn, Alan 149
Fiol *et al* 56, 57
Fog *et al* 99–100
Fombrun, Charles J. 5, 9, 34, 99, 122, 158, 159, 160–161, 164
Forman, Janis 5
Forston, Robert F. 127
Fournier, Susan 185–186
Fraser, Benson P. 118

Freeman, Edward R. 82, 88
Friedman, Andrew L. 84, 89–90, 118
Friedman, Linda 118
Frooman, Jeff 85, 89

Gaertner, Karen N. 200
Gapp, Rod 53
Garbett, Thomas F. 143–144
Gardner, Wendi 183
Garud, Raghu 164
Giddens, Anthony 165
Gilliland, David I. 202
Gilly et al 125
Gioia et al 27
Glynn, Mary Ann 189
Godes, David 128
Godfrey, Paul C. 56, 57
Goffman, Erving 99
Goldberg, Marvin E. 164
Goldsmith et al 164
Golob, Urša 66–67, 68, 69, 72, 74
Gønhaug, Kjell 167
Goslar, Marjan 58
Gotsi, Manto 159
Gray, Edmund R. 5
Gray, Rob 82
Grayson, Kent 166
Greenbaum et al 6
Greenberg et al 168
Greene, Robert 85
Greyser, Stephen A. 159–160, 164
Gruen, Thomas 188
Gruen et al 201–202
Grunig, James E. 7, 82, 149
Gundlach et al 198
Gwinner, Kevin 118

Hallahan, Kirk 99
Halliday, Sue Vaux 190
Han, Jian 123
Handy, Charles B. 8
Harris, Fiona 52, 55, 57
Harris Stanley G. 102
Hart et al 126
Hartwick, Jon 164
Hatch, Mary Jo 36, 56, 57
Hayward et al 117
He, Hong-Wei 24
Heany, Donald, F. 21
Heath, Robert Lawrence 104, 105
Heide, Mats 103
Herbig, Paul 158
Herr et al 126
Herscovitch, Lynne 202

Heugens, Pursey 101
Highhouse, Scott 51
Ho et al 118
Holten Larsen, Morgens 97
Homer, Pamela M. 118
Hooley, Graham J. 37
Hopkins, Michael 65
Hosmer, Larue Tone 166, 167
Hunt, Shelby D. 167, 202, 203
Hunt, Todd 7, 82
Huston, Ted L. 168
Hwang et al 124

Ind, Nicholas 142
Iniesta, M. Angeles 200, 203
Ivanevich, John M. 6

Jackson, Peter 4–5
Jančič, Zlatko 50, 83
Joachimstahler, Erich 38
Johansson, Catrin 103
Johansson, Ingrid 105
Johnson, Devon 166
Johnson, Scott A. 179–180, 181, 183
Jones et al 164

Kagan, Jerom 179
Kahle, Lynn R. 118
Kamins et al 118
Kammerer, Jürgen 41
Kapferer, Jean-Noel 127
Kaptein, Muel 183
Kelley, Harold H. 117
Kennedy, Sherril H. 142
Kennedy et al 165
Kenning, Peter 165
Kim et al 190
Kirchmeyer, Catherine 203
Klein, Naomi 68
Kline, Miro 7
Klonoski, Richard J. 65
Knox, Simon 33, 36, 37–38
Kotler, Philip 70–71, 143
Kotler et al 24
Kramer, Roderick M. 162
Kuenzel, Sven 190
Kumar et al 168

Laforet, Sylvie 38
Lagadec, Patrick 104
Lampel, Joseph 164
Langer, Roy 103
Lantos, Geoffrey P. 69
Larson, Gregory S. 182

Larzelere, Robert E. 168
Leblanc, Gaston 142
Lee, Nancy 70–71
Lee, Young Lyoul 124
Lerbinger, Otto 104
Levy, Margaret F. 147
Levy, Sidney J. 186
Lewis, Philip V. 8
Lievans, Filip 51
Linksold, Svenn 168
Longman John P. 118
Luhmann, Niklas 165
Lux, Peter G. C. 26–27

Maathuis, Onno Johannes Maria 141
Macleod, Jennifer 142
Madrigal, Robert 141
Mael, Fred A. 179, 182, 183, 188–189
Mahnert, Kai F. 53, 55
Mahon, John F. 65, 108
Maignan, Isabelle 68
Maklan, Stan 37
Malešič, Marjan 105, 106
Manktelow, R. 84
Mannari, Hiroshi 199, 203
Margulies, Walter P. 120
Marquis, Harold H. 17, 120
Marsh, Robert M. 199, 203
Martin et al 98
Martineau, Pierre 159
Mathieu, John E. 203
Matteson, Michael T. 6
Mayer et al 168
Maynard, Roberta 104
Mayzlin, Dina 128
McAlexander, James H. 188
McCracken, Grant 118, 119, 120
McDonald, John P. 122–123
McDonald, Malcolm 32
McFarlane Shore, Lynn 203
McGowan, Richard A. 65
McHugh, David 9
McLellan, Hilary 97
McLuhan, Marshall 114
Melewar, T. C. 120
Merrilees, Bill 42, 43, 53
Mesner-Andolšek, Dana 57
Meyer, John P. 198, 200–201, 202, 203
Michelson, Grant 125
Miles, Samantha 84, 89–90
Milewicz, John 158
Millar, Dan Pyle 104, 105
Miller, Dale 42, 43
Mindak, William A. 146
Mitchell et al 81, 82, 85–86

Mithen, Stephen 138
Mohr et al 68, 169
Moloney, Deirdre 43
Monsen, Joseph R. 68
Moore, Susan A. 205
Morgan, Robert M. 167, 202, 203
Morgan, Sandra 98, 101
Moriarty, Sandra E. 7
Morris, H. James 198, 199
Morrow, Paula C. 179
Morrow et al 165
Morsing, Mette 63, 72
Mosley, Richard W. 50
Mouly, Suchitra V. 125
Mowday et al 199
Muniz, Albert M. Jr. 187–188

Neilson, Ellerup Anne 75
Newlove et al 105
Newman, William H. 21
Nguyen, Nha 142
Nollen, Stanley D. 200

Obermiller, Carl 169
Oetting, Martin 128
Ogilvy, David 124
Ogorelec Wagner, Vida 65
O'Guinn, Thomas C. 187–188
Ohanian, Roobina 120
Olins, Wally 18, 38
Oliver, Richard L. 203
Osgood et al 146
Ottensmeyer, Edward 108

Paine, Lynn Sharp 68
Palazzo, Guido 63
Papadatos, Caroline 100
Parasuraman, A. 166
Patti, Charles H. 122–123
Peirce, Charles Sanders 120
Pepper, Gerald L. 182
Perryman, Alexa A. 118
Peteraf, Margaret 189
Plummer, Joseph T. 186
Podnar, Klement 7, 8, 10, 17, 24, 71, 83, 119, 140–141, 158, 164, 184, 186, 197, 201
Podnar et al 7
Polkinghorne, Donald E. 101
Porras, Jerry I. 53
Porter et al 198–199
Postman, Leo 127
Pratt, Michael G. 182, 189, 197
Preston, Lee E. 82
Punjaisri et al 53
Putnam, Linda 8

Rajagopal 38, 40
Reddy, Srinivas K. 186
Reichers, Arnon E. 179
Reinsch, Lamur N. 6
Rempel et al 168
Repovš, Jernej 122
Repper, Fred C. 82
Riley, John W. 147
Rindova et al 116
Ring, Peter Smith 166
Roberts, Peter W. 164
Rothschild, Michael L. 123
Rotter, Julian B. 165
Russo, Tracy Callaway 179, 198
Ruyter, Ko de 126

Sahlin-Andersson, Kerstin 204, 205
Sako, Mari 167
Sanchez, Manuel 200, 203
Sanchez, Romulo 38, 40
Sano, Yoko 198
Saparito et al 166
Saunders, John 38
Savage et al 88
Schein, Edgar H. 57
Scholl, Richard W. 198
Schouten, John W. 188
Schroeder, Robert F. 204–205
Schultz, Majken 56, 57, 63, 72
Schultz and Schultz 7
Schumann et al 123, 124
Schwer, Keith R. 118
Scott, Craig R. 179
Selame and Selame 17, 121
Selnes, Fred 167
Sen, Sankar 70, 163, 179
Sethi, Prakash S. 123, 124
Shanley, Mark 158, 161, 164, 189
Sheinin, Daniel A. 123
Shenkar, Oded 158, 164, 165
Sherman, Daniel J. 198, 199
Shultz, Majken 36
Siegel, Philip H. 198
Sillanpää, Maria 84
Simmons, John Aydon 49
Sisaye, Seleshi 198
Skoglund, Per 105
Smidts et al 162
Smith, Craig N. 68
Smith, Gareth 118
Sobol et al 159, 164, 165
Söderlund, Magnus 126
Soenen, Guillaume B. 22–23, 25
Song, Seokwoo 124
Spangenberg, E. R. 169

Speck et al 118
Spector, Aaron J. 139
Spekman, Robert E. 168
Srivastava et al 164
Stadler, Marinus 9, 10
Stanley, Edmund 166, 167
Starik, M. 82
Steiner, George A. 68–69
Stephens et al 104
Stevens et al 198
Stinnett, Nick 166
Stone, W. Robert 21
Strong et al 91
Stuart, Helen 72
Sturken, Marita 120
Sullivan,, John 50, 51
Swerdlow and Swerdlow 119, 120
Szwajkowski, Eugene 91

TerraChoice Environmental
    Marketing Inc 64
Tetrick, Lois E. 183
Thompson, Paul 9
Thomsen, Christa 75
Thorelli, Hans B. 167
Thorup, Signe 103
Tikoo, Surinder 51
Tildesley, Amy E. 190
Topalian, Allan 19
Torres, Ann M. 53, 55
Treadway et al 116, 117
Tyagi,, Pradeep 57
Tyler, Katherine 166, 167
Tyler, Tom R. 205

Underwood et al 187

Vallentin, Steen 68
van den Bosch et al 120, 121, 122
van der Laan, Sandra L. 74
van Halderen, Mignon D. 150
van Laer, Tom 126
van Rekom,, John 57
van Riel, Cees B. M. 5, 9, 17, 34, 41–42,
    97–98, 99, 122, 145, 150, 160–161, 164
van Vuuren, Mark 103
van Woerkum, C. M. J. 90
Vardi et al 199–200
Viklund, Mattias J. 165

Waddock, Sandra A. 108
Walker, Derek H. T. 85
Wall, Toby 168
Walsh et al 161
Walters, James 166

Waltzer, Herbert 124
Wang, Weiquan 168
Wan-Huggins *et al* 182
Watzlawick, Paul 4
Wayne, Sandy J. 203
Wempe, Johan 183
Westbrook, Robert A. 125
Wheeler, David 84
Whetten, David A. 56, 57, 67, 181
Wiener, Yoash 201
Wilkins, Alan L. 98
Will, Markus 34
Williamson, Oliver E. 166
Wilson, Alan 159
Winick, Charles 144–145
Wolfe *et al* 205

Wood, Donna J. 65
Woodward *et al* 74
Woolward, Iain 124

Yaniv, Eitan 52
Yoon *et al* 164, 198
Yuchtman-Yaar, Ephrainm 158, 164, 165
Yukl Gary A. 84–85

Zaheer *et al* 56
Zajac, Dennis M. 203
Zarantonello, Lia 33
Zemke, Ron 98
Zenisek, Thomas J. 65
Zucker, Lynne Goodman 166
Zutshi, Ambika 74, 75

SUBJECT INDEX

References to figures are in **bold**

acceptance 204
accreditation process 158
ACID test 25
acquisitions, corporate identity 20–21
adaptive instability 27, 30
advertising 122–123, 131, 164
advocacy 123
affective commitment 200, 202, 203, 207
anthropomorphism 138, 193
anthropomorphization 138, 153, 186
association techniques 145
attribution theory 117
audience management programme 23
autonomy of organization 8, 14

Barilla Group 91–92
belonging 198
benevolence 168, 172
bluewashing 64
BMW group 12–13
BP 169–171
branch, definition 24, 30
branch identity 23–25, 30
brand architecture 38–40, 46
brand communities 187–188, 193
brand equity 33–34
brand promise 55
brands: consumer identity 185–186;
    definition 32, 45; interactivity 187;
    marketplace recognition 32; positioning
    strategy 186
Burson-Marsteller 115–116
business communication, definition 6, 14

business strategy 9
business units 39, 41

calculative commitment 200–201, 208
cause promotion 70
cause-related marketing 70
celebrity: definition 130; endorsement
    118–120, 186; management 116–117
centralization 11
chair of the board: as personification of
    organization 11, 115; reputation 115, 117
change management: corporate rebranding
    42–43; corporate story 101–103, 212;
    employer branding 55
charity partnerships 69, 70
'cobweb' method 25–26
Coca-Cola 206–207
cognitive apathy 182
cognitive maps 139
cognitive schemes 138, 153
cognitive scripts 138, 153
commitment 189, 198
    see also organizational commitment
common operational system 42
common starting points (CSPs) 41–42
communications see also corporate
    communication; corporate story:
    competitors 26; consistency 101;
    corporate social responsibility (CSR)
    71–74; crisis situations 104–108;
    employer branding 52; as identity
    projectors 18; informal 125–28, 131;
    stakeholders 86–87, 90–91

communication skills 6 *see also* business
communication
community partnerships 69, 70
community volunteering 71
competence 167–168
competitive advantage *see also* strategic
advantage: branch identity analysis 25;
corporate brand 34; corporate identity
20, 22; internal branding 53; positioning
strategy 23; reputation 164; social
responsibility 68
competitors: communications 26; corporate
image mesurement 145–146; positioning
strategy 37–38
completion techniques 145
congruity 52
consistency 18, 101, 122, 150–151, 162, 212
construction techniques 145
consumers: brand communities 187–188;
celebrity endorsement 119–120,
186; corporate advertising 123;
corporate brand 35, 185–186; informal
communications 128; interactivity 187;
loyalty 188, 202, 203; organizational
commitment 198, 201–202, 203;
organizational identification 184–187,
190; reputation 161, 164; social
responsibility 68, 72
continuance commitment 200–201,
202, 208
corporate, meaning/definition 2, 5
corporate advertising 122–124, 131
corporate associations 136–137, 141,
151, 153
corporate brand *see also* corporate identity:
attributes 36–37; brand architecture
38–40; cognitive approach 33; costs 34;
definition 32–33, 45–46; disadvantages
35; employees 49–50, 53–54; experiential
approach 33; historical development 1–2;
management process 35–36; management
responsibility 33–34; organizational
identity 57; organizational structure
40–42; positioning strategy 37–38, 186;
purpose 34–35, 185; rebranding 42–43;
relational approach 33; as social actor 33;
strength 33; usage 35
corporate communication
see also communications: definition
4–5, 13–14; framework 5–6; historical
development 1; organizational behaviour
10; purpose 114–115; relationship to
other disciplines 10; stakeholders 212;
tasks 11–12, **116**

corporate governance 69
corporate identification 183, 184, 193
corporate identity *see also* corporate brand;
corporate visual identity; organizational
identification: acquisitions and mergers
20–21, 121–122; components 18–19,
22–23; consistency 150–151; corporate
advertising 122–124; credibility 211–112;
definition 17, 18, 22, 29; diversity
outwards 19, 29; goals relationship
20–22; historical development 2;
reputation 161–162; as social actor 19;
strategic advantage 20; symbol usage 17;
uniformity inwards 19, 30
corporate identity management: articulation
20, 25–27, 36–37; communication 27;
definition 30; tasks overview 21
corporate image: accreditation process
158; approaches 147; Boorstin 147–149;
consistency 150–151, 212; definition
141–142, 154, 157–158; factors
143–144; hierarchical model 142;
honesty 149–150; literature review
141–142; measurement 144–147; sources
143; structure **140**; transparency 150
corporate philanthropy 70–71
corporate positioning, definition 46
corporate rebranding 42–43, 46
corporate reputation *see* reputation
corporate social marketing 70
corporate social responsibility (CSR):
communications 71–74; definition
65–67, 77; expectations 67–69; explicit
67, 77; implementation 69–71; implicit
67, 72, 77; reporting 74–75, 78
corporate spokesperson 115–117, 130
corporate story *see also* crisis communication:
coherence 9; comprehensiveness 11;
context 99; corporate advertising
124–125; definition 97–98, 110;
framework 99; importance 96–97;
informal communications 126;
management 97, 103; narration 114, 115,
212; organizational changes 101–103, 212;
plurality 101; structure 98; types 97, 98
corporate visual identity (CVI) 120–122, 130
corrective actions 107
costs, brand architecture 34, 39
credibility 211
crises 104, 111
crisis communication 104–108, 111, 212
CSR report 78
CVI *see* corporate visual identity
cynicism 169

de-identification 182
differentiation 20
dis-identification 181–182
diversity outwards 19, 29
Domino's Pizza 108–110
duality of organization 7–9, 14

emotional values 33, 56, 96, 139, 142, 160, 166, 203
employees: change management 103–104; commitment 189; corporate brand 34, 35–36, 43, 49–50, 53–54; corporate identity 18, 20, 21; organizational commitment 198, 200–201, 203; organizational identification 179, 180–181, 182–184, 188–189; reputation management 161, 162–163, 164; social responsibility 68, 69, 72–74
employer brand 50, 51, 59 see also internal branding
employer branding 50–53, **54**, 60
endorsed structure 39, **40**
endorsement 39, 118–120, 186
ethical branding 63–65, 77
    see also corporate social responsibility (CSR)
explicit corporate social responsibility 67, 77
expressivity 9, 10

framing 99, 110
functionalism 8

Gorenje 129–130
gossip 125, 126
greenwashing 64
group identification 8, 183–184, 188, 189, 192

Harley-Davidson 190–192
Harris/Fombrun Corporate Reputation Quotient (RQ) 160
hidden trade-offs 64
Hidria 28–29
holistic approach 4, 5–6, 10
honesty 149–150, 168, 172, 205, 211

identity see also corporate brand; organizational identification: corporate communication relationship 5, 10; definition 9, 178; dynamics 10; hierarchies 179–180; projected 10
identity traits 139–141, 153
image see corporate image

implicit corporate social responsibility 67, 72, 77
individuals as part of group 14
industrial identity see branch identity
industry, definition 30
informal communications 125–128, 131
information flows 6 see also organizational communication
information transfer 127–128, 150
institutional advertising 122–124
internal branding 53–58, 60
    see also employer branding
internal communications 11, 69
internal marketing mix 50
issue advertising 123
issue management see crisis communication

Krka 75–77

'laddering' method 26
language designations 139
Lasswell's model 3, 213
legal frameworks for social responsibility 66, 74–75
legitimacy 85–86, **87**, 205
Lego Group 44–45
Likert scale 146

management communication: corporate identity 21; definition 6–7, 14
management reputation 115–117
mandatory disclosure 74–75
marketing communications 7, 14, 40
meaning transfer 119–120
measurement techniques: corporate image 144–146; reputation 159–161
media communications: celebrity 116–117; corporate advertising 124–125; crisis management 105–106
medium is the message 114
Mercator 58–59
mergers, corporate identity 20–21, 121–122
modes of action 18
mono brand structure 39, **40**
monolithic structure 38, **40**, 41
moral branding see ethical branding
mortification 107
motivation 20, 51

neural networks 138
non-communication 4
normative commitment 199–200, 201, 202, 208

opinion leaders 127, 128, 171
ORC model 159–160
organization: autonomy 8, 14; duality 7–9, 14
organizational change: corporate story 101–103, 212; definition 110–111
organizational climate 56, 57, 60
organizational commitment: consumers 198, 201–202, 203; definition 197, 207; dimensions 200–203; effects 203–204; employees 198, 200–201, 203; exchange approach 199, 200; identification 197–198; instrumental-calculative approach 199; normative approach 199–200, 201, 202; psychological approach 198–199, 200; relational 200; transactional 200
organizational communication 6, 14 *see also* corporate communication
organizational culture 36, 56–57, 60
organizational dis-identification 192
organizational identification *see also* corporate identity: categories 183–184; cognitive apathy 182; commitment 197–198; consumers 184–187, 190; cross-cutting 181; definition 177–178, 192, 197, 199; de-identification 182; dis-identification 181–182; employees 179, 180–181, 182–184, 188–189; generalization 181; nested 180–181; process 178–179
organizational identity 56, 57, 60
organizational structure: corporate brands 40–42; corporate identity 18

perception *see also* reputation: bias 138; branch identity effect 24; corporate associations 136–137; corporate image 141–142; credibility 211; crisis communication 105; definition 137–138, 153; discrepancies 27; employer branding 51, 55–56; identity traits 139, 141; image theory 147–149; informal communications 125–126, 127; organizational climate 57; perceived external prestige 162–163, 171; schemes and scripts 138
personification 186, 193
plurivocity 110
positioning strategy 23, 37–38, 186
power 84–85, 89
pressure groups 68
prestige 162–163
proactive endorsement 72–73
products: positioning strategy 37, 186; reputation 164

projected identity 10
Propp model 99–100
pseudo-events 147–148
psychological contract 50–51, 60
public, definition 82–83, 93, 204
public image: crisis communication 106–107, 212; definition 171
public relations *see also* communications; corporate image: definition 7, 14; image theory 147–149
public sphere 83, 93

range scale measures 146
rebranding 42–43
recruitment: corporate identity 21; employer branding 51–52, 55–56
reliability 167–168, 172
reporting, corporate social responsibility 74–75, 78
Reptrak model 160–161
reputation *see also* corporate identity; corporate image; public image: benefits 163–165; consistency 162, 212; corporate brand 34; corporate identity 21, 23; definition 9, 157, 158; dimensions 159, **160**, 161; management 115–117, 161–162; measurement techniques 159–161; mistrust consequences 168–169; perceived external prestige 162–163; projected identity 10
risk management 108
RQ (Harris/Fombrun Corporate Reputation Quotient) 160
rumour 125, 126–128

scepticism 169
semantic differential scale 146
shadow endorsement 39
SIDEC model 41
Si.mobil 151–153
situational identification 179
situation analysis 43
social acceptance 204–205, 208
social contracts 68–69
social identity 163, 189
social network analysis 147
social responsibility 67, 77–78 *see also* corporate social responsibility (CSR)
Soenen, Guillaume B. 25
solicited disclosure 74
specialization 11
specific trust 165–166
spokesperson 115–117, 130

stakeholder management 87–89, 93
stakeholder maps 88
stakeholder power 84–85, 89, 93
stakeholders: audience management
    programme 23; behaviour 89; categories
    83–84, 93; celebrity endorsement
    118–119; classification 85–87;
    communications 9, 86–87, 90–91, 212;
    compared to public 82–83; corporate
    advertising 123, 124–125; corporate
    brand 34, 35, 42, 43; corporate identity
    20–21, 23, 27, 150–151, 161; corporate
    story 97, 98, 100, 103; credibility 211;
    definition 81–82, 93; legitimacy 85–86,
    87, 93; public relations 7; reputation
    158, 159, 161, 169; satisfaction 91; social
    acceptance 204–205; social responsibility
    67–68, 70, 71–73; urgency 86, 93
storytelling 96–97, 99–100, 110, 114
    see also corporate story
strategic advantage see also competitive
    advantage: branch identity analysis25;
    corporate brand 34; corporate identity
    20, 22; positioning strategy 23
strategic vision 36
structural identification 179

supported structure 39, **40**
sweatwashing 64
symbolic values 51
symbol usage 1–2, 10, 17, 23, 122

transparency 91, 105–106,
    108, 150
trust see also reputation: commitment 203;
    definition 166–167, 172; dimensions
    167–168; forms 165–166; mistrust
    consequences 168–169

unbound structure **40**
uniformity inwards 19–20, 30
urban legends 125
urgency, stakeholders 86, 93
usage strategy 89

value analysis 23, 51
verbal messages 10
visibility 21, 38, 118, 121, **160**, 186
visual representation 1–2, 10, 17, 23, 33
    see also corporate visual identity
voluntary disclosure 74

withholding strategy 89